Palgrave Studies in the Enlightenment, Romanticism and Cultures of Print

Palgrave Studies in the Enlightenment, Romanticism and Cultures of Print will feature work that does not fit comfortably within established boundaries—whether between periods or between disciplines. Uniquely, it will combine efforts to engage the power and materiality of print with explorations of gender, race, and class. By attending as well to intersections of literature with the visual arts, medicine, law, and science, the series will enable a large-scale rethinking of the origins of modernity.

Titles include:

Scott Black
OF ESSAYS AND READING IN EARLY MODERN BRITAIN

Claire Brock
THE FEMINIZATION OF FAME, 1750–1830

Brycchan Carey
BRITISH ABOLITIONISM AND THE RHETORIC OF SENSIBILITY
Writing, Sentiment, and Slavery, 1760–1807

E. J. Clery
THE FEMINIZATION DEBATE IN 18TH-CENTURY ENGLAND
Literature, Commerce and Luxury

Adriana Craciun
BRITISH WOMEN WRITERS AND THE FRENCH REVOLUTION
Citizens of the World

Peter de Bolla, Nigel Leask and David Simpson (*editors*)
LAND, NATION AND CULTURE, 1740–1840
Thinking the Republic of Taste

Ian Haywood
BLOODY ROMANTICISM
Spectacular Violence and the Politics of Representation, 1776–1832

Anthony S. Jarrells
BRITAIN'S BLOODLESS REVOLUTIONS
1688 and the Romantic Reform of Literature

Tom Mole
BYRON'S ROMANTIC CELEBRITY
Industrial Culture and the Hermeneutic of Intimacy

Mary Waters
BRITISH WOMEN WRITERS AND THE PROFESSION OF LITERARY CRITICISM, 1789–1832

David Worrall
THE POLITICS OF ROMANTIC THEATRICALITY, 1787–1832
The Road to the Stage

Palgrave Studies in the Enlightenment, Romanticism and Cultures of Print
Series Standing Order ISBN 1–4039–3408–8 hardback 1–4039–3409–6 paperback
(outside North America only)

You can receive future titles in this series as they are published by placing a standing order. Please contact your bookseller or, in case of difficulty, write to us at the address below with your name and address, the title of the series and the ISBN quoted above.

Customer Services Department, Macmillan Distribution Ltd, Houndmills, Basingstoke, Hampshire RG21 6XS, England

Byron's Romantic Celebrity

Industrial Culture and the Hermeneutic of Intimacy

Tom Mole

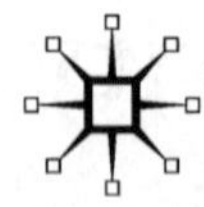

First published 2007 by
PALGRAVE MACMILLAN
Houndmills, Basingstoke, Hampshire RG21 6XS and
175 Fifth Avenue, New York, N.Y. 10010
Companies and representatives throughout the world

PALGRAVE MACMILLAN is the global academic imprint of the Palgrave Macmillan division of St. Martin's Press, LLC and of Palgrave Macmillan Ltd. Macmillan® is a registered trademark in the United States, United Kingdom and other countries. Palgrave is a registered trademark in the European Union and other countries.

ISBN-13: 978–1–4039–9993–1 hardback
ISBN-10: 1–4039–9993–7 hardback

This book is printed on paper suitable for recycling and made from fully managed and sustained forest sources. Logging, pulping and manufacturing processes are expected to conform to the environmental regulations of the country of origin.

A catalogue record for this book is available from the British Library.

A catalog record for this book is available from the Library of Congress.

10 9 8 7 6 5 4 3 2 1
16 15 14 13 12 11 10 09 08 07

Printed and bound in Great Britain by
Antony Rowe Ltd, Chippenham and Eastbourne

'To my Mother and my Father'

Contents

List of Figures

Acknowledgements

This book was conceived in Bristol, developed in Glasgow and finished in Montreal. Along the way I have accumulated many debts. I would like to thank Stephen Cheeke, who supervised my doctoral thesis with unfailing intelligence and good humour. I would also like to thank my teachers and colleagues at Bristol, especially Timothy Webb, Andrew Bennett, David Punter and Andrew Nicholson; my friends and colleagues in Glasgow, especially Robert Miles, Clifford Siskin, Janet Todd and Richard Cronin; and my new colleagues at McGill. I have received financial support from the Arts and Humanities Research Council, the Leverhulme Trust, the University of Bristol and the Fonds Québécois de la Recherche sur la Société et la Culture. An earlier version of Chapter 2 appeared as 'Byron's "An Ode to the Framers of the Frame Bill": The Embarrassment of Industrial Publishing', *The Keats-Shelley Journal*, 52 (2003), 97–115. An earlier version of Chapter 6 appeared as 'The Handling of *Hebrew Melodies*', *Romanticism*, 8, no. 1 (2002), 18–33. I gratefully acknowledge the editors of those journals for granting permission to reprint that material here.

Abbreviated Titles

BLJ — *Byron's Letters and Journals*, ed. Leslie A. Marchand, 13 vols (London: John Murray, 1973–1994).

CMP — Lord Byron, *The Complete Miscellaneous Prose*, ed. Andrew Nicholson (Oxford: Clarendon Press, 1991).

CPW — Lord Byron, *The Complete Poetical Works*, ed. Jerome J. McGann, 7 vols (Oxford: Clarendon Press, 1980–1993). All quotations from Byron's poetry are from this edition.

HVSV — *His Very Self and Voice: Collected Conversations of Lord Byron*, ed. Ernest J. Lovell (New York: Macmillan, 1954).

Preface

In 2002, a British newspaper ran a story under the headline 'Celebrity is Nothing New', in which a Romantic poet made an awkward bow. 'Lord Byron drew hordes of screaming young women', it claimed, '[h]is readings drew crowds of adoring women.'[1] Byron certainly attracted the impassioned interest of large numbers of women. But they didn't gather in crowds, and they certainly didn't scream. He never gave a public reading, and neither did anyone else until later in the century.[2] Those hordes of women were spliced into Byron's story from an entirely different cultural memory. They screamed not for Byron but for the Beatles.

Celebrity *is* nothing new, but this is no way to write its history. Contemporary culture is so saturated with celebrities that their very ubiquity makes it difficult to see their historical and cultural significance. It's time to pay them some more rigorous attention. This book presents one case study in a history that has yet to be written of a phenomenon that has yet to be adequately theorised. The vast and complex apparatus that sustains modern celebrity culture is now so familiar that it seems to be either a unique characteristic of our contemporary moment or an expression of universal, ahistorical ambitions and desires.[3] Although we live in a culture obsessed by celebrities, we lack a history of celebrity. I argue that modern celebrity culture began in the Romantic period and that Lord Byron should be understood as one of its earliest examples and most astute critics. I understand celebrity to be a cultural apparatus, consisting of the relations between an individual, an industry and an audience, that took shape in response to the industrialised print culture of the late eighteenth century. Under that rubric I investigate the often strained interactions of artistic endeavour and commercial enterprise, the material conditions of Byron's publications, and the place of celebrity culture in the history of the self.

The modern vocabulary for talking about celebrity emerged with the phenomenon it described. The original meanings of the word *celebrity*, concerning pomp, solemnity and the conduct of ceremonies, were obsolete by the Romantic period, although *OED* records that the use of *a celebrity* to mean a rite or celebration lingered until 1774. In 1751 Samuel Johnson recalled in *The Rambler* a time when he 'did not find [him]self yet enriched in proportion to [his] celebrity'.[4] He used the word to name a desirable personal attribute for the professional man of letters. Johnson acquired celebrity before he accrued any money. A century later, in 1849, the novelist Dinah Mulock Craik had one of her characters ask another, 'Did you see any of those "celebrities," as you call them?'[5] using a form of the word that was evidently still unfamiliar, Mulock employed it as a concrete noun. Her character was eager for reports of people who were recognizable on sight as celebrities. The Romantic period witnessed the transition between Johnson's usage and Mulock's, when the noun concretised, becoming an individual's definitive condition. Celebrity was no longer something you had, but something you were. In the year of Byron's death another important word in the modern celebrity lexicon appeared. *Star* is first cited by *OED* as meaning 'a person of brilliant reputation or talents' in 1824. By the end of the Romantic period, one could meaningfully speak of a celebrity or a star as a special kind of person with a distinct kind of public profile. The lexical shifts acknowledge, define and help to shape the emergence of a specifically modern way to enter the public sphere. A new form of public life had appeared.

It was also in the Romantic period that celebrity first came to be understood as a distinctly inferior variety of fame. In an age when, according to Maria Jane Jewsbury, 'to read ten thousand volumes and to write a hundred, [was] scarcely a distinction', it became important to classify what kinds of public profile were worth having.[6] Hester Thrale, writing to Samuel Johnson in 1784, used the word to indicate the modesty of her ambitions and her gendered sense of propriety. 'Perhaps by my fame (and I hope it is so)', she wrote, 'you mean only that celebrity which is a consideration of a much lower kind. I care for that only as it may give pleasure to my husband and his friends.'[7] Although he did not use the word, Hazlitt made a comparable distinction between 'fame' and 'popularity' in his lecture 'On the Living Poets' (1818). 'Fame is the recompense not of the living, but of the dead', he asserted, 'for fame is not popularity, the shout of the multitude, the idle buzz of fashion, the venal puff, the soothing flattery of favour or of friendship; but it is the spirit of a man surviving himself in the minds and thoughts of other men, undying and imperishable.'[8] John Hamilton Reynolds worried in 1816 that, as paper money drove gold out of circulation, 'popular poetry' drove out 'genius'.[9] And Samuel Taylor Coleridge confirmed both the association between celebrity and commerce and the tone of condescension when he asserted in *Biographia Literaria* (1817) that 'money and immediate fame form only an arbitrary and accidental end of literary labour'.[10] Thrale, Hazlitt, Reynolds and Coleridge used different terms for the same end: to identify an inferior kind of fame, and quarantine true fame from its contamination.

Once this understanding took hold, writing appreciatively about Byron often meant rescuing him from his own celebrity. When the great living poets come to mourn the dead Keats in Percy Shelley's 'Adonais' (1821), Byron appears among them as 'The Pilgrim of Eternity, whose fame / Over his living head like Heaven is bent, / An early but enduring monument' (264–6). Shelley accepted the hierarchy proposed by Hazlitt, Coleridge and Reynolds that placed true fame above transient celebrity, but he refused the implication that they were mutually exclusive. Shelley insisted that, far from being a passing fad, Byron's celebrity was an early sign of lasting greatness. Byron's immortality, Shelley suggested, had simply arrived prematurely. Working hard against a Romantic celebrity culture with which Byron was synonymous, Shelley was at pains to assert that his friend's fame would endure. Taking their cue from Shelley, critics from Thomas Macaulay to Matthew Arnold elaborated the orthodoxy that merit is to be sought where celebrity cannot penetrate. In 1831, Macaulay felt 'a generation must pass away before it will be possible to form a fair judgement of [Byron's] books, considered merely as books. At present they are not only books, but relics.'[11] A generation later, in 1881, Arnold wrote:

> The hour of irresistible vogue has passed away for him; even for Byron it could not but pass away. The time has come for him, as it comes for all poets, when he must take his real and permanent place, no longer depending upon the vogue of his own day and upon the enthusiasm of his contemporaries.[12]

From Shelley onwards, serious criticism of Byron has often defined itself by turning away from celebrity's meretricious glitter to weigh the 'real' merits of his poetry.

This book reverses that procedure by making Byron's celebrity its subject. I begin by tracing the emergence of modern celebrity, before film or photography, in the industrialised print culture of the late eighteenth century. Referring to the careers of David Garrick, Laurence Sterne, Sarah Siddons, Mary Robinson, Ann Yearsley, Edmund Kean, Thomas Moore and Letitia Landon, I offer a new account of celebrity culture's beginnings. I then turn to Byron's career in detail. I take 'An Ode to the Framers of the Frame Bill' as a starting point to think about Byron's place in industrial culture and his aspirations to activist writing. In chapters on *Childe Harold's Pilgrimage* and the verse tales Byron published from

1812 to 1815, I investigate the development of the reading paradigm that characterises celebrity culture – which I call the 'hermeneutic of intimacy' – and examine the understanding of subjectivity on which it was based. After tracing the crucial visual dimension of Byron's public profile, I turn to his attempts to rethink his own celebrity in *Hebrew Melodies* and *Childe Harold*, Canto Three. Finally, I argue that in *Don Juan* Byron exploited his position in Romantic celebrity culture in order to critique its understanding of subjectivity just as that understanding was becoming the modern norm. Throughout, I aim to contribute to the project of writing celebrity's history and theorising its significance. That task obliges us to re-evaluate an idea about Romanticism that is as old as the urge to theorise Romanticism itself: the claim that it is a poetics of self-expression, which gains its potency from personality. The cultural history of celebrity provides a new lens through which to view that notion, by showing how commercial collaboration and creative compromise made a public profile possible.

One of Borges's narrators remarks, '[f]ame is a form of incomprehension, perhaps the worst'.[13] Even as he ironises a scholarly preference for the obscure, the narrator reinforces the assumption that understanding literature means ignoring celebrity culture. That assumption has prevented us from asking important questions: how and why did the modern culture of celebrity emerge; what cultural problems did it solve; whose interests did it serve; and how does it continue to shape our public discourse? As celebrity colonises new areas of endeavour and pleasure, from sports and business to politics and the academy, as it becomes an ever more powerful force for structuring public information and private imagination, the assumption that celebrity culture is none of the scholar's business is one we can no longer afford. As an increasing number of thinkers acknowledge this fact, celebrity is emerging as an interdisciplinary area of study. Understanding Byron's career as an early chapter in the still unwritten history of celebrity culture offers a new way to situate his poetry in context while relating it to pressing contemporary concerns.

1
Romantic Celebrity

Celebrity culture does not want to be understood. It functions best when consumers remain mystified by it, attributing a celebrity's success to his or her magical star quality. Only recently have cultural theorists begun to map celebrity's structures, and scholars of literature, theatre and the visual arts to trace its historical contours. This chapter elaborates a theory and a history of celebrity, which not only underpin my reading of Byron's career, but are also, I hope, more widely applicable. Celebrity is a cultural apparatus consisting of three elements: an individual, an industry and an audience. Modern celebrity culture begins when these three components routinely work together to render an individual personally fascinating. This kind of fascination is unlike the pre-modern interest with an individual's public role, and its genesis is historically specific. I argue that we've had celebrities since the late eighteenth century and a celebrity culture since the beginning of the nineteenth.

Reviewing *Childe Harold* Canto Three in 1816, the *Portfolio* knew what kind of text it was dealing with, and dissected the new 'species of distinction':

> Indeed it is the real romance of [Byron's] life, immeasurably more than the fabled one of his pen, which the public expects to find in his pages, and which not so much engages its sympathy, as piques its curiosity, and feeds thought and conversation. The Noble Poet, in the mean time, is content with – it should be said is ambitious of – this species of distinction; the booksellers, printers, and stationers, all profit by the traffic to which the exhibition gives rise; and thus every party is a gainer in this remarkable phenomenon of the time.[1]

First, the reviewer identified an audience that was fascinated by the author's life, which seemed to be a 'real romance' operating on a more remarkable plane than the lives of his readers. They enjoyed contemplating the celebrity's subjectivity through the lens of his (and elsewhere her) poems, and their fascination fed both private 'thought' and sociable 'conversation'. On one hand, that fascination enabled a retreat from social life into thoughts about the poet. On the other, it provoked controversy, unifying and dividing Byron's readers into accusers and defenders of his personal motives, admirers and condemners of his private conduct, lovers and haters of his poetry. Providing a topic about which anyone could take a view, celebrity structured social intercourse and supplied a ligament of group identity.

Having diagnosed readers' expectations, the reviewer proceeded to join them in peering behind the text to glimpse an individual whose motives could be discerned. The author, he claimed, was ambitious for a particular kind of public profile – an implicitly inferior 'species of distinction' – and was responsive to the demands of his audience. His ambitions and their demands coalesced into a particular kind of text. It was not simply an autobiography, although the emergence of a vocabulary for autobiography is part of celebrity culture, but a laminar text that overlaid revelation and concealment.[2] On the surface it was a fabled romance, a doubly fictive construction. But the enterprising and curious reader could 'find in his pages' a 'real romance' which was both remarkable and yet routinely expected from the author's texts. Once it was uncovered or decoded, this layer not only offered a superior kind of satisfaction, but also 'pique[d]' the reader to search for a further, extra-textual layer of authenticity, where the 'real romance' would give way to reality itself.

This torrid partnership of confessional author and curious reader was supplemented and mediated by a third term: an industry of 'booksellers, printers, and stationers' whose primary motive was pecuniary. Availing themselves of technological developments in papermaking, printing and engraving, of improvements in infrastructure and the new promotional opportunities afforded by an enlarged market for newspapers, magazines and literary journals, this industry promulgated 'the traffic to which the exhibition gives rise'. It produced celebrity texts in unprecedented numbers by industrial means and distributed them rapidly around the country, the continent and – before long – the world. When the individual, the industry and the audience clicked into place to form the celebrity apparatus, it seemed to the *Portfolio* that no one could lose. '[E]very party [was] a gainer': the author gained cultural distinction and often financial reward, the industry sustained and expanded a profitable business, and the audience enjoyed both private pleasures and social amusements in exchange for the price of a book. These authorial activities, readerly rewards and industrial enterprises were worth commenting on because they were new. When the *Portfolio* identified this as a 'remarkable phenomenon of the time' it did so because the reviewer thought it was a decidedly modern and significant development.

1. History and theory

I contend that any analysis of celebrity culture should be built on the three pillars of an industry, an individual and an audience. An *industry* arranges the available technology, labour and skill in order to produce and distribute multiple copies, in large numbers, of a commodity which need not refer back to any 'original'. The celebrity apparatus embraces both the primary industry which produces the celebrity's work (such as literary publishing or Hollywood cinema) and several secondary industries which promote and distribute it (such as newspapers and engravings, or photography and television). In this book I am concerned with the industries that produce and distribute verbal and visual printed matter.[3] These industries were displaced, but not simply made redundant, by the later flourishing of celebrity through lens-based media, which continue to work hand in hand with print. The celebrity *individual* enters a feedback loop in which being a celebrity affects his or her self-understanding, so that neither self nor celebrity can be conceptually quarantined from the other. The non-celebrity does not survive unchanged within the celebrity apparatus, but neither does the apparatus operate without reference to the subject at its core. The individual may, however, be concerned to defend a kernel of subjectivity that appears to be untouched by celebrity. An *audience* – massive, anonymous, socially diverse, geographically distributed – consumes and interprets celebrity, often in creative ways. These responses are unauthorised by the celebrity individual or the industry, and beyond their control, although the industry may attempt to police them in various ways. The audience's responses are acts of self-fashioning: definitions and declarations of individual and group identity which may entail both emulation and critique. The nature of each element in the celebrity apparatus – the individual, the industry and the audience – may change over time. But particular characteristics of each, and particular relations between them, are necessary for celebrity culture to get going in the first place. I argue that the crucial changes that produced modern celebrity culture occurred in the Romantic period.

In the story that celebrity culture tells about itself, the celebrity's public profile appears as the well-deserved reward for talent and determination and the seemingly magical crystallisation of personal qualities. A priority for critics of celebrity culture, therefore, has been to demystify its ideological work. Daniel Boorstin began this process with a notable jeremiad that characterised celebrity as recognition without substance. For Boorstin, celebrities were 'human pseudo-events' symptomatic of a lamentable inauthenticity in American life.[4] Richard Dyer limited his analysis to film stars, but provided a useful way of thinking about the star as a 'sign'.[5] Critics such as Joshua Gamson, Tyler Cowen and P. David Marshall performed a strategic shift, bracketing the experience of the celebrity individual in order to focus on the phenomenon's cultural and economic scaffolding. Gamson offers a sociological account based on participant observation and on interviews with media professionals and audience members, concluding that at least some people in both camps have a highly developed sense of irony.[6] Cowen analyses the economics of celebrity culture, arguing that it is a non-zero-sum business with potential trickle-down benefits.[7] Marshall, in the most sophisticated study to date, employs a 'double hermeneutic' that considers both 'intention' and 'reception'.[8] He locates intention not in the individual but in the culture industry, and looks to reception aesthetics and social psychology for insights into audience response. Graeme Turner surveys the existing work on the subject, paying attention to production (the industry) and consumption (the audience).[9] These studies all tend to avoid discussing the experience of individual celebrities and to concentrate on the industry and/or the audience. They represent celebrities as what Marshall, Gamson and Moran variously call a 'bridge of meaning', 'built on major [...] fault lines' or 'a contested area of cultural production'.[10] Forming an important node of cultural concerns, celebrities connect producers and consumers, elite and popular pursuits, high and low culture, bourgeois individualism and proletarian collectivity, cultural capital and hard cash.

Bracketing the individual out of the investigation made a critical theory of celebrity possible. But it also made it difficult to develop an account of the limits that impose on the celebrity's agency and the tactics he or she develops to function within those limits. These issues are important because the celebrity experiences the subjective trauma of commodity capitalism in a particularly acute fashion. He is both a producer of commodities and himself, in a sense, a commodity.

Seeing his or her image return in industrially mediated forms, the celebrity's experience goes beyond the standard Marxist diagnosis of alienation to become self-alienation.[11] Bracketing celebrity subjectivity may give the impression that identity remains unchanged by celebrity. But subjectivity is not an extrinsic component for the critic to plug in once his or her understanding of the celebrity apparatus is complete. The subjectivity of the individual and the apparatus of celebrity may in fact be mutually constitutive. Moreover, the historical emergence of celebrity is connected, I believe, to the normalisation of certain modern ideas about subjectivity. Celebrity impacts not only on the selfhood of the celebrity, but on conceptions of selfhood itself.

Such conceptions must be understood in relation to a history of private life and the public sphere. The historical emergence of modern celebrity culture contributes, in an early and pervasive fashion, to the disintegration of the Habermasian public sphere. Habermas suggests several factors that contribute to this disintegration, from the intrusion of state power to the inclusion of previously excluded groups, but celebrity also plays its part in two ways.[12] First, the growth of celebrity culture helps to blur the boundary between the private and the public experiences of individuals; secondly, it contributes to the colonisation of the public sphere by the market. The Habermasian public sphere passed off the interests of its limited membership as universal and representative, but historians have also identified a variety of counter public spheres, occupied by women, radicals and other disenfranchised groups.[13] The celebrity apparatus does not set up another counter public sphere in which celebrity discourse circulates. Rather, celebrity is a tendency that cuts across all public and counter public spheres, emphasising not just the permeability of private and public, but their commercialised interpenetration.

A similar caveat applies to the doctrine of separate spheres for the genders. The notion that 'separate spheres' ever described a historical reality is now routinely questioned. The doctrine is better understood as a prescriptive discourse which tried to regulate women's participation in either the Habermasian public sphere or a feminised counter public sphere.[14] The existence of female celebrities shows that the doctrine of separate spheres is not an accurate description of gender roles in the Romantic period, but nonetheless female celebrities often fell foul of the *prescriptive* discourse of separate spheres, and had to adjust or excuse their practice accordingly. Studying celebrity culture requires us to look again at the public sphere's history. Rather than argue that private overtook public, or vice versa, it would be more accurate to say that a liminal space between the two expanded to take over both public and private, with the result that, in the experience of both the celebrity and the fan, public and private aspects are constantly referred to one another.[15]

I use the term *apparatus* to give my theory a historical dimension.[16] The term encompasses the individual, the industry and the audience that combine to produce the celebrity phenomenon and acknowledges that these elements come together at a specific historical moment. Brecht uses the term (*apparat* in German) to refer to the physical conditions of production in the opera, the theatre or the press, which proceed unquestioned and impose their logic on the work produced.[17] Foucault extends the term (*dispositif* in French) to refer to 'a thoroughly heterogeneous ensemble' whose elements are 'the said as much as the unsaid' and which consists of 'the system of relations that can be established between these elements.'[18] Foucault also insists that an apparatus has a history, and is tied to a particular genesis. It is a 'formation which has as its major function at a given historical moment that of responding to an *urgent need*'.[19] The elements that make up celebrity's heterogeneous ensemble are modified over time, as I have suggested. But I will argue that the *urgent need*, which leads to the apparatus becoming a cultural norm, should be located in the Romantic period and has not yet been studied.

There is little consensus about when modern celebrity culture began. For Leo Braudy, fame is a 'constant theme in the history of Western society', and he acknowledges no decisive break inaugurating modern celebrity.[20] Chris Rojek invokes the 'major interrelated historical processes' of 'democratisation', 'decline in organised religion' and 'the commodification of everyday life', before claiming that 'celebrity must be understood as a *modern* phenomenon, a phenomenon of mass-circulation newspapers, TV, radio and film'.[21] Several film historians date modern celebrity culture from the story of Florence Lawrence. Her fans knew her as the 'Biograph Girl' until 1910, when her employers apparently planted a false newspaper report of her sudden death. A few days later they placed an advertisement in *Moving Picture World*, with a photo, refuting the first story and confirming that Lawrence now worked for them at IMP.[22] Neal Gabler and Charles L. Ponce de Leon, by contrast, argue for the emergence of celebrity in twentieth-century human-interest journalism.[23] With the exception of Braudy, all these critics share Richard Schickel's 'first basic assumption' that 'there was no such thing as celebrity prior to the beginning of the twentieth century'.[24]

However, a number of critics have recently argued for a longer view of celebrity culture's history. Investigating late-nineteenth-century celebrity, Richard Salmon has cited as evidence the proliferation of photographs, the rise of interviewing as a journalistic form, a tendency to conduct interviews in the subject's home and the fashion for authors to give public readings.[25] Film historians studying Sarah Bernhardt (1844–1923) have argued for her importance as a transitional figure between theatrical and cinematic celebrity.[26] Lenard R. Berlanstein has examined gendered aspects of celebrity in the nineteenth-century French press and Claire Brock has drawn attention to the 'feminization' of fame in the Romantic period.[27] Art historians have argued that Joshua Reynolds (1723–1792) was a pivotal figure in cultivating celebrity for himself and his sitters.[28] Frank Donoghue and David Higgins have argued for the importance of periodical writing to eighteenth- and nineteenth-century literary celebrity.[29] Mary Luckhurst and Jane Moody have suggested that theatrical celebrity can be traced back to 1660.[30] And Antonin Careme (1783–1833) has been claimed as 'the first celebrity chef'.[31]

Clearly, careful distinctions are required to make a history of modern celebrity culture compelling. Elements of celebrity culture are certainly visible by the early 1700s, but I will argue that the cultural apparatus did not start to function in earnest until the end of the century. David Garrick (1717–1779) is my first example. His London debut, as Richard III at Goodman's Fields Theatre in 1741, aged 24, was hailed as a revolution in acting style. Garrick aimed 'to bring the Sock & Buskin down to Nature', replacing a stylised representation of the passions with a 'natural' acting style.[32] He became famous for his facial expressions, which were indebted to Charles Lebrun's scheme for portraying emotions in painting.[33] Having drawn on painterly conventions, Garrick's style lent itself to pictorial representation, which consolidated his public profile.[34] His efforts to promote and control his public image foreshadow many later celebrity strategies, but take place in a largely pre-industrial culture.

The Farmer's Return is a good example of Garrick's practice. He wrote this short interlude in 1762 and played the title role at Drury Lane. He got Hogarth to draw the scene and hung the drawing in his London house. Then he arranged for Johan Zoffany, who had already painted four pictures of Garrick and his family enjoying the domestic comforts of the gentry, to paint the same scene. Zoffany exhibited his painting at the Society of Artists before it too was hung in Garrick's house. Finally, Garrick got Hogarth's drawing engraved and used it as a frontispiece when the play was published later in the year. Neither script, performance, drawing, painting nor engraving is a significant work of art on its own. But taken together they represent a multimedia effort to promote Garrick's career, which exploits the permeability of domestic and public spaces to boost his cultural visibility. At the same time, Garrick was being portrayed not only in his roles, but as himself. In Joshua Reynolds's painting *David Garrick Between Tragedy and Comedy* (1761), Garrick appears in an allegory of his own career. Equally talented in tragic and comic roles, Garrick is wooed by both muses, and must choose between the soft delights of a comely Comedy and the stern virtues of the matriarch Tragedy. Reynolds's 1784 portrait of Sarah Siddons (1755–1831) as the tragic muse treads similar ground, and Thomas Lawrence's 1804 portrait shows her out of costume, giving a dramatic reading.[35] Rather than commemorating particular productions, these portraits show actors enacting their ability to act. Reynolds presents Garrick and Siddons as heightened versions of themselves, propagating a fascination with them as individuals which would flower with the advent of celebrity culture at the end of the century.

David Garrick would also play his part in promoting another versatile eighteenth-century performer: Laurence Sterne (1713–1768). Armed with a provincial printer and a metropolitan distributor, Sterne was keen to leave his Yorkshire parishes behind and make a stir in London. After a pre-publication advertisement appeared in the *London Chronicle*, he wrote a letter in praise of *Tristram Shandy*, which he got his mistress Catherine Fourmantel to copy out and send to Garrick, as though it came from her.[36] Garrick subsequently befriended Sterne, and is mentioned by name four times in *Tristram Shandy*. Meanwhile, Sterne's first biographer, John Hill, was keen to tell a different story: one about merit making good. 'Here were none of the common arts of making a reputation practised', he wrote, 'no friend before hand told people how excellent a book it was [...] A parcel of books were [*sic*] sent up out of the country; they were unknown, and scarce advertised; but thus friendless they made their own way, and their author's.'[37] Here a parcel of books stands as a metonym for the author, in a now-familiar story of the unknown aspirant who comes to the big city and waits for someone to scout out her star quality. There was a backlash when it emerged that Sterne was a clergyman, but he cemented his success on his visits to London, where, Hill wrote, '[e]very body is curious to see the author; and, when they see him, every body loves the man'.[38] Peter Briggs suggests that Sterne positioned himself 'not as a literary candidate for slow fame but as a theatrical candidate for sudden fame'.[39] Sterne went on to circulate his portrait as a frontispiece engraving, and enjoyed a more limited success with the publication of his sermons. Garrick and Sterne operated on the cusp of modern celebrity culture, but I will argue that technological innovations and social changes were necessary before celebrity became a cultural norm.

Garrick's experience in the 1760s suggests that the three elements which make up the celebrity apparatus were not yet working in concert. While visiting Paris, Garrick wrote to his brother that he was 'plagu'd here for my Prints or rather Prints of Me', and asked him to send '*six* prints from Reynolds's picture [...] & any other prints of Me, if tolerable'.[40] But it seems that prints of the Reynolds portrait were already circulating in Paris – it's just that no one knew they were of Garrick. Just a few months later, George Colman the Elder wrote to Garrick from Paris, 'There hang out in every street, pirated prints of Reynolds's Picture of you, which are underwritten "L'homme entre le Vice et la Virtu".'[41] Mistaking the identities of Garrick and his allegorical co-stars, the Paris printsellers marketed the image as a moral emblem rather than a celebrity spin-off. The pirates, knowingly or otherwise, detached the picture from the individual in order to promote it in abstract terms to a wider audience. In celebrity culture the opposite approach will dominate. Texts that do not originate with the celebrity individual will be associated with him or her in order to enhance their circulation and boost their market value.

Sterne's strategies of self-promotion closely resemble those of later celebrities. But the same reservations apply.[42] His success relied on ceaselessly collecting subscriptions; he secured six hundred and fifty of them for *The Sermons of Mr Yorick*, and for a later volume of sermons he aimed to compile 'the largest, and most splendid list which ever pranced before a book, since subscriptions came into fashion'.[43] Sterne's tireless dining-out won his books a large audience among the 'splendid' social and ecclesiastical elite. But without the later industrial developments in print technology, the growth of the periodical market to which they gave rise, the improvements in infrastructure which enabled wider distribution of printed matter to the increasing number of literate people among a rapidly enlarging population, and the shift from subscription publication to unmediated commercial publication, Sterne could not reach the mass audience of modern celebrity, nor reach his audience with such speed. When Walter Scott reflected on the impact of *Childe Harold's Pilgrimage*, it was this sense of the audience's size and social diversity, and the speed with which new works could reach it, that seemed to him to mark off his generation from that of Sterne:

> Reading is indeed so general among all ranks and classes, that the impulse received by the public mind on such occasions is instantaneous through all but the lowest classes of society, instead of being slowly communicated from one set of readers to another, as was the case in the days of our fathers.[44]

Although the self-presentation of individuals such as Sterne and Garrick included celebrity characteristics, it required the growth of a modern industry of production, promotion and distribution, and a modern audience – massive, anonymous, socially diverse and geographically distributed – before these elements combined to form a celebrity culture in the modern sense.

2. Personality overload and readerly alienation

Celebrity became a modern cultural phenomenon because it answered an '*urgent need*' created by the industrialised print culture of the Romantic period. Industrial publishing functioned as the primary industry for literary celebrities such as Byron, and as the secondary industry which promoted celebrities from other media, such as the theatre. Industrialisation combined with new intellectual property regimes, population growth, urbanisation and rising literacy to drive the explosive, unprecedented growth in the annual output of printed items from the late eighteenth century, which is visible in statistics from the English Short Title Catalogue (Fig. 1.1). After a phase of slow growth in the 1700s (possibly a fall in real terms) during what William St Clair calls the 'high monopoly period', we see an exponential growth curve begun by Donaldson v. Beckett in 1774, sustained by industrialisation and augmented by rising demand.[45] These statistics should be treated with caution, but the overall picture is unmistakable. By the turn of the century there were not only more readers in Britain than ever before, but also a great deal more for them to read.

The explosion of printed matter threatened both to reach a disturbingly radical popular audience and to swamp those readers who by remaining *au courant* might have checked and guided the tide of popular opinion. The overwhelmingly large and exponentially growing body of text called for strategies of selective reading. By 1795, the flood of new material had already overwhelmed Isaac D'Israeli:

> When I reflect that every literary journal consists of 50 or 60 publications, and that of those, five or six at least are capital performances,

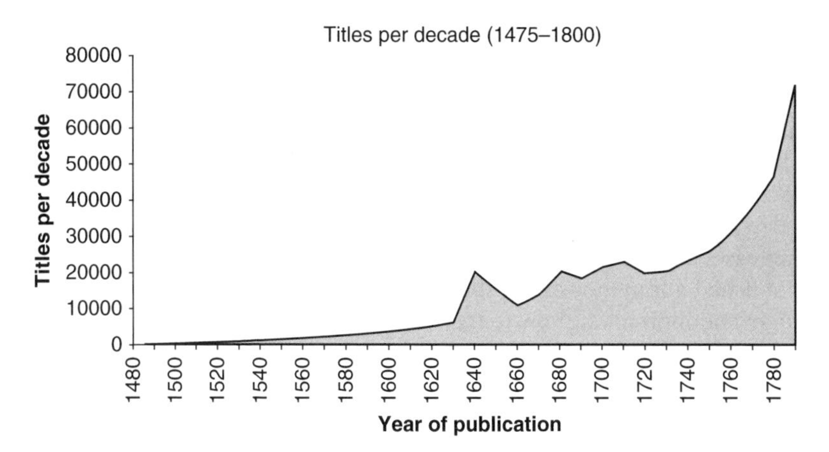

Figure 1.1 Graph showing publication totals from the English Short Title Catalogue.

Source: Alain Veylit, 'Some Statistics on the Number of Surviving Printed Titles for Great Britain and Dependencies from the Beginnings of Print in England to the year 1800', http://www.cbsr.ucr.edu/ESTCStatistics.html consulted 11 November 2003. Veylit notes that 'This [...] chart gives us a global picture of the printed material from Great Britain, dependencies and North America that has survived in public libraries organised by number of titles per decade. The overall mathematical shape is clear: it is an exponential curve. Even if we compensate for the fact that more items are likely to survive from the 18th than they are from the 16th century, and are cautious about the distorting lens of cataloguing procedures, it is very unlikely that historical reality could have been very much different.' See Note 47 for further comments on interpreting these data.

> and the greater part not contemptible, when I take the pen and attempt to calculate, by these given sums, the number of volumes which the next century must infallibly produce, my feeble faculties wander in a perplexed series, and as I lose myself among billions, trillions, and quartillions, I am obliged to lay down my pen, and stop at infinity.[46]

After the turn of the century, the *Edinburgh Review* (founded in 1802), and its rival the *Quarterly* (1809), abandoned the ambition of earlier journals such as the *Gentleman's Magazine* (1731) to notice every new publication. Their radically selective and evaluative approach helped to mediate between this glut of text and its audience.[47] But it was not simply a surge in the amount of printed matter that assaulted Romantic readers; it was also a deluge of proper names.

It is now possible to calculate the percentage of poetry and novels in the Romantic period that appeared anonymously. The results shed a new light on the received idea that this is an age of personality. Not only were there more printed items to read, but, for these two literary forms, an increasing proportion of them emerged with a proper name attached. More books, more names. Both novels and poetry volumes show a marked and rapid drop in percentage anonymity until 1807 (Fig. 1.2). After that year the downward trend continues steadily for poetry volumes, while the percentage of novels published anonymously increases once again.[48] In 1770, over 60 per cent of poetry volumes were published anonymously. In the years that followed, it became increasingly common for authors to fix names to their books, and when Byron was born in 1788 only 36 per cent of poetry books were anonymous. When he died in 1824 the figure was only 22.7 per cent and it went on to reach a low point of 16.7 per cent in 1834: only 22 volumes out of

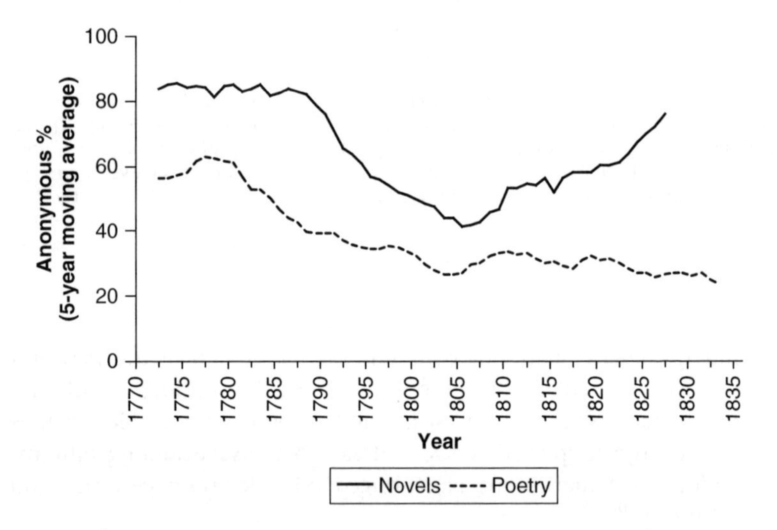

Figure 1.2 Graph showing percentage of new novels and poems published anonymously in the Romantic period.

Source: My calculations for poetry volumes are based on Lee Erickson's data in his article '"Unboastful Bard": Originally Anonymous English Romantic Poetry Book Publication, 1770–1835', *New Literary History*, 33 (2002), 247–78. Erickson's figures are drawn from J. R. de J. Jackson, *Annals of English verse, 1770–1835: A Preliminary Survey of the Volumes Published* (New York: Garland, 1985) and supplemented by additional titles from J. R. de J. Jackson, *Romantic Poetry by Women: A Bibliography, 1770–1835* (Oxford: Clarendon Press, 1993). For the novel, I have drawn on *The English Novel 1770–1829, a Bibliographical Survey of Prose Fiction Published in the British Isles*, ed. James Raven, Peter Garside and Rainer Schöwerling, 2 vols (Oxford: Oxford University Press, 2000), using data from tables on I, 46–7 and II, 73. For the graph, a 5-year moving average has been used to smooth out peaks and troughs in the data.

132 recorded.The strength of the general trend away from anonymous poetry in the period is striking.

The less anonymous writing there was, the more names had to compete for attention in the increasingly overcrowded public sphere. Mary Robinson – herself celebrated as a poet, novelist, actress and sometime mistress of the Prince of Wales – listed the aspirants in 1795:

> Poets, painters, and musicians;
> Lawyers, doctors, politicians:
> Pamphlets, newspapers, and odes,
> Seeking fame by diff'rent roads.[49]

In an Augustan descriptive catalogue, she linked an emerging professionalism with the varieties of print that propelled all kinds of people towards the common goal of individual celebrity. Print culture thronged with named individuals promoting their products and policies, their ideas and ideals – themselves. Proper names circulated along newly formed distribution networks, jostling for public notice. The numbers point to a Romantic surfeit of public personality.

This surfeit required people to develop new strategies for discriminating between the claims on their attention made by different individuals. And once print culture had redrawn the map of public life, strategies of self-promotion took on a new significance. When the surge in public profiles combined with the historic power shifts that were underway, established ways of working out who mattered would no longer hold. Paralleling the shift from inclusiveness to selectivity in the reviews, biographical encyclopaedias in the period show the difficulty of assimilating all the information circulating about personalities. Granger's *Biographical History of England* marks the failure of attempts to be comprehensive. Its first edition in 1769 was in three volumes and bore the long-winded title:

> A BIOGRAPHICAL HISTORY OF ENGLAND, FROM EGBERT the GREAT to the REVOLUTION: CONSISTING OF CHARACTERS disposed in different CLASSES, and adapted to a METHODICAL CATALOGUE of Engraved BRITISH HEADS: INTENDED AS An ESSAY towards reducing our BIOGRAPHY to SYSTEM, and a Help to the Knowledge of PORTRAITS: INTERSPERSED WITH Variety of ANECDOTES, and MEMOIRS of a great Number of PERSONS, not to be found in any other Biographical Work: With a PREFACE, shewing the Utility of

> a Collection of ENGRAVED PORTRAITS to supply the Defect, and answer the various Purposes of MEDALS.

Granger produced a second edition in 1775, a third edition 'with large additions and improvements' in 1779 and a fourth edition in 1804, each in four volumes.[50] By the fifth edition in 1824, the original three volumes had swelled to six 'with upwards of a hundred additional lives'. Granger's effort 'towards reducing our BIOGRAPHY to SYSTEM' required a comprehensive classification scheme. He arranged the catalogue historically by the reigns of English monarchs and hierarchically within each reign into 12 classes. The royal family came at the top, followed by 'Great Officers of State', peers, churchmen and so on. 'Ladies, and others, of the Female Sex' were grouped in the eleventh category, and at the bottom came 'Persons of both Sexes, chiefly of the lowest Order of the People, remarkable from only one Circumstance in their Lives; namely [...] deformed Persons, Convicts, &c.'[51] Bibliomaniacs collected the engraved portraits that Granger catalogued, and bound them into his book, in a practice that became known as *Grangerizing*. In the process, a single copy of Granger's book might expand into a multi-volume set containing thousands of illustrations.[52] Such unwieldy and hubristic attempts at comprehensiveness were bound to fail once the Romantic personality overload set in. No matter how fast Granger's *History* grew with each edition, it couldn't hope to keep pace with the increasing number of names that demanded inclusion in its pages and made its system seem hopelessly dated.

Instead of comprehensiveness, selectivity was required. While the *Edinburgh Review* took the flood of printed matter in hand, deigning to notice only a tiny fraction, another kind of biographical collection aimed to sift through the surfeit of public personality. Nobility provided the obvious tool for selection, and 75 different guides to the peerage were published between 1770 and 1830, including the first edition of Debrett's in 1802 and Burke's in 1826.[53] But in a changing political climate, rank was no longer such an effective rule of thumb. Claims to public notice could no longer rest solely on heraldic devices, inherited titles or inalienable estates. These historic shifts both displaced the authority of the old codes and made it all the more urgent to find new ones for winnowing claims on the public's attention. Lord Byron, as both an aristocrat and a celebrity, eased the transition to a new form of personal distinction.

In the shadow of the French Revolution, it also seemed vital to assert British individuality over French collectivity. Jerome Christensen suggests that the French Revolution was characterised in Britain as the 'collective subordination of manifold, contingent life courses to the idea of an inevitable historical event'. The British reacted by looking for a 'new man' whose individual strength of character would oppose the Revolutionary 'supersession of biography by typology' and reassure them that revolution was an exclusively Continental trauma.[54] But a personality vacuum occupied the political power centre after the deaths of Pitt and Fox in 1806, and the ironically named Ministry of All the Talents (1806–1807) failed to fill the gap; moreover, the Regency crisis of 1811 only made things worse.[55] The British seemed to be deluged with personalities, yet lacking a way to work out who really mattered.

What was true for public life in general was true for literature in particular. 'This truth at least let Satire's self allow', Byron wrote, 'No dearth of Bards can be complained of now.'[56] And Thomas Moore raised a laugh by pretending that the opposite was true, in an 'Announcement of a New Grand Acceleration Company for the Promotion of the Speed of Literature'.[57] The company would feed the newly enlarged reading public's demand for books, 'Loud complaints being made, in these quick-reading times, / Of too slack a supply, both of prose works and rhymes' (1–2). The company had established a literature factory where 'We keep authors ready, all perch'd, pen in hand, / To write off, in any giv'n style, at command' (40–1). It thus aimed to profit from the importance of proper names in the literary market. '[O]n th' establishment' were to be found:

> six Walter Scotts,
> One capital Wordsworth, and Southeys in lots; –
> Three choice Mrs. Nortons, all singing like syrens,
> While most of our pallid young clerks are Lord Byrons.
> Then we've ***s and ***s (for whom there's small call),
> And ***s and ***s (for whom no call at all).
>
> (44–9)

There was no call for authors with no names. Meanwhile, named authors flooded the market with writing that seemed to be churned out of the factories that were appearing across the English countryside.

The rise of industrially produced books interposed an impersonal mediating layer between writers and readers. With 'general commercial publishing of the modern kind', in Raymond Williams's classic characterisation, came 'the institution of "the market" as the type of a writer's actual relations with society'.[58] As more published writers became known to their readers by name, writers could know the names of a smaller fraction of their readership. The audience became anonymous and unknowable, creating a new alienation between writer and reader. Many authors despaired of finding a sympathetic audience, and denigrated the marketplace and the reading multitude as a result.[59] Readers likewise felt estranged from authors: how were they to find among the mass of new reading material an author who shared their assumptions and concerns? Thomas De Quincey recalled his childhood experience of this estrangement in *Suspiria de Profundis* (1845). Having contracted a debt with a local bookseller, De Quincey recalled how he seemed to have stumbled into a 'vast systematic machinery' for the industrial production of innumerable books and their distribution into every corner of England.[60] He imagined an endless 'procession of carts and waggons' emanating from the mysterious and impersonal metropolis to jettison piles of books at his door.[61] 'De Quincey's fantasy', writes Lucy Newlyn, 'figures the reader as the helpless consumer of books and as the humiliated victim of a powerful machinery of literary production designed precisely to remind him of his anonymous unimportance.'[62] The apparatus of celebrity was among the structures that Romantic culture developed to mitigate this sense of information overload and alienation. It responded to the surfeit of public personality by branding an individual's identity in order to make it amenable to commercial promotion. It palliated the feeling of alienation between cultural producers and consumers by constructing a sense of intimacy.

3. The branded identity

In order to boost the celebrity individual's visibility over that of other aspirants, the celebrity apparatus turned his or her proper name into a brand name.[63] The words 'Edmund Kean', printed in red on the first two-colour playbills, were bound to draw an audience.[64] Theatregoers could rest assured that, whatever the play, they would witness another lightning flash of Kean's genius. When the *European Magazine* received a 'new volume of poetry, bearing the noble name of Byron as it's [*sic*] passport to celebrity' it knew that the noble name acted as a guarantor of certain marketable qualities and connotations.[65] Byron's name commanded notice, even when his writing did not. The volume in question included *Sardanapalus*, which had 'so very few claims upon our attention, that were it not the work of the author of "*Childe Harold*," it might be very readily permitted to pass unnoticed'.[66]

A branded identity was the product of many mentions in the Romantic print media such as these. Being connected to a particular newspaper or journal was invaluable. Mary Robinson was promoted through the pages of the *Morning Post*, where she was poetry editor from 1799. Judith Pascoe notes that a reader of the *Post* would often have seen 'a front-page advertisement for a subscription to a new Robinson volume, a poem, a puff, a promotion for a soon-to-be-published poem', a report on her health or a poem addressed to her by an admirer.[67] Robinson also promoted herself by including her name in the 'List of British Female Literary Characters', which concluded her initially pseudonymous *Letter to the Women of England on the Injustice of Mental Subordination* (1799). Her efforts combined with sometimes-unwelcome attention from others to create a celebrity identity. Branded as Perdita after the Shakespearean role in which she caught the Prince of Wales's eye, she would later try to escape this branded identity by appearing under several pseudonyms, from the Della Cruscan Laura Maria to the thornier Tabitha Bramble.[68] While Robinson used multiple pseudonyms to escape her branded identity, Letitia Landon (1802–1838) was moulded into the compelling and mysterious initials L.E.L. in the pages of the *Literary Gazette*. Edward Bulwer Lytton recalled sharing with his undergraduate friends 'a rush every Saturday afternoon for *The Literary Gazette*, and an impatient anxiety to hasten at once to the corner of the sheet which contained the three magical letters of "L.E.L." '. Having read Landon's weekly contribution to the paper, they joined in the twin pursuits of literary appreciation and celebrity fascination: 'all of us praised the verse, and all of us guessed at the author. We soon learned it was a female, and our admiration was doubled, and our conjectures tripled. Was she young? Was she pretty?'[69]

Robinson and Landon were sophisticated literary performers, but the mechanisms for branding identity were so crucial to Romantic celebrity culture that they functioned even when most strenuously disavowed. Ann Yearsley (*bap.* 1753, *d.* 1806), with little effort on her part and against the moralising intentions of her patrons, found herself branded as Lactilla, milkmaid poet of Bristol. Having 'discovered' Yearsley, Hannah More embarked on a promotional scheme which, whatever its charitable intentions, effectively turned her protégée into a celebrity. More began by writing about Yearsley to literary friends such as Mary Hamilton, Horace Walpole and Elizabeth Montagu. The latter had already been the patron of James Woodhouse (*bap.* 1735, *d.* 1820), the 'shoemaker poet', and so brought valuable experience to More's project. More then arranged for Yearsley's *Poems on Several*

Occasions to be published in 1785 and supplied a 'Prefatory Letter' addressed to Montagu.[70] The volume received pre-publication publicity from two letters to the *Gentleman's Magazine*, possibly written by More herself. It was also advertised in *Felix Farley's Bristol Journal*, and More collected over one thousand subscribers, assuring the volume's commercial success and Lactilla's celebrity profile.[71] In each of these cases, the circulation of poems by Byron, Robinson, Landon and Yearsley was accompanied by information (or speculation) about their authors, fostering celebrity culture's fascination with personalities who became the subjects of discourse once their identities were branded through a variety of mutually supporting texts.

The 'texts' that branded an identity could be visual as well as verbal. Mary Robinson's flamboyant dresses and carriages appeared in popular prints, and such distinguished artists as Gainsborough, Reynolds and Romney painted her.[72] Byron's image also permeated Romantic visual culture. The celebrity apparatus cultivated visual trademarks, making Byron recognisable from a few repeated features: a curl of hair, a high forehead, an open collar. These were depicted in portraits which circulated via the new technology of steel plate engraving, creating almost endlessly reproducible prints whose features were then picked up in illustrations and cartoons.[73] These images, which are the subject of Chapter 5, helped to create a fascination with seeing celebrities in the flesh. Byron experienced the sharp end of this fascination when he went to dinner at Madame de Staël's and 'found the room full of strangers, who had come to stare at me as at some outlandish beast in a rareeshow'.[74] And Landon encountered it when *Blackwood's Magazine* printed directions to her house in its review of *The Improvisatrice*.[75]

The visual and verbal texts that constructed the branded identity were bolstered by the celebrity's social appearances. Mary Robinson's performances didn't stop when she stepped off the stage. One of her neighbours noted her 'remarkable facility in adapting her deportment to her dress':

> To-day she was a *paysanne*, with her straw hat tied at the back of her head, looking as if too new to what she passed, to know what she looked at. Yesterday she, perhaps, had been the dressed *belle* of Hyde Park, trimmed, powdered, patched, painted to the utmost power of rouge and white lead; to morrow, she would be the cravatted Amazon of the riding house[.][76]

Robinson complained in her *Memoirs* that the high visibility her celebrity brought her was nothing but trouble. When she went out shopping in her trademark carriage, 'I scarcely ventured to enter a shop without experiencing the greatest inconvenience. Many hours have I waited till the crowd dispersed, which surrounded my carriage, in expectation of my quitting the shop.'[77] Those readers who crowded Robinson's carriage, stared at Byron or went to Chelsea for a glimpse of Landon took their cue both from the poems those celebrities produced and from the texts, images and appearances that surrounded them and produced a branded identity.

Robinson began her career as an early example of a new breed of theatrical celebrity. Star actors became literally more visible in the Romantic period when stage lighting improved greatly: smoky tallow candles were replaced with high-quality wax ones, and in 1817 Drury Lane theatre introduced gas lighting. The invention of limelight in 1816 meant that a star performer could be spot lit, while the rest of the stage remained in darkness. While spectators had traditionally sat on the stage, from 1763 onwards (at Drury Lane) they were banished to the increasingly dim auditorium.[78] Star actors, meanwhile, had minimal rehearsal with the rest of the company, who were expected to accommodate their performances. They toured alone, working with local companies each night and, without a modern conception of the director, they were entirely responsible for their own interpretation of a role. Their salaries reflected their increased status; they greatly exceeded those paid to other members of the company, and they might be doubled by a successful benefit performance. At the same time, the rise of a distinct genre of thespian biography fed the audience's interest in their private lives.[79] At the beginning of the eighteenth century, spectators came and went throughout the evening's entertainment, in a lighted auditorium where they would look at, and converse with, other audience members as much as the actors. At the beginning of the nineteenth century, they tended to sit in silence, in a darkened auditorium, watching a star actor on a brightly lit stage: a trip to the theatre now seemed like an interpersonal interaction between audience member and star. As a result, actors like Sarah Siddons and Edmund Kean functioned as Romantic celebrities. Something comparable happened to concert music, with the rise of the *virtuoso* – a word which, like *celebrity*, changed its meaning in this period to denote a new way to enter the public eye.

While his appearance became recognised for a few distinctive features, Byron's poetry played with several formulae, which were repeated with variations. The Byronic hero enabled readers to project ideas and emotions connected with the author onto his characters, functioning as a further tool for increasing his personal visibility in Romantic culture. By shaping his poems into an integrated oeuvre, repeated formulae like the Byronic hero enhanced their cumulative effect of increasing Byron's celebrity. Landon also created a variety of heroines, poets or lovers like Erinna, Eulalia or the Improvisatrice, who appeared to her readers as avatars of L.E.L.[80] Byron's use of series to which he could return at crucial moments provided touchstones of public prominence, ways in which he could remind his readers of his characteristic qualities. *Childe Harold* and *Don Juan* kept readers coming back to purchase the next instalment and kept Byron's branded identity in the public eye so long as he continued to write them. The result, as John Scott noted in 1821, was that Byron 'awakened, by literary exertion, a more intense interest in his person than ever before resulted from literature.'[81] Although the process of branding identity began by fixing on existing features of Byron's style, it quickly became implicated in shaping that style, making Byron's celebrity not simply an adjunct to his writing but a component of it. Critics of Romanticism have traditionally preferred poetry that could be detached from contingencies of patronage or promotion, in the belief that authentic poetry did not lay waste its powers in getting and spending. Byron's poetry reveals that distinction between a poet's writing and his or her promotion as a celebrity to be an artificial one. Celebrity is folded back into literary creation.

Celebrities often found themselves trapped in that fold. The mechanisms for branding identity were wonderfully effective, but they also left Byron committed to a logic of celebrity which could be constraining. Having risen to public prominence, he felt the burden of public expectation. Too often, it seemed, he had to produce what a correspondent of the *Brighton Magazine* called 'the paltry impostures and *tours de finesse* to which a popular writer is obliged to resort in order to preserve what, in modern cant, is called the ear of the public'.[82] Such constraints were often gendered. The existence of female celebrities reveals existing narratives about female 'anxiety of authorship', and the 'vanishing acts' that turned women writers into 'nobody', to be only part of the historical story.[83] Subject to the same fascination with private lives that turned actresses of the period into 'sexual suspects', Landon's reputation was dogged by rumours about her love life and untimely death.[84] She objected humorously to biographical readings of her poetry in the 'Preface' to *The Venetian Bracelet* (1829):

> With regard to the frequent application of my works to myself, considering that I sometimes pourtrayed [*sic*] love unrequited, then betrayed, and again destroyed by death – may I hint the conclusions are not quite logically drawn, as assuredly the same mind cannot have suffered such varied modes of misery. However, if I must have an unhappy passion, I can only console myself with my own perfect unconsciousness of so great a misfortune.[85]

Mary Robinson made a similar claim in her Preface to *Sappho and Phaon* (1796). She imagined that Sappho's audience, unlike her own, had 'an unprejudiced enthusiasm for the works of genius' which prevented them from turning Sappho into a celebrity: 'when they paid adoration to Sappho, they idolised the MUSE and not the WOMAN'.[86] Yearsley, doubly disempowered by her gender and social status, found herself trapped in a promotional apparatus that apparently worked independently of her poetry. Mary Waldron suggests that, like other 'primitive' poets, her work was characterised as wild, natural and unschooled, whilst in fact she was keen to display her classical knowledge and stylistic polish.[87] Yearsley, Robinson and Landon might all have joined in the complaint of Landon's heroine Eulalia: 'I am a woman: – tell me not of fame.'[88] But it would be wrong to present the celebrity apparatus as something that constrained women while it empowered men. It constrained and empowered celebrities of both genders in gender-specific ways, but neither gender had a monopoly on constraint or empowerment. Despite having every advantage of class and gender, Byron was also constrained by his celebrity. As I show in Chapter 6, the limits of his branded identity obstructed his efforts to move his work in a new direction. A century later, Rudolph Valentino expressed the same problem succinctly. 'A man should control his life,' he said. 'Mine is controlling me. I don't like it.'[89]

The branded identity's commercial success was ensured because it was easily recognisable in the crowded marketplace, continually developing to offer new satisfactions but remaining reassuringly familiar. It rose to public prominence because it circulated effectively, and this circulation was guaranteed by the ease with which it could be appropriated. 'A star', writes Andrew Wernick, 'is anyone whose name and fame have been built up to the point where reference to them [...] can serve as a promotional booster in itself.'[90] Sterne was at first delighted and then unsettled by the outpouring of Shandeana, which left him with a 'sense that he was competing with his imitators for the right to speak authoritatively in Tristram's voice'.[91] While Byron's noble name acted as a passport to celebrity for each new volume on its first appearance, Murray appropriated his branded identity to sell other products. These included collected editions, which contrived to sell the same poems in other formats, illustrations, which traded on Byron's visual familiarity, and opportunities for synergy, such as the publication of Moore's *Jacqueline* in the same volume as *Lara*. Byron's celebrity could also be appropriated to sell other products, for example magazines, over which Byron and even Murray had little control. Letitia Landon helped to sell copies of the *Literary Gazette* not only by supplying poems for the editors to print over her trademark initials, but also because her persona generated the large numbers of poems addressed to L.E.L. which appeared in its pages.[92] Mary Robinson's celebrity identity was appropriated to provide commercial profit or cultural currency every time a newspaper (including her own *Morning Post*) published a story about her, a caricature of her, or a poem addressed to her. Authors of the latter ranged from Robert Merry to Samuel Taylor Coleridge, knitting Robinson into complex intertextual relationships with male authors, in which each tried to gain by association with the other.[93]

On the one hand a commercial asset constructed with the help of a single publisher, the celebrity's branded identity garnered cultural prominence and commercial success because it was also impossible to maintain a monopoly over its exploitation. In the undeveloped copyright conditions of the Romantic period, a celebrity identity took on a life of its own in the marketplace, where it was appropriated and redeployed by both entrepreneurs and consumers. This set of practices for branding an individual's identity in order to boost his or her cultural visibility and create a fascination with his or her personality and private life enabled certain individuals to rise to prominence above the Romantic surfeit of public personality. These practices were not controlled by any individual celebrity or svengali, but they shaped the public profiles of many individuals. They established the structures that governed a Romantic celebrity culture which is the ancestor of our own.

4. The hermeneutic of intimacy

The growth of celebrity culture also eased the sense of industrial alienation between readers and writers. The celebrity apparatus relied on the concealed use of new cultural technologies to construct an impression of unmediated contact. Instead of appearing as industrial productions competing for attention in a crowded market made up of increasingly estranged readers and writers, the poems fostered a hermeneutic of intimacy. Mary Robinson forged an apparently intimate connection with her readers in ostensibly confessional poems. In 'Stanzas' ('When the bleak blast of winter') she hints to her readers that she's brooding over a secret amorous sorrow, for which fame and talent are no consolation. 'What the laurel of Fame, or the song of the Muse,' she asks, 'When the heart bleeds in silence, the victim of woe?' (19–20). But although she will not lament the loss of her lover in verse, her sorrow will apparently make itself visible on her body:

> Yes, in silence, proud silence, I'll muse o'er his worth,
> Though reflection shall steal the faint Rose from my cheek,
> Though my eye's faded lustre its poison shall speak,
> And my heart-bursting sighs bend my frame to the earth!
>
> (29–32)

While suggesting that her sorrow lies too deep for words, the speaker invites us to read it in her cheek, her eyes and her sighs. Using a strategy similar to Byron's (see Chapter 4), Robinson constructs a speaker who's associated with herself, hints at a hidden pain and suggests that readers can understand that pain by gazing at her, at the same time as she was being represented in frontispieces and portraits. While seemingly reluctant to reveal her intimate concerns in her poetry, Robinson suggested that those who learned how to read and where to look could share them.

Byron would elaborate this hermeneutic of intimacy more systematically and potently. It worked by suggesting that his poems could only be understood fully by referring to their author's personality, that reading them was entering a kind of relationship with the author and that that relationship resembled an intimate connection between individuals. As a result, in Peter Manning's words, the poems 'furnished the simulacrum of intimacy the new readership craved'.[94] John Wilson, reviewing *Childe Harold* Canto Four in the *Edinburgh Review*, described the effect:

> Each of us must have been aware in himself of a singular illusion by which these disclosures, when read with that tender or high interest which attaches to poetry, seem to have something of the nature of private and confidential communications. They are not felt, while we read, as declarations published to the world, – but almost as secrets whispered to chosen ears. Who is there that feels, for a moment, that the voice which reaches the inmost recesses of his heart is speaking

> to the careless multitudes around him? Or, if we do so remember, the words seem to pass by others like air, and to find their way to the hearts for whom they were intended, – kindred and sympathizing spirits, who discern and own that secret language, of which the privacy is not violated, though spoken in hearing of the uninitiated, – because it is not understood. There is an unobserved beauty that smiles on us alone; and the more beautiful to us, because we feel as if chosen out from a crowd of lovers.[95]

Wilson figures Byron's poems not as broadcasts but as billets-doux, coded messages for those readers sympathetic enough to receive them.[96] Bypassing the careless multitudes, the poems avoid the Romantic sense of alienation by appearing as communications between intimates. Those communications are 'disclosures', referring back to a pre-textual Byron and revealing the details of his subjectivity. Twin engines drove the hermeneutic of intimacy. Firstly, it relied on the belief that Byron revealed himself in his poetry, though this revelation was never stable or complete. A large part of the poems' attraction for their first readers was the evidence they offered of an ur-Byron, a non-textual or pre-textual George Gordon with hidden subjective depths. Secondly, it gave the impression that his poems were not only the effusions of a particularly fascinating individual, but that they could also offer a kind of access to him.[97]

For many of Byron's first readers, buying, reading, reading aloud, lending, borrowing, copying into commonplace books, annotating and discussing Byron's poetry were the central activities among a group of practices aimed at investigating Byron the man in order to know more about him or relate more intimately to him. One of the many readers who wrote Byron a fan letter was anxious that 'Your Lordship may perhaps smile, and with a smile not wholly free from satire, that one to whom you are personally entirely unknown should thus take the liberty of addressing you.' But she was also certain that 'he who is known through the medium of his works, cannot be uninteresting even to a stranger'.[98] The poems fostered this impression, as I will show, by figuring reading as a form of relationship, a 'para-social interaction' that enabled an intimate bond.[99] When they also suggested that bodies could be read like texts and that texts could metonymically substitute for bodies, they charged that encounter with erotic undertones. Landon worked in similar ways, as Emma Francis suggests. She 'arouses but then holds off sexuality', creating 'a huge sexual tension which is never fully released'.[100] Reading Byron's poems was supplemented by such activities as buying and looking at portraits of Byron, or illustrations in which the Byronic hero was represented as the poet, soliciting introductions to Byron, writing to him, dressing in Byronic fashion, reading newspapers, cartoons or reviews, and falling in love, either with the noble lord or violently, passionately and hopelessly, as his characters were wont to do. The hermeneutic of intimacy, then, is an intertextual paradigm for reading celebrity texts, seeded by the texts themselves and the ways in which they were published, propagated by a wider print culture, and variously enacted by individual readers, which, although it may not be consciously articulated or adopted, is difficult to avoid.

The hermeneutic of intimacy succeeded commercially because it marketed as a commodity an escape from the standardised impersonality of commodity culture. It therefore had attractions for both entrepreneurs and consumers, and answered the problem of individuation through consumption. If our patterns of consumption define us as individuals, how will we remain convinced of our own uniqueness while consuming mass-produced standardised products? The hermeneutic of intimacy allows readers to imagine that those endlessly copied poems are for them alone, not for the careless multitude.[101] This kind of reading then becomes the basis for claiming cultural distinction. Laying claim to the virtues of sympathy and perspicuity enables discriminating readers to distinguish their understanding of a celebrity from that of those around them, making them 'feel as if chosen out from a crowd of lovers'. While the rest read merely adequately, discerning readers have 'chosen ears'. Sympathy touches 'the inmost recesses' of their hearts. They are the 'kindred and sympathising spirits' who hear meaning in words that 'pass by others like air'. Numbered among the 'initiated', they feel as though the poems' 'secrets' are intended for them.

These techniques of branding and reading relied on assumptions about subjectivity which the celebrity apparatus played an important part in sponsoring. Branding an identity that would be amenable to commercial promotion required subjectivity to be understood as self-identical over time, but continually developing towards greater self-expression or self-fulfilment. This enabled the brand to remain immediately recognisable in the crowded market and yet to be always newly interesting. The hermeneutic of intimacy required subjectivity to be understood as structured around a private interior. That interior was hidden from the view of the undiscerning, but was also continually making itself legible, expressing itself in poems where its secrets could be read by the discerning few. One commentator found this 'something quite new and peculiar, indeed, in the whole career of Byron', claiming that 'his poetry, at least a considerable portion of it, is a mirror in which are reflected the movements of his soul'.[102] Landon endorsed this Romantic understanding of poetics and subjectivity in her essay on Felicia Hemans, writing, 'Nothing is so strongly impressed on composition as the character of the writer.'[103] Critics have suggested that these ideas were among those to coalesce into a recognisably modern model of the subject in the Romantic period. What has not been understood is the role of the celebrity apparatus in normalising that model. The celebrity apparatus, I contend, championed this understanding of subjectivity not because it was 'natural', but because it fitted the commercial need for a kind of identity that could be reliably branded and consistently marketed.

As I show in the final chapter, Byron chafed against these conventions. So did Robinson and Yearsley. Both of their careers can be better understood as discontinuous series of experiments with varied models, forms and styles than as linear narratives of development. And both would foreground the difficulty of knowing anything about another individual's mind or heart. In 1793, at the height of her celebrity, Robinson stressed the impossibility of truly knowing another's pain in 'The Maniac'. The poem is a long series of questions to the maniac about his psychological distress, groundless speculations about its source and requests for him to 'tell me all thy pain' (115) so that the speaker can 'share thy pains, and soothe thy woes' (117).[104] But the maniac never answers, the speaker learns nothing and the poem remains unresolved. After several years in a celebrity apparatus that routinely assumed that secrets of her subjectivity were legible in her poems and her social performances, Robinson chose to represent an illegible subject who revealed nothing at all. Likewise, Yearsley claimed that those who accused her of ingratitude could no more understand the divinely hidden workings of the universe than they could 'scan the feelings of Lactilla's soul'.[105] These examples suggest that, whilst celebrity culture was crucial in shaping modern understandings of subjectivity, it also produced a strain of resistance to those assumptions in the writings of celebrities who found them intrusive and constricting. In Chapter 8, I examine evidence of that resistance in *Don Juan*.

Taken together, this assemblage of industrial technologies, driving ambitions and private pleasures, with its attendant techniques for branding identity and constructing intimacy, constitutes a still-unexamined strand of modernity. We will not understand why celebrities fascinate and trouble us so much until we have a more fully elaborated history of celebrity culture. Writing that history and theorising its significance means turning back to Byron, whose celebrity seemed to Thomas Macaulay to be something new and strange. 'It is certain', he wrote, 'that the interest which he excited during his life is without a parallel in literary history.'[106] I site that unparalleled interest at the historical emergence of a modern obsession not in order to immure it in its two-hundred-year-old strangeness, but to allow it to resonate with the present. If Byron's works absorb your interest, as they absorb mine, you may be experiencing a kind of fascination that refuses to be over and done with, that is not an episode in the history of literature, but an element in the historicity of the present.

2
'An Ode to the Framers of the Frame Bill': The Embarrassment of Industrial Culture

Most of Byron's critics skip over 'An Ode to the Framers of the Frame Bill', understandably eager to get to *Childe Harold's Pilgrimage,* which was published only eight days later, when Byron awoke to find himself famous.[1] To linger on the 'Ode' is to hold Byron on the threshold of fame, to capture him in a freeze frame just before his career takes off. Doing so enables us to glimpse him before it becomes clear what direction his life will take, and gives us a chance to peer behind the scenes at some of the machinery that will drive Byromania, propelling its star to the pinnacle of Romantic celebrity. Byron wrote to his political mentor Lord Holland that he was 'apprehensive that your Lordship will think me [...] *half* a *framebreaker myself*' (*BLJ*, II, 166). In this chapter, I too am half a framebreaker. The frames that I aim to break are those chronological and conceptual frames that have led critics to ignore or dismiss the 'Ode'. Incomplete understandings of legal definitions and parliamentary procedures have led critics mistakenly to frame the poem chronologically, representing it as a peevish comment on a completed legislative process. This characterisation is part of a conceptual frame in which Byron's political engagement with Luddism can be dismissed as a failed effort in self-promotion, designed to launch his career in the House of Lords. These are the frames I would break.

But I am only half a framebreaker; I will also construct three new frames in which to view the poem. The first is the corrected chronology of the Frame Bill's passage through parliament, which made it law. The second is the industrialisation of textile manufacture, on which the poem comments. The third is the industrialisation of printing, on which the poem relies for its reproduction. Byron's poem benefits from industrial printing by being published in a large-circulation newspaper produced by rapidly advancing print technology. Since that technology made Romantic celebrity culture possible, it is an essential context for studying that culture. I site 'An Ode to the Framers of the Frame Bill' where my three frames – two trajectories of technological advance and one instance of oppressive legislation – intersect. On these frames I would weave an argument for understanding 'An Ode to the Framers of the Frame Bill' as one example of Byron's activist writing. That argument will be supported by my discovery of a previously unknown reprint of Byron's poem in a Nottingham newspaper. But the argument will also oblige me to address the issue of whether the ethical effectiveness of Byron's poem on the industrialisation of textile manufacture is compromised by its complicity in the industrialisation of printing. To do so, I will draw a distinction between two kinds of poetic agency, which has implications for the broader frame in which critics of Romanticism work: on one hand, the agency of a poet over the production and distribution of his poems, which William Blake maintained in the highest degree; on the other, the agency of a text in the world, which Byron aspired to mobilise. The ode's example suggests that although Byron should perhaps have been embarrassed by industrialisation, he could also embarrass industrialisation by annotating its abuses.

Having returned from his travels, Byron fixed on the Frame Bill for his maiden speech in the House of Lords.[2] The Bill, introduced into the House of Commons by Richard Ryder, the Home Secretary, on 14 February 1812, prescribed the death penalty to people breaking weaving frames. Breaking frames was already an offence punishable with transportation for 14 years, but the Government proposed a more exemplary punishment. This was a response to the civil disturbances in the Midlands, where weavers were vandalising weaving frames in protest against wage-cuts which had reduced them to a state of near-starvation. Ryder told the Commons that 'the ground on which he proposed the bill, was this, that if the offence were permitted to be perpetrated as it had been, it would threaten serious danger to the state'.[3] The Tory ministry was trying to prevent the rioting from turning into a full-scale insurrection and, as D. N. Raymond dryly asserts, 'the easiest method of procedure was, in their opinion, so to terrorise the weavers that they would submit with more amenity to unemployment and starvation'.[4] The Commons passed the Bill on 20 February.

Lord Liverpool introduced the Bill to the House of Lords, where it received its first reading on Friday, 21 February 1812; as was customary at a first reading, no debate took place that day.[5] The following Monday, 24 February, it was ordered that the Bill receive its second reading the following day, but in fact there was no time, and the last thing the Lords did before adjourning on Tuesday was to postpone the second reading until Thursday. On Thursday, 27 February, there were two attempts further to postpone the second reading, either for 3 weeks or until the following Monday, but those motions fell, and the debate began with Byron's speech.[6] Journalists reported the speech 'very incorrectly', and Byron wrote, 'I could not recognise myself or anyone else in the Newspapers' (*BLJ*, II, 167). No Tory Lord responded to Byron, and the Lords voted to allow the Bill to pass to the committee stage on the following Monday. Lord Lauderdale, a prominent Scottish Whig, moved that the 12 common-law judges of the realm, who give judicial advice to the legislature, be summoned to attend on Monday, but this was negatived. On Friday, the Bill was again raised when the Earl of Rosslyn and Lord Lauderdale asked for a protest which they had lodged against it to be 'vacated' as 'informal and irregular'. Their request was granted, and they remade their protest the following Monday, 2 March (it was a leap year) when the Bill came up again, to be put into committee.

The committee stage is a 'committee of the whole House' and takes place in the main chamber of the House. All Lords are entitled to attend, and it is at this stage that the bill is debated in detail and amendments are proposed. It was on this Monday that Byron's 'An Ode to the Framers of the Frame Bill' was published in the *Morning Chronicle*, a London daily newspaper. After the committee stage, the House hears a report of what happened at that stage, for the benefit of those Lords who did not attend. This usually takes place some weeks later except for bills that are felt to be urgent. For the Frame Bill it happened the very next day, Tuesday, when Lord Walsingham reported amendments to the Bill. Byron scholars have described this stage incorrectly. Both D. N. Raymond in *The Political Career of Lord Byron* and, following her, Jerome McGann in his commentary to Byron's *Complete Poetical Works* write that the offence of framebreaking was reduced from a felony to a misdemeanour.[7] But according to *Cobbett's Parliamentary Debates*, which is the forerunner of *Hansard*:

> Earl Grosvenor moved an amendment, making the *attempt* to destroy frames only a misdemeanor instead of a felony without benefit of clergy, which was agreed to.[8]

The editor of the fifteenth edition of Blackstone's *Commentaries on the Laws of England*, which was standard in 1812, noted that 'misdemeanors comprehend all indictable offences, which do not amount to felony; [such as] attempts and solicitations to commit felonies'.[9]

The attempt to commit a felony was 'in many cases a misdemeanor', according to Tomlins' *Law Dictionary* of 1835, which drew extensively on Blackstone.[10] Moreover the distinction between a felony and a misdemeanour was crucial in this case, since, according to Blackstone:

> The idea of felony is indeed so generally connected with that of capital punishment, that we find it hard to separate them; and to this usage the interpretations of the law do now conform. And therefore if a statute makes any new offence felony, the law implies that it shall be punished with death [...] And, in compliance herewith, I shall for the future consider it also in the same light, as a generical term, including all capital crimes below treason[.][11]

As such, an amendment that reduced the offence of framebreaking to a misdemeanor would have wrecked the Bill, since it would have made capital punishment all but impossible, and making the offence capital was the Bill's whole point. No such amendment was proposed, but nonetheless, since Luddites could mount a defence on the grounds that they were guilty only of the lesser offence of *attempting* to destroy weaving frames, this amendment still made a substantial difference. On Thursday 5 March 1812, the amended bill was given its third reading and passed. Following parliamentary protocol, a message was sent to the House of Commons, desiring its concurrence. The Bill received the Royal assent and became law on 20 March. So, 'An Ode to the Framers of the Frame Bill' was published while the parliamentary process was still going on, but after Byron's formal contribution to it had ended. This is a poetic event and a political intervention. By framing the poem against the background of the textile industry, which inspired it, and the newspaper industry, which disseminated it, we can understand the nature of that intervention.

The first technological innovation from which the newspaper industry benefited in this period was not a printing press but a machine for making paper. The Fourdrinier papermaking machine automated the manufacture of paper, which had previously been made laboriously and expensively by hand. The machine was developed by brothers Henry and Sealy Fourdrinier and patented in England in 1803. It made paper from rags.[12] This was much faster and more efficient than hand-making paper, and the machine was widely adopted in the first decade of the century. Cheap paper meant cheaper books, journals and newspapers, which could then reach a wider and less elite audience. But the development of papermaking would have been of little value without a correspondent development in printing. Until the end of the eighteenth century, printing presses were made of wood and driven by hand. The pressman pulled a bar, which turned the screw and pressed the paper onto the inked forme (where the type was set). 'The major improvements needed to make the hand press more efficient', writes James Moran, 'were greater stability of structure; ability to print a forme at one pull; a reduction in manual effort; and an automatic return of the bar after pulling.'[13] The invention of the Stanhope press, the first printing press to be built entirely from iron, solved these problems. Charles, Third Earl of Stanhope (1753–1816) was dedicated to the advancement of science, and was able to devote considerable resources to his investigations. He invented his press around 1800 (the earliest surviving example is from 1804) but, in a politically charged act of philanthropy, he never patented it, preferring to make it as widely available as possible. He teamed up with the ironsmith Robert Walker to manufacture it. It is essentially a screw press on which the screw's leverage is compounded many times over by a system of levers. This greatly reduced the effort needed, and made it possible to print a sheet at one pull.

The Stanhope press was rapidly adopted by newspapers, which particularly needed fast printing. Even with the much faster Stanhope press, it was still necessary to set several formes in order to get the paper out on time. *The Times* purchased what it described as a 'battalion' of Stanhope presses, operated by a small army of pressmen, on which the paper was printed for the first 14 years of the nineteenth century.[14] The newspaper's circulation increased dramatically, and the same technology enabled the growth of the whole periodical market. Even before this growth there was considerable anxiety among the Establishment about popular reading and its potential for demagoguery. The Government responded to this anxiety about mob reading by raising advertisement duty and the stamp tax.[15] This made papers costing 6–7 d too expensive for all but the wealthier individuals, but coffee houses, gentlemen's clubs, barbers' shops and pubs took in large numbers of papers, and in the pubs they could be read out to those who could not read them for themselves.[16] Its larger circulation enabled *The Times* to increase from four pages to twelve in 1803 and to increase its advertising revenue as more manufacturers realised the advantages of tapping into the emerging mass consumer market.[17] Increased circulation meant increased political clout, and during the alarm of Luddism, a writer in the *Quarterly Review* asserted that 'anarchist journalists' were 'inflaming the turbulent temper of the manufacturer (i.e. the labourer in manufacturing industry), and disturbing the quiet attachment of the peasant to those institutions under which he and his fathers have dwelt in peace'.[18]

The *Morning Chronicle*, which published Byron's poem, had become famous for its political reporting since it was founded in 1769. Its first proprietor, William 'Memory' Woodfall, would sit in the public gallery of the House of Commons, where note taking was forbidden, and listen to the debates. At the end of the day he would go back to the office and write 'sixteen columns of word-for-word report', pioneering a now-familiar style of parliamentary reportage.[19] James Perry became editor in 1789 and under his direction the paper became the leading Whig journal in London.[20] Perry was not afraid of controversy; he was charged with seditious libel in 1793 and 1798, and was sentenced to 3 months in prison on the second occasion. Byron's choice of this paper as a medium through which to publish his poem is an important part of the creation of that poem's meaning. As I will shortly suggest, the way in which the newspaper framed the poem was both empowering and embarrassing.

Like the printing industry, the textile industry had developed new technologies and had grown rapidly at the end of the eighteenth century.[21] But it went into crisis in the early nineteenth century, when economic depression at home and the loss of export markets in Napoleonic Europe and Revolutionary America hit hard. Wage cutting was endemic in the industry, and many workers suffered drastic hardships as wages fell or failed to keep pace with rising prices. A parliamentary committee investigating the situation in 1812 heard that wages were on average one-third lower than they had been in 1807 and before.[22] The workers' distress was exacerbated by at least three other factors, including the practice of payment in truck; the introduction of cheaply produced low-quality stockings known as 'cut-ups'; and the possibility of hiring juvenile and unskilled labourers owing to the lapsed apprenticeship laws, which flooded the labour market and further depressed wages in a practice known as 'colting'.[23] The use of new wide weaving frames, which weavers were forced to rent from their employer or from an independent entrepreneur, often at exorbitant rates, also had its part to play in the industry's degradation. It was this factor that Byron particularly stressed in his speech. Between 1780 and 1830 workers were reduced from comparative prosperity and independence to crippling poverty and complete dependence on their employer.

The situation reached a crisis in 1811–1812, when what E. P. Thompson calls 'the supreme grievance of continuous hunger' was added to existing grievances.[24] The weavers petitioned Parliament for relief, establishing a prototype Trade Union.[25] The Government's refusal to intervene marks 'a crisis between paternalism and *laissez-faire*' which grew from the new science of political economy.[26] The degradation had begun first in the cotton industry, then in wool and worsted, but Luddism first appeared among the framework-knitters of Byron's Nottinghamshire, who wove stockings and lace. In March 1811, a riot in the Nottinghamshire village of Arnold saw 60 weaving frames broken, and sparked a series of disturbances in the area that lasted several weeks. But it was in November that, according to E. P. Thompson, 'Luddism appeared in a much more disciplined form':

> Frame-breaking was no longer the work of 'rioters' but of smaller, disciplined bands, who moved rapidly from village to village at night. From Nottinghamshire it spread to parts of Leicestershire and Derbyshire, and continued without intermission until February 1812.[27]

The Government, fearing Jacobinism and mob violence, moved to quell the disturbances and restore what was for the weavers an intolerable order, with the introduction of the Frame Bill.

Byron seems to have placed more weight on the role of new technology in producing the Luddite disturbances than recent historians do.[28] He noted to Lord Holland, in the letter in which he begins to work out the argument for his speech, that 'by the adoption of a certain kind of frame 1 man performs ye. work of 7 – 6 are thus thrown out of business' (*BLJ*, II, 165). Byron learned his speech by heart, and practised some parts of it in front of Robert Charles Dallas, who reported that 'he altered the natural tone of his voice, which was sweet and round, into a formal drawl, and he prepared his features for a part – it was a youth declaiming a task'.[29] But regardless of how effective Byron's oratory was, the Whigs were in opposition, and it was unlikely that they could block the Bill's passage. Byron, however, had other methods of resistance. We don't know when he wrote 'An Ode to the Framers of the Frame Bill'; there is no extant manuscript, and the only letter that refers to the poem is one to Perry, the editor of the *Morning Chronicle*, dated 1 March, which contains a correction to the poem (which Perry had presumably received in a previous and now lost letter). Perry had therefore accepted the poem within 2 days of Byron's speech. The poem has left no trace in the memoirs or letters of Byron's circle, so it seems likely that he didn't tell many people about it.[30] It was published anonymously, and not known to be Byron's until 1880. 'I wish you could insert it tomorrow for a particular reason', Byron directed the editor (*BLJ*, II, 166). On the following day the Bill was due to be raised in the House again, and put into committee. Lauderdale and Rosslyn would enter their protest against it, as Byron may well have known. He wanted the poem's stinging satire to be ringing in their Lordships' ears as they debated.

The ode satirically celebrates the achievement of the Lord Chancellor, Lord Eldon, and the Home Secretary, Richard Ryder, in coming up with such a solution to the problem of the troublesome weavers. Byron adopts the voice of a Tory, but the mask is always slipping to reveal his satirical intent. He obliquely engages with the discourse of political economy in the following lines:

> Men are more easily made than machinery –
> Stockings fetch better prices than lives –
> Gibbets on Sherwood will *heighten* the scenery,
> Showing how Commerce, *how* Liberty thrives!
>
> (13–16)

This mocks a Malthusian fear of the rate at which the poor breed and a dilettantish regard for sublime landscapes. The Government attempts in the Frame Bill to safeguard the rule of law, enforcing the harsh (so-called) laws of political economy on a population who, it is felt, would submit contentedly if only they could understand that a *laissez-faire* approach made for the long-term good. The Tory ministers draw a line beyond which the weavers may not step on pain of death. Byron criticises them for stepping beyond the pale of responsible and benevolent governance. Men must not be sacrificed to technological advances, nor commerce pursued at the expense of liberty. By putting 'Commerce' and 'Liberty' together, Byron suggests that for his imagined speaker, they are synonyms. The free market makes the free man. In fact, the poem argues, there is considerable friction between the two terms, and the Government is on the wrong side.

But not everyone takes the Government's view; as the poem goes on to make clear:

> Some folks for certain have thought it was shocking,
> When Famine appeals and when Poverty groans,
> That life should be valued at less than a stocking,
> And breaking of frames lead to breaking of bones.

> If it should prove so, I trust, by this token,
> (And who will refuse to partake in the hope?)
> That the frames of the fools may be first to be *broken*,
> Who, when asked for a *remedy*, sent down a *rope*.
>
> (25–32)

If framebreaking is to result in violence against individuals, Byron argues from the safety of his anonymity, let it be against the framers of the Bill, not against the framebreakers. The pun on 'frames', as both weaving technology and bodies, suggests the threat of personal violence which is just beneath the surface of Luddism (and which would, in fact, shortly burst out) and the hypocrisy of a legal system that would put down violence with violence. A Government which would deploy against its own people 'Grenadiers, Volunteers, Bow-street Police, / Twenty-two Regiments, a score of Jack Ketches', and in fact more troops than had been engaged in the Peninsula War, twelve thousand in all, is shown to be scared and unforgivably callous (18–19). Such violence defends not the rule of law but the interests of the factory owners and the ruling oligarchy. The fools will get their comeuppance, 'I trust, by this token'. '[B]y this token' means both 'by the logic that leads from framebreaking to personal violence (judicial or otherwise)' and 'by means of this poem'. The ode itself is a token, with currency in the framebreaking debate, with political clout.

Discerning and evaluating the nature and extent of that clout – the poem's agency – is the challenge for a historical criticism committed to finding meaning in poetic events and the intersections of power-relations that they crystallise. The token of the ode will be *only* a token gesture unless it is inscribed within a frame which gives it a degree of power. Malcolm Kelsall, in one of the few critical responses to the ode, argues that it appropriates the crisis for an attack on the Government, without proposing any remedy, 'that being the classic Whig strategy'.[31] As such 'this jingle' fails completely for Kelsall as a political poem, in line with his argument that 'the life of Byron is of no political significance'.[32] However, Kelsall writes that the poem appeared 'subsequent to the debate', and was Byron's 'verse account of what had happened'.[33] This mistakes the chronology of the Bill's passage through Parliament, inaccurately suggesting that Byron is powerlessly commenting on a completed event, whereas in fact he is intervening in an ongoing process, in a poem that may well have influenced the important amendment that reduced attempted framebreaking to a misdemeanour. Byron had large ambitions for his own agency as a peer and a poet, and Kelsall underestimates the agency of this poem. To understand that agency, I need to turn back to the context in which the poem was published and republished.

Newspaper publication empowered Byron in several ways. He could respond quickly to the Bill through that medium, speaking on Thursday and publishing the poem the following Monday. He could also guarantee a large, politically concerned and well-informed audience. The *Morning Chronicle* had reported the parliamentary debate on Friday's front page, including a one-paragraph précis of Byron's speech, so regular readers of the paper were familiar with the issues. Since it appeared in the leading Whig journal of the day, many of the Lords must have read the poem before they went to the House that morning to consider the Bill again and, although no records exist, it seems likely that the House of Lords itself took a copy of the paper.[34] But the way the paper framed the poem may have undercut its chance to make a difference. The *Morning Chronicle* consisted of only four pages (i.e. a single sheet folded in half), each of which had five columns. Since 2 March was a Monday, and there was no Parliamentary news to report from the previous day, the front and back pages were entirely devoted to advertising. Page one contained advertisements for a variety of goods and services, including announcements of lectures, bankruptcies, usurers, 'New-invented folding round hats' and 'Bradberry's patent spectacles'. Most of the reportage was on page two and the first column of page three. Page three also contained a gossip column, including a report on the King's health, theatre reviews, a report on Humphry Davy's recent lecture and a note on ladies' fashions for March. At the bottom of the third column readers were informed of an 'extraordinary circumstance':

> A few days ago a cat, belonging to Mr Merle, auctioneer, of Brighton, gave birth to three kittens, each of which has two heads! – They are all alive at the present moment, and free to the inspection of the curious.[35]

Byron's poem was at the top of the next column. It was immediately followed by two epigrams, also by anonymous contributors, who exercised their wit on 'the recent loppings in Bushy Park' and on the unlikely subject of a legal case for slander being fought between two Jews. Framed by such light comedy on both sides, Byron's political ode was not in auspicious company.

The one thing that would have made it blaze out of the page and into every eye – his name – he withheld, writing to the editor, 'of course, do *not* put *my name* to the thing' (*BLJ*, II, 166). Even before his authorial celebrity began in earnest, the poetic comment of a Lord on the business of the House of Lords would have drawn attention to the poem, not least from the legislators themselves. A public pledge of support for the Luddites' version of direct action would have confirmed the workers' belief that the disturbances were 'countenanced by individuals of a higher class and description, who are to declare themselves at a future time'.[36] Yet Byron's name did feature in that day's *Morning Chronicle*. The last paragraph on page two read:

> Lord BYRON, who spoke on the Nottingham Felony Bill on Thursday, evinced considerable eloquence. – His talents have been already established by his literary productions, but it does not always happen that able writers are gifted with the powers of elocution.[37]

Although James Perry kept his promise not to put Byron's name to the poem, he inserted a compliment to his noble contributor which drew attention to his poetry and his politics. The *Morning Chronicle*, then, enabled Byron's poem to reach the eyes of the legislators before the end of the debate, but framed it between light-hearted squibs which detracted from its interventionist potential.

But while this was the only printing of the poem that Byron authorised, it was not the only printing to occur. In Nottinghamshire, where the insurrectionary action was taking place, there were two local newspapers: the *Nottingham Journal* and the *Nottingham Review and General Advertiser*. The *Nottingham Journal* came out weekly on Saturday and was broadly Tory in its political allegiance. It reported on Luddite disturbances and the Frame Bill debates throughout this period, mentioning Byron by name on 7 March 1812 in its account of the House of Lords debates. It did not regularly publish any poetry. Its rival, the *Nottingham Review*, was published weekly on Friday and had a broadly Whig allegiance. In the issue for 6 March 1812, the first to appear after Byron's poem was first published, there were extensive reports on the Frame Bill debates. On page four the editors wrote that they had left out their regular comic column of 'lucubrations' in order to make room for more information on this important bill. The Frame Bill, they noted, 'met with a formidable opposition in the House of Lords, and by no member of that august assembly more than by a Noble Lord from this neighbourhood'.[38] On the same page they printed an 'abstract' of the Frame Bill, and immediately below that they reprinted Byron's ode.

The ode appeared on a different page from the only other poem printed in that issue of the *Review*, which was also a political poem that mentioned Luddism.[39] Framed by political reportage and editorial, it was presented in the context of informed political debate, and not in the company of comic epigrams, as it had been in the *Morning Chronicle*. Geographically closer to the riots that occasioned it, the poem must have been read out in Nottingham's pubs, and may have circulated orally among the weavers there. When it was reprinted, 'An Ode to the Framers of the Frame Bill' took a step closer to being a genuine working-class ballad, of which there are many examples associated with the Luddites.[40] The reprinted text appeared as eight quatrains instead of four octaves, presenting the poem in a modified ballad stanza. The fact that this reprinting appears to have been unknown to all previous critics of the poem may have led them to underestimate its agency. But, as with its first appearance, this republication constrained the poem even as it empowered it. In the penultimate line, the word 'frames' in the phrase 'the frames of the fools, may be first to be *broken*' was replaced with a long dash.[41] The editors of the *Nottingham Review* took fright and tried to take the sting out of the poem's tail. They were almost certainly unaware that the poem was by the 'Noble Lord from this neighbourhood' whose speech they had praised, and Byron, in London, was almost certainly unaware that his poem had been reprinted. The infrastructure of industrial publication that made Byron's intervention felt in both the House of Lords and the mills of Nottinghamshire also drastically curtailed his control over the text of his poem.

As a political intervention, Byron's poem benefited greatly from the rapid printing and wide circulation of newspapers in the period. This was made possible by advances in technology which paralleled those in the textile industry. Industrialisation's upheavals came slightly later to printing, when the Stanhope press was superseded by the powerful cultural technology of the steam press. Friedrich Koenig, the inventor of the cylinder press, which harnessed the power of steam to printing for the first time, came to London in 1806, where he began to develop his press for the printer Thomas Bensley. Koenig teamed up with Andreas Bauer, an engineer, and they developed the cylinder press over a number of years. In 1810 they were still working on the Stanhope screw and platen model, but by 1813 they had a cylinder machine ready to show to newspaper proprietors.[42] James Perry of the *Morning Chronicle* didn't buy, but John Walter II of *The Times* ordered two 'double' machines, which took Koenig another year to develop and build.[43] The first issue of *The Times* to be printed by steam was that of 29 November 1814. Walter had installed the new presses in secret in a building adjacent to *The Times'* office. He told the pressmen, who worked the battalion of Stanhope presses, to wait for late news from the Continent. This was not an unusual occurrence, as *The Times* prided itself on its foreign correspondents. In fact there was no late news. At 6 o'clock in the morning, Walter went into the press room and told the men that the whole issue had already been printed by steam and that the entire printing workforce was redundant. No doubt mindful of the Luddite disturbances in the Midlands, he went accompanied by a force of men to control the pressmen if they turned violent, and promised to continue their wages until they could be found similar employment.[44] It must have been a tense moment. The pressmen, astonished, departed peacefully.

The Times editorial for that day declared, 'Our journal of this day presents to the public the practical result of the greatest improvement connected with printing, since the discovery of the art itself.' Describing printing as an art and Koenig as 'the artist', the editorial presented the new technology as 'a system of machinery almost organic', deploying a rhetoric of the natural in support of technological advance. Such an advance 'relieves the human frame of its most laborious efforts' so that 'little more remains for man to do than to attend upon and watch this unconscious agent in its operations'. The steam press is presented as a labour-saving device, freeing men from the troublesome business of working at the hand press. The redundant pressmen, looking for other work, are not mentioned. Finally, the editorial figures the paper's economic speculation on the new machine and the successful return on its investment as a primarily emotional matter:

> Our share in this event has, indeed, only been in the application of the discovery, under an agreement with the Patentees, to our own particular business; yet few can conceive – even with this limited interest – the various disappointments and deep anxiety to which we have for a long course of time been subjected.[45]

Describing how the invention of the engineer Koenig has superseded that of the aristocratic philanthropist and radical Stanhope, *The Times* overlooks the fact that the press could not have been developed without investment from speculative publishers, eager to make money from it; suggests that more than a business deal this has been an adventure 'few can conceive'; and foregrounds, with the tone of a new father, the 'deep anxiety' 'we' felt. Again, that 'we' does not include the redundant pressmen. So Walter deployed a three-pronged strategy in managing his workmen: to threaten them with a force of men who would answer their violence with violence; to conciliate them with a promise to continue their wages for the time being; to elide their distress from public notice in his editorial.

Following the story of publishing's industrialisation this far enables us to see the parallels between the industries of textile production and printing, and to locate 'An Ode to the Framers of the Frame Bill' at the intersection of my three historical frames: the process by which the Frame Bill became law; the industrialisation of textile manufacture and its adoption of new technology; and a similar process in printing. There are two ways to theorise the position, at this nexus, of Byron's poem. The first way is to view the poem as part of the problem with which it deals. In this view, Byron's poem about the dangers of industrialisation is tainted by its contact with industrial publishing. The poem is itself an industrial production in a technologically developing industry and therefore cannot be a neutral place from which Byron can comment on the issue. As such, Byron becomes complicit in the process of dehumanising industrialisation that he deplores when he benefits from the march of technology. Out on a limb, Byron buys the poem's political clout only by incurring the culpable cost of involvement with the enemy. In this view, Byron is embarrassed by industrial publishing. Indeed, Byron's celebrity would continue to be closely bound up with the introduction of the steam press as that technology made possible new forms of public life. When the 'Ode' came out, *Childe Harold's Pilgrimage* was already at the printers. Just eight days later it would burst forth, firmly associating Byron's celebrity with the new printing technologies that met the demand for that poem and the tales that appeared in rapid succession afterwards. 'I am persuaded', James Webster told him, 'that you must write by steam.'[46] The problems with this aggressive characterisation, however, are severe. Byron would have known very little about the developments in printing, and even if he had known more, this is a situation he could do very little to avoid. Blake had produced books by hand that remained completely within his control and outside the sphere of industrial publishing. But Blake's disciplines were not available to Byron, and Blake's books could not be produced as fast or distributed as widely as the *Morning Chronicle* or the *Nottingham Review*, and therefore could not have the same impact. And the ode did make an impact, reaching a large and informed audience before the end of the Lords' debate.

The second way to characterise this nexus of forces is to see the poem as part of the solution. In this view, Byron appropriates the technology of the press, repossessing it from those who, like Walter, would use it without compassion for the men who worked in the industry, and following the example of Stanhope, who sponsored technological advance for all. Championing the Luddites, Byron puts industrial printing in the service of the workers. He asserts that the problem is not technology itself, whether in weaving or in printing, but the uses to which technology is put. As such the poem provides an example of how industrialisation can be turned to humane ends. Seen from this angle, Byron does not 'buy' the poem's agency at any price, but takes it right from under the nose of the industrial revolution. He is a fifth columnist, redirecting the energies of early industrial capitalism from within. He embarrasses industrial publishing. There are also problems with this position, but less fatal ones. The trouble is that, as I've already suggested, this is not the expression of Byron's untrammelled agency, as it might appear to be. Byron can't control the text of his poem, or the text that surrounds it, in the newspapers, nor maintain his anonymity uncompromised.

There is a trade-off here between two kinds of agency: first the poet's agency over the production of his text, which Blake strove to maintain; secondly, the agency of the text in the world, its ability to make a difference. Byron relaxes his control over his text in order to guarantee it greater worldly agency. Most historicist criticism has been sceptical about the political agency either of individuals or of texts. Having inherited the Foucauldian idea that power is all-pervasive and endowed with an unending capacity to stage, contain and co-opt its own subversion, critics have been profoundly pessimistic about the possibility of a political intervention that would avoid unwitting collusion with its opponent. Distinguishing between the kinds of agency helps to temper that pessimism. The infrastructure of industrial publication, then, both empowers and compromises Byron in very specific ways.

Although 'An Ode to the Framers of the Frame Bill' is in many ways untypical of Byron's work, the complexities of the poem's position in Romantic political and print culture are representative of the complexities of the interpretative field that stretches between the poles of Lord Byron the cultural producer and Lord Byron the cultural product. Byron is constantly in motion between these two poles, on the axis between producer and product, actor and acted-on. The example of 'An Ode to the Framers of the Frame Bill' suggests that the attempt to map his movements on that axis should be a central concern of Byron's critics. Reframing the ode makes visible the enabling, but potentially embarrassing, industrial technologies that will be a crucial component of the modern celebrity apparatus.

3
Childe Harold's Pilgrimage: Beginning the Hermeneutic of Intimacy

I would begin at the beginning, if I knew where *Childe Harold's Pilgrimage* began.[1] But the poem begins at least three times. The prefatory poem 'To Ianthe' and the first two stanzas dramatise Byron's attempt to figure out a relationship with his readers and to figure it into his writing. In the first two stanzas, written a year and eight months apart, Byron ironically employed two sets of opening conventions, each of which signalled a generic affiliation, identified a literary tradition and targeted a specific audience.[2] When he added 'To Ianthe' in the seventh edition, he adopted a third set of conventions and rethought the poem's opening once again. This chapter investigates how Byron configured and refigured the relationship between writer and reader at the beginning of *Childe Harold's Pilgrimage*. In the process, the collaborative, encoded intimacy of a coterie was replaced by the constructed, hermeneutic intimacy between producer and consumer in industrial culture. Byron began adding to the poem's opening in response to several painful bereavements, but his revisions helped to construct the hermeneutic paradigm that would govern his celebrity career.

In Byron's fair copy manuscript, the poem opens with the received second stanza, beginning 'Whilome in Albion's isle there dwelt a youth / Who ne in virtue's ways did take delight' (1. 2). This recalls *The Faerie Queene*'s first line and, along with the stanza's form and archaic diction, signals a burlesque Spenserianism. There was a revival of interest in Spenser by both scholarly commentators and poetic imitators in the second half of the eighteenth century, which spawned, and was reinforced by, editions, anthologies and educational practices that appeared in mid-century and substantially shaped the poet's subsequent reception.[3] While Spenser's eighteenth-century imitators revived interest in his poetic practice, they did not necessarily endorse his ideology. By Byron's time, Spenserianism instead connoted Whiggism, a somewhat quaint and burlesqued antiquarianism and, given Spenser's difficulty, a degree of erudition.[4] Greg Kucich has shown how pervasive this tradition's influence on Romanticism was, and Byron's preface makes his debt explicit, mentioning James Thomson and James Beattie as his most immediate antecedents.[5] Drawing on this tradition, the stanza prepares us for a burlesque Spenserian romance centred on Harold and narrated with ironic moralising.[6]

But when Byron revised the poem for publication, he added a new first stanza which drew on a different set of conventions. The new first stanza employs the conventions for invoking the muse while maintaining a sophisticated, ironic detachment:

> Oh, thou! in Hellas deem'd of heav'nly birth,
> Muse! form'd or fabled at the minstrel's will!
> Since sham'd full oft by later lyres on earth,
> Mine dares not call thee from thy sacred hill:
> Yet there I've wander'd by thy vaunted rill;
> Yes! sigh'd o'er Delphi's long deserted shrine,
> Where, save that feeble fountain, all is still;
> Nor mote my shell awake the weary Nine
> To grace so plain a tale – this lowly lay of mine.
>
> (1. 1)

The muse is self-consciously presented as a poetic fiction; faith in her inspiration occurs elsewhere and at other times, in 'Hellas'. This invocation comes after the (imaginary) age of faith in the muses; muses are now created by poets and do not create them.[7] But it isn't doubt about the muse's existence that stops the poet calling on her. Instead, Byron turns away from the sceptical position of the first two lines and adopts the conventional stance of playing down his poem's claims on the goddess's attention. He arrives belatedly, in a debased and mundane age, with only a 'lowly lay' to sing. And yet Byron claims an alternative authority, because he has been to the home of the muses himself. The stanza's twists and turns display an ambivalent attitude towards the conventions of public poetry. In an uneasy combination of self-assertion and *diminutio*, the self-authorising poet, when coming before the public, feels the need to invoke a muse in whom he professes not to believe. Each of the first two stanzas, then, is shaped in ironic relation to two generic sets of opening conventions. They form two examples of what Edward

Said calls 'transitive beginnings', each of which inaugurates a project 'with (or for) an anticipated end, or at least expected continuity'.[8] Part of the difficulty in beginning to read *Childe Harold's Pilgrimage* lies in the effort to orientate oneself in relation to these potentially contradictory signals and work out what kind of poem this is.[9]

Byron's preface implies a Spenserian line of descent via Ariosto to Thomson, Beattie and Byron. But a genealogy of poets will not stand alone; it requires a genealogy of readers. James Thomson's *The Castle of Indolence* (1748), Byron's most important model, addressed a double audience. Written over a period of 15 years, it began as a private poem and only later evolved a public dimension. Thomson's friend and biographer Patrick Murdoch wrote that 'It was, at first, little more than a few detached stanzas, in the way of raillery on himself, and on some of his friends, who would reproach him with indolence, while he thought them, at least, as indolent as himself.' 'But he saw very soon', Murdoch continued, 'that the subject deserved to be treated more seriously, and in a form fitted to convey one of the most important moral lessons.'[10] Thomson's poem therefore had a dual readership, with a coterie of friends standing between the poet and the public. Byron's Spenserian second stanza imagines a similarly split audience. On the one hand, a faceless public; on the other, a limited, sophisticated and sympathetic audience of friends. This coterie would match the poet's claim to step into a tradition of writing by stepping into a tradition of reading, taking their place as descendants of Thomson's coterie.[11] These were the young men who would recognise their 1809 party at Newstead Abbey in the description of Harold's ancestral home:

> Monastic dome! condemned to uses vile!
> Where Superstition once had made her den
> Now Paphian girls were known to sing and smile;
> And monks might deem their time was come agen,
> If ancient tales say true, nor wrong these holy men.
>
> (1. 7)

The mock-sententiousness, signalled by the exclamation marks and the comically archaic spelling of 'agen', enlists the shared memory of dressing up as monks at Newstead.[12] This mode, signalled by the second stanza, may raise hackles among the staid public, but is certain to raise a laugh among Byron's friends.

But when Byron wrote a new first stanza for the poem, he turned away from this convivial coterie and towards a public audience familiar with the conventions of epic invocation. Unlike the audience implied by stanza two, this audience is not divided into those who get the in-jokes and those who don't. While both conventions require the competence of Stanley Fish's 'informed reader', Byron also demanded a second kind of knowledge from some of his readers, as Thomson had done.[13] This was the specific initiation to otherwise hidden meanings, which they gained through knowledge of the poet's life. I contend that when Byron began writing *Childe Harold's Pilgrimage*, he imagined a small audience of friends who would mediate between him and the unpredictable reaction of a larger and more public audience. The loss of that sense of a mediating audience deprived Byron of the protective intimacy of a coterie and precipitated him into the constructed intimacy of celebrity.

This argument requires that the poem be viewed neither as an ahistorical conceptual unity nor as a single publication event. Rather, following Jack Stillinger's textual pluralism, I understand the poem as existing in several states, extending through stages of composition, revision and publication in multiple editions.[14] The received view of Byron's manuscript revisions is that he began writing a burlesque Romance in a broadly comic and satiric style, which set out to recount his travels and attack various aspects of British policy. When he returned to England, however, a series of deaths caused Byron to rework the poem, making it more despondent, and ending it on an elegiac note close to despair.[15] This account's limitation is that it views the poem as developing towards the point of publication in response to the effects of events on Byron's state of mind. This truncates the poem's evolution, which continued beyond its first publication. It also mistakes the significance for the poem of the deaths of Matthews and Edleston. These deaths left Byron feeling not only bereft of friends, but also deprived of a coterie audience. Between his first draft and his final revision, Byron lost one set of readers (whose spokesman would have been Charles Skinner Matthews) and found another (whose projection is Lady Charlotte Harley). This movement from one audience to another is the movement into celebrity, where the difference between a spokesman who can answer back and a projection who enables fantasies marks the start of a new relationship between Byron and his audience.

Facing the common Romantic experience of alienation between author and audience, Byron targeted a coterie with his private references and ironic Spenserianism. This arrangement would guarantee that someone would read the poem sympathetically and would offer some compensation in the face of widespread hostility or indifference. As Lucy Newlyn suggests, creating restricted and sympathetic audiences such as this was 'a crucial component in the protective armoury of authorship at this time'.[16] Byron's reading-circle formed in Cambridge, where he met John Cam Hobhouse, Scrope Berdmore Davies, Francis Hodgson, Douglas Kinnaird and Charles Skinner Matthews. Byron wrote, '[Matthews], Hobhouse, D[avies], and myself, formed a coterie of our own at Cambridge and elsewhere' (*BLJ*, II, 93).[17] This circle of friends formed through the Cambridge Whig club, the party at Newstead in 1809 and their shared fascination with classical homoerotica.[18] The leading light of the group, both intellectually and socially, was Matthews. The son of a Hertfordshire MP, Matthews was a brilliant scholar, a sparkling wit, a sceptic, a sodomite and a radical. He occupied Byron's Cambridge rooms while Byron was away and led the revelry at Newstead – pretending to be a ghost to frighten Hobhouse and threatening to throw the tedious Webster out of the window.[19] 'There was the stamp of immortality in all he said or did', wrote Byron, 'I was indeed so sensible of his infinite superiority that though I did not envy, I stood in awe of it' (*BLJ*, II, 93). Matthews was at the centre of a close-knit group of university contemporaries who shared similar views and experiences. The coterie's reading of *Childe Harold's Pilgrimage* would stand reassuringly alongside its more uncertain reception by a wider audience. These cognoscenti could be relied upon to lend a sympathetic ear.

This group developed a shared vocabulary of playfully coded references, which revolved around their necessarily secretive sexual interests. This collective discourse appears clearly in the exchange of letters between Byron and Hobhouse, in Falmouth awaiting a passage to the Continent, and Matthews, in Cambridge. 'My dear Mathieu,' Byron wrote on 22 June 1809:

> I take up the pen which our friend has for a moment laid down merely to express a vain wish that you were with us in this delectable region, as I do not think Georgia itself can emulate in the capabilities or incitements to the 'Plen. and optabil. – Coit.' the port of Falmouth and parts adjacent. – – We are surrounded by Hyacinths & other flowers of the most fragrant [na]ture, & I have some intention of culling a handsome Bouquet to compare with the exotics we expect to meet in Asia. – One specimen I shall certainly carry off, but of this hereafter. – Adieu Mathieu! (*BLJ*, I, 206–7)

The abbreviated Latin phrase, from a passage in Petronius' *Satyricon* describing the seduction of a boy, was identified by Gilbert Highet and translated as 'complete intercourse to one's heart's desire' (*BLJ*, I, 207n). Matthews's response shows how much he enjoyed cracking Byron's codes and creating new ones of his own:

> In transmitting my dispatches to Hobhouse, mi carissime *βυρον* [Byron] I cannot refrain from addressing a few lines to yourself: chiefly to congratulate you on the splendid success of your first efforts in *the mysterious*, that style in which more is meant than meets the Eye. I shall have at you in that style before I fold up this sheet.
>
> Hobhouse too is uncommonly well, but I must recommend that he do not in future put a *dash* under his mysterious significances, such a practice would go near to letting the cat out of the bag, should the tabellarians [i.e. postmen] be inclined to peep: And I positively decree that every one who professes *ma methode* do spell the term wch designates his calling with an e at the end of it – *methodiste,* not method*ist*, and pronounce the word in the French fashion. Every one's taste must revolt at confounding ourselves with that sect of horrible, snivelling fanatics.[20]

The mysterious style holds the group together in shared and unwritten understandings encoded in a sophisticated and esoteric vocabulary of French, Italian, Greek and Latin terms. The code is a mark of distinction both because it displays their class and education and because their sexual identity prevents them from being 'confounded' with the common crowd. It's unclear whether John Edleston, the Cambridge chorister to whom Byron was passionately attached at this time, was in on this game, but he and Byron had codes of their own, and Byron wrote at least one note to Edleston in cipher (*BLJ*, XI, 173). After his death, Edleston would appear in the Thyrza poems as the most sustained and mysterious of Byron's codes.

Louis Crompton suggests that Byron's Cambridge circle shared a 'gay identity' reinforced by these codes.[21] This description risks overstatement and anachronism, but if not a shared identity, these letters do reveal a set of shared sexual interests and a coded exchange of sexual stories. These exchanges take place in a semi-public sphere, where postmen may peep at letters, and the methodistes delight in smuggling hidden meanings past the prying eyes of the world. Amending Crompton's claim, Jerome Christensen asserts that 'this bit of correspondence describes the deliberate formation of a *literary* sense of identity'.[22] At a basic level, the number of Byron's circle who counted authorship among their avocations confirms this collective literary identity. This was not only a group of readers; it was also a group of writers of the kind that Jeffrey Cox has urged us to see as an important locus of cultural production in this period.[23] Francis Hodgson published his novel *Sir Edgar* in 1810, and John Galt was then circulating his Greek poem 'The Fair Shepherdess' ('appears to be damned nonsense', concluded Byron (*BLJ*, II, 22)).[24] Hobhouse was writing a book about his travels, and the poor sales of his miscellany are a constant topic of Byron's letters at this time.[25] He wrote to Edward Ellice:

> I do exhort you and all your acquaintance who may be possessed of a dormant half-guinea to purchase [the miscellany], and he himself (when he is worth so much money) will in return buy rhyme at the same rate from any of the said persons who shall please to be poetical. (*BLJ*, I, 255)

Byron was also planning to launch a journal to which they could all contribute, to be called *La Bagatelle* or *Lillabulero*. This scheme would bring the methodistes before the public as writers. The journal would not be a 'common magazine or review' and they wouldn't need other contributors 'if we set seriously about it'.[26] The planned journal would distinguish Byron and his friends as men of discernment, 'clubable persons with a sufficient tincture of literature' apart from the common herd (*BLJ*, II, 49). Here, then, Byron was collaboratively creating a circle of literary men who were ready to lend a sympathetic ear to each other's writings and who were well accustomed to playfully coded homoerotic communications.

In the manuscripts of *Childe Harold's Pilgrimage*, Louis Crompton identifies three points where Byron encoded meanings for these cognoscenti: in the characterisation of Harold's page, the stanzas on William Beckford and the mention of pederasty at the court of Ali Pasha.[27] The page addressed in 'Childe Harold's Good Night' was originally 'a <guilty> henchman page / a <dark-eyed> peasant boy who <loved> served his master well' (*CPW*, II, 10). The stanzas on Beckford were also revised, removing the line '<By one fair form> Gainst Nature's voice seduced to deed accurst' (*CPW*, II, 18). But although this explicit reference to Beckford's notorious homosexuality was cancelled, Byron left the description of 'wild flowers' which 'breathe' around Beckford's now-deserted house intact (1. 22). This recalls the code words in Byron's Falmouth letter, where desirable boys are 'Hyacinths & other flowers'.

The description of Ali Pasha's court originally included the lines 'For boyish minions of unhallowed love / The shameless torch of wild desire is lit, / Caressed, preferred even to woman's self above' (*CPW*, II, 63). But Byron cancelled these too after the deaths of Edleston and Matthews. There are three likely reasons for the suppressions: firstly, that Byron simply had second thoughts, perhaps after the Vere Street scandal in 1810 and the subsequent executions for sodomy in 1811, which whipped up English homophobia; secondly, that he responded to the urging of Robert Charles Dallas and John Murray to tone down elements of the poem that were likely to prove controversial; thirdly, and most importantly for my argument here, that once the audience Byron hoped to titillate with these references could no longer read them, they no longer served their purpose.

But these examples, I contend, are the textual trace of a primarily oral conception. While Byron was writing *Childe Harold's Pilgrimage*, he thought of the poem as the bare bones of the stories that he would tell *viva voce* when he was back in England. What could safely be written could then be embellished in different directions for different auditors: with urbane modesty for the folk of Southwell or racy detail for the methodistes. During the first year or so of *Childe Harold's* existence, when Byron was writing the poem on his travels but not writing about it in his letters, he repeatedly declined to give his correspondents the full story of his escapades, deferring the detail until they met on his return.[28] Unlike Hobhouse, who was 'scribbling' long letters and a book of travels with the 'two gallons Japan Ink, and several vols best blank' that he had taken with him, Byron claimed to have 'laid down [his] pen' (*BLJ*, I, 208). Instead, he planned to 'reserve all account of my adventures till we meet' (*BLJ*, I, 235). Byron's letter to Hodgson from Lisbon exhibits this deferral motif:

> Thus far we have pursued our route, and seen all sorts of marvellous sights, palaces, convents, &c. – which, being to be heard in my friend Hobhouse's forthcoming Book of Travels, I shall not anticipate by smuggling any account whatsoever to you in a private and clandestine manner. (*BLJ*, I, 215)

Here Byron set up the terms that would continue to govern his attitude towards accounts of his travels, including the poem that he was privately writing. Hobhouse is associated with writing, formality and absence, conscientiously and industriously recording his impressions and prudently investing them in a future book. Byron sets himself against this characterisation, associating himself here and elsewhere with speaking, friendship and presence, writing 'you must be satisfied with simple detail till my return, and then we will unfold the floodgates of Colloquoy [*sic*]' (*BLJ*, I, 239). Unlike Hobhouse's responsible efforts to enhance his reputation with a travel book, Byron's account of his tour is figured as contraband. Although he defers them for the present, he promises to smuggle clandestine stories back into England.

Once it transpired that Hobhouse would arrive home before Byron and get a head start on the storytelling, Byron dispatched letters to bolster his own claim to conversational authenticity. Hobhouse was 'bursting with his travels', and Byron jokingly wrote to Henry Drury that:

> I shall not anticipate his narratives, but merely beg you not to believe one word he says, but reserve your ear for me, if you have any desire to be acquainted with the truth [...] *I* am to be referred to for authenticity; and I beg leave to contradict all those things whereon he lays particular stress. But, if he soars, at any time, into wit, I give you leave to applaud, because that is necessarily stolen from his fellow-pilgrim. (*BLJ*, I, 246)

With Hobhouse back in England, Byron lost a restraining influence and gained a new correspondent. 'Give my compliments to *Matthews*', he wrote, 'I have a thousand anecdotes for him and you, but at present τι *να καμω?* [τι *να κανω?* = what to do?] I have neither time nor space, but in the words of Dawes, "I have things in store"' (*BLJ*, II, 10). From Patras he reiterated, 'I am in possession of anecdotes that would amuse you and the Citoyen, but I must defer the detail till we meet' (*BLJ*, II, 16). And he reminded Hobhouse again from Malta that 'My fantastical adventures I reserve for you and Matthieu and a bottle of Champagne' (*BLJ*, II, 46).[29] It is significant that all these promises of a commentary on his travels include Matthews, who wrote to Byron in eager anticipation of getting all the details:

> A thousand thanks for your letter, of which I had given up all hopes. Cam did me a great injustice when he said I was particular. Twould be the height of impudence in me, who am so indulgent towards myself. In one sense of the word, I would you were a little more *particular*; that is to say, minute. In some of your passages I desiderate volumes of commentary. Not that there is any obscurity – the commentary I should require would be illustrative not explanatory.[30]

Given the deferral motif in Byron's correspondence, I suggest that he intended to supply an illustrative verbal commentary not only to his letters, but to some passages of *Childe Harold's Pilgrimage*. His commentary would have embellished the coded homosexual references, and part of its pleasure would have come from the sense that his audience of cognoscenti had access to meanings denied to the public at large. By definition, we who are not initiates to that circle of erotic storytellers and codebreakers cannot claim to know which passages of *Childe Harold* Byron might have glossed, or what he might have said. But the notes, which allude frequently to Byron's travels, the Romaic materials appended to the poem, many of which were untranslated, and the mysterious Thyrza poems published in the same volume all seem to invite glosses and explanations from Byron.[31] These elements, when considered alongside the deferral motif in Byron's letters, suggest that *Childe Harold's Pilgrimage* was designed to be supplemented, and in a sense completed, by a verbal commentary for a privileged audience to whom the poem would mean more, in different ways, than it did to the commercial readership.

Shortly after he arrived back in England, with the manuscript of *Childe Harold's Pilgrimage* and the host of stories that would embellish it, Byron learnt of the deaths of his mother and of his school friend John Wingfield, of Charles Skinner Matthews and of John Edleston.[32] Byron was 'almost desolate – left almost alone in the world' (*BLJ*, II, 69). For want of anyone else to address, he apostrophised himself:

> For thee, who thus in too protracted song
> Hast sooth'd thine idlesse with inglorious lays,
> Soon shall thy voice be lost amid the throng
> Of louder minstrels in these later days:
> To such resign the strife for fading bays –
> Ill may such contest now the spirit move
> Which heeds nor keen reproach nor partial praise;
> Since cold each kinder heart that might approve,
> And none are left to please when none are left to love.
>
> (2. 94)

The public arena which Byron aimed at in the first stanza of Canto One ('the strife for fading bays') is here presented as a crowded and clamorous market, a 'throng / Of louder minstrels'. But the privileged private readership which he aimed at in the second stanza, the 'kinder heart[s]', cannot provide an alternative audience whose approbation would be worth having, because 'none are left to please when none are left to love'. The loss of 'the parent, friend, and now the more than friend' leaves Byron feeling unloved, unregarded and in a sense non-existent (2. 95). Uncertain of his audience, he is uncertain of his abilities, even his identity. 'What is my being?' he asks, 'thou hast ceased to be!' (2. 96). The deaths deform the teleological structure of the pilgrimage by making Byron figuratively homeless and therefore making homecoming impossible. He returns only 'to find fresh cause to roam' (2. 95). Byron is left feeling bereft of the mediating audience that would have come between him and the potentially hostile public.[33] There is now no one between him and 'the crowd', and he is left with no choice but 'to plunge again into the crowd' (2. 97). The end of the poem presents Byron living on after the end, having prematurely reached 'the worst of woes that wait on age' with his whole life still before him (2. 98).[34] When he turned back to revise the beginning of the poem, Byron faced the problem of trying to begin once he had arrived beyond the end. How was he to start speaking, when there was no one left to listen?

This trauma traumatised the poem. Byron added the final disconsolate stanzas of Canto Two and the first stanza of Canto One, with its implied public audience. He also inserted an elegy for Wingfield and a tribute to Matthews in a note, where he writes, 'In the short space of one month, I have lost *her* who gave me being, and most of those who had made that being tolerable' (1. 92n). The deaths of Edleston and especially Matthews – the master cryptanalyst of methodisme – deprived Byron of the sense that an audience of friends would welcome his poem. Robert Charles Dallas remembered that 'he felt himself ALONE. The town was now full; but in its concourse he had no intimates whom he esteemed, or wished to see.'[35] Byron wrote, 'my friends are dead or estranged, and my existence a dreary void' (*BLJ*, II, 92). Revising the poem for publication in this mood, Byron was placed against his will into an unmediated relation with the anonymous audience of the Romantic period. Alone in the crowd, and without any clear sense of who would read his poem, Byron grappled emotionally with the loss of his friends and poetically with the loss of his audience. But in losing one audience, Byron discovered another, creating the apparently unmediated relationship between poet and reader that characterised the hermeneutic of intimacy. That apparently unmediated relationship was in fact mediated by the intervention of industrial publication methods, under the direction of John Murray.

Dallas offered Murray *Childe Harold's Pilgrimage* after Byron had declined to send it to Cawthorn, who had published *English Bards and*

Scotch Reviewers, and Miller, having read the manuscript, had turned it down.[36] While Byron lacked any clear sense of who was going to buy the poem, Murray knew his market. He produced the first edition of five hundred copies in quarto, priced 30 s., making the book a luxury item.[37] Murray spent the relatively small amount of £19 3 s. 6 d. on newspaper advertising, but since he was only committed to five hundred copies, he could afford to rely on word of mouth.[38] Murray's biographer notes that before the day of publication, 'the publisher had already taken pains to spread abroad the merits of the poem'.[39] The target audience for the first edition, then, was few in number but very rich and very fashionable. It was not a social group in which Byron felt comfortable at this time. Murray must have had his eye on possible future editions in cheaper formats, which would reach a much wider audience, but this would be a knock-on effect from the poem's niche-success with an elite group of trendsetters.[40] William St Clair puts it succinctly:

> When the Duchess of Devonshire wrote that *Childe Harold* was 'on every table', she meant on about 12½ per cent of the tables of the few thousand families who could afford 30 shillings or 50 shillings from their weekly budget.[41]

That Byron did not understand this plan to niche-market the poem and then capitalise on its success with an elite audience by sales of cheaper editions is clear from his comment: 'He wants to have it in quarto, which is a cursed unsaleable size; but it is pestilent long, and one must obey one's bookseller' (*BLJ*, II, 113). When writing *Childe Harold's Pilgrimage*, then, Byron imagined an amenable and friendly audience who would emotionally mediate between him and the mass reading public. He targeted this group with homoerotic references which he planned to gloss verbally. When publishing *Childe Harold's Pilgrimage*, on the other hand, Murray identified an affluent and fashionable audience who would commercially mediate between the poet and the mass reading public.[42] He targeted this group with the price and format of the first edition and with word-of-mouth publicity.

But 10 March 1812, the publication date of the first edition, is not the end of the story. Byron revised the poem in 1814, adding ten new stanzas to Canto Two and 'To Ianthe'. At the height of his celebrity Byron returned once again to the beginning of the poem and added a lyric that identifies and idealises a specific reader. If the first stanza addresses a public and the second identifies a coterie, 'To Ianthe' 'hail[s]' an individual within the crowd (43). The name 'Ianthe' masks Lady

Charlotte Harley, the 11-year-old daughter of Byron's lover Lady Oxford. 'To Ianthe' begins with a flattering comparison:

> Not in those climes where I have late been straying,
> Though Beauty long hath there been matchless deem'd;
> Not in those visions to the heart displaying
> Forms which it sighs but to have only dream'd,
> Hath aught like thee in truth or fancy seem'd[.]
>
> (1–5)

Byron's 'straying' among the 'matchless' beauties of the East may suggest that Ianthe is being compared to the boys he encountered on his tour. While they were 'Hyacinths', she is a 'lily' (36). Ianthe is described in Oriental terms; her eye is compared to the gazelle's (28), like Leila's in *The Giaour* (474), and she's dubbed 'Young Peri of the West' (19). She is an Oriental beauty rediscovered at home, disproving Byron's previous strictures about the 'paler dames' of England ('How poor their forms appear! how languid, wan and weak!' (1. 58)) and making possible the homecoming that was previously denied to him. Ianthe had both personal and literary uses for Byron. Personally, he made her into a consolation for the loss of Edleston. Literarily, he used her to refigure the relationship between reader and writer once he became a celebrity. Writing his new-found readers into the poem, he cultivated the hermeneutic of intimacy.

Ianthe is praised in terms which align her with Edleston and yet distinguish her from him. She is young like Edleston and she is compared to cupid, the boy god ('Love's image upon earth without his wing' (13)). But whereas Edleston died young, Ianthe's youth is carefully linked to her longevity. She will not 'unbeseem the promise of [her] spring' (11). She is 'hourly brightening' and the speaker can 'safely view [her] ripening beauties shine' because she will outlive him, and he 'ne'er shall see them in decline' (16, 22, 23). Her youth also preserves the speaker from the pain of loving her: 'while all younger hearts shall bleed, / Mine shall escape the doom thine eyes assign' (24–5). Addressing Ianthe, then, Byron is doubly protected from the pain caused by the death of Edleston, whom she resembles. He claims not to desire her because the difference in their ages makes it impossible, and he is certain that she won't die, because her youth assures him of her longevity. These are both consoling fictions. Edleston taught Byron that age is no barrier to desire, and that youth is no guarantee of longevity. While Byron initially looked to

Edleston to be an especially privileged reader, he now looks to Ianthe. While Edleston died before reading the poem, Ianthe's future reading is assured.

But Ianthe is more important as a literary convention than she is as a psychological consolation. Unlike the Greek boys, whose desirability was linked to the possibility that their attractions could later be communicated to the methodistes, Ianthe's beauty is said to be beyond the limits of language:

> Nor, having seen thee, shall I vainly seek
> To paint those charms which varied as they beam'd –
> To such as see thee not my words were weak;
> To those who gaze on thee what language could they speak?
>
> (6–9)

Ianthe's charms won't stay still long enough to be painted, and they beggar Byron's words. This pose of inadequacy is a highly conventional one, marking the poem as an orthodox lyric in praise of a young girl. According to these conventions, the girl must be beautiful beyond description and supremely innocent ('guileless beyond Hope's imagining' (14)). The poet wishes she could always remain so ('may'st thou ever be what now thou art' (10)), and her youth leads him to meditate on mortality ('My years already doubly number thine' (20)). If that were all that the poem contained, then Ianthe could be identified as the descendant of Marvell's Little T.C. and the ancestor of Hopkins' Margaret. But the ease with which Byron can deploy these conventions indicates another reason why Ianthe displaces the Greek boys. She trumps the boys as a suitable object of desire for a celebrity poet because the representation of her beauty relies not on a clandestine conversation, but on a publishable poetic convention. Once Byron is fixed in a poetic career, he shifts his attention from a love that speaks its name only in private conversations or in codes, to one that writes its name in public verses with the support of a literary tradition.[43]

Byron departs from convention when he represents Ianthe as desirable not because she is an indescribable beauty but because she is a sympathetic reader. The terms in which her reading is imagined indicate why she is so desirable:

> Oh! let that eye, which, wild as the Gazelle's
> Now brightly bold or beautifully shy,

> Wins as it wanders, dazzles where it dwells
> Glance o'er this page; nor to my verse deny
> That smile for which my breast might vainly sigh,
> Could I to thee be ever more than friend:
> This much, dear maid, accord; nor question why
> To one so young my strain I would commend,
> But bid me with my wreath one matchless lily blend.
>
> (28–36)

Having adopted the pose of being immune from desiring Ianthe, Byron is denied the smile of assent she would give to a suitor. Since Byron cannot have that smile for himself in the present, he solicits it for his poem in the future, eroticising the act of reading. Ianthe reads with her seductively winning eye (30), bestowing her smile of assent on the poem and drawing fresh music from Byron's 'lyre' (42). Her 'fairy fingers' trail over his book, in lieu of his body, bewitching both (42). Caroline Franklin describes the effect: '[t]his powerfully intimate address to Ianthe, and through her his female reader, invites her to read the poem as a mode of relationship with him'.[44]

'To Ianthe' fantasises that although *Childe Harold's Pilgrimage* is sold to a faceless commercial audience, it is received by a single special reader, who accepts it as a billet-doux inviting her to a reading which is a kind of tryst. The commercial significance of this rhetoric is that Ianthe provides an enabling projection for a whole section of Byron's readership. Byron's female readers could imagine their own readings in the intimate terms in which Ianthe's was presented. Having lost the 'kinder heart[s]' of his coterie (2. 94), Byron opens his book to the 'kinder eyes' of a new audience (38). Their 'kinder eyes', unlike Ianthe's, are not too young to be desirable. The poem thus encodes a flirtatious doubleness. On the one hand, Ianthe is praised from a distance in terms of chivalric chastity. On the other, the poem's purchasers are implicitly invited to look through her eyes and smile her smile as they participate in the hermeneutic of intimacy.

The difference between how Byron imagined this reading and how he imagined that of the methodistes shows how he refigured his sense of audience when becoming a celebrity. Ianthe's reading is based not on knowing the code, but on the construction of an imaginary intimacy in which the poem becomes a conduit providing access to the poet. Whereas the methodistes' reading was deferred until Byron could be present to add a verbal commentary, Ianthe's begins in Byron's absence with her sexualised smile. Her reading differs from that of the methodistes because instead of resulting from something Byron adds to the text from outside, an authorial supplement that modifies and completes the poem, it is produced by the extent to which he is embodied in or by the text and by the idea that reading functions as a form of relationship with him. As such, the shift in Byron's sense of an audience that is signalled when Ianthe displaces Edleston or Matthews as a privileged reader marks a significant step in his creation of the textual erotics of *Childe Harold's Pilgrimage*.

The methodistes' pleasure, I have argued, would have lain in using the poem as a starting point for the erotic retelling of past sexual encounters, saying what could not be written in order to conjure up acts done elsewhere and previously that could not (or not so easily) be done here and now. The pleasure of Ianthe's eroticised reading, by contrast, lies in the action of reading the poem and the access it provides to a seductive but absent Byron. This kind of reading does not rekindle eroticism from another place and time, it produces eroticism now – and reproduces it with each rereading and every new poem. As such, the pleasure of Ianthe's reading is not limited to cognoscenti, but is available to anyone who can project their own desires onto her. The difference between the methodistes and Ianthe is the difference between keeping the commercial readership at bay with privileged mediating individuals and trying to shape that readership's response by presenting it with an exemplary figure. 'To Ianthe', 'first beheld, forgotten last' presents an image of reading in which all female readers can invest (40). Celebrity requires that a relationship between the celebrity and his audience be created which sustains the appearance of being intimate and special, but which is also indefinitely marketable. When Byron started writing *Childe Harold's Pilgrimage* in 1809, he tried to protect himself from the anonymous and potentially hostile commercial readership of the Romantic period by addressing a select group of friends. When he returned to the poem in 1814 to add 'To Ianthe', he seduced that commercial audience by constructing the hermeneutic of intimacy, inviting them to imagine reading as a meeting of intimates and turn a blind eye to the industry which produced, distributed and sold the poem endlessly.

4
Scopophilia and Somatic Inscription in Byron's Verse Tales

After *Childe Harold*'s dazzling success, all eyes were on Byron. The upper echelons of Regency society welcomed him into their drawing rooms and showered him with invitations to balls and dinners, not to mention trysts and assignations. Byron now faced the challenge of consolidating his position in the Romantic celebrity culture that he was helping to create, sustaining the attention he had attracted and proving that his fame was more than a flash in the pan. Between them, Byron and Murray needed to turn the remarkable singularity of *Childe Harold's Pilgrimage* into a sequence providing a reliable income for the publisher and fuel for the poet's fame.

In response to this challenge, Byron's verse tales aroused a kind of desire that took its pleasure in looking and elaborated a kind of characterisation in which information of narrative import could be read on bodily surfaces. These techniques established the poems as relays of desire, conduits channelling readers' attention back to the poet. They had three far-reaching consequences. Firstly, they franchised a secondary industry which supplemented celebrity's letterpress texts with the engraved portraits and illustrations that soon circulated both alongside and independently of Byron's poems. Where 'To Ianthe' figured reading as a potentially eroticised relationship between reader and poet, the tales extended that relationship from reading to looking, adding a visual dimension to Byron's celebrity. Secondly, Byron's entry into an industrialised visual culture embedded him more securely in overlapping capital and libidinal economies where his agency was severely circumscribed.[1] As Byron's celebrity identity circulated in ways he could not control, he began to experience the sense of self-alienation that would be crucial to his later poetry. Thirdly, the tales' concern with scopophilia and somatic inscription helped to promulgate ideas about subjectivity, resting on certain assumptions about gender roles and cultivated sensibilities, which would become central to modern celebrity culture and modernity in general.[2]

All this began in the ingenious folds of *The Giaour*'s non-linear narrative. Linear narratives rely on their ability to arouse the reader's desire to get to the end. While we luxuriate in narrative obstacles, the end is always comfortably just out of sight, somewhere between the bookmark and the back cover. As Frank Kermode has suggested, linear narratives are read with reference to postulated closure: the ending may be unpredictable, but we can predict that there will *be* an ending which will make sense of the story.[3] The desire for more of a linear story is therefore paradoxically also the desire for the story to end. Peter Brooks presents narrative desire 'diminishing as it realises itself, leading to an end that is the consummation (as well as the consumption) of its sense-making'.[4] But narratives also generate desires that remain after the end and that they themselves cannot satiate. 'It could be that we always need more stories because in *some* way they do *not* satisfy' according to J. Hillis Miller. 'Each story and each repetition or variation of it leaves some uncertainty or contains some loose end unravelling its effect'.[5] *The Giaour*'s fragment form left plenty of loose ends, disrupting the sense of an ending that drives more conventionally linear narratives, and leaving its readers' desires in search of an extra-textual object.

Avoiding a linear exposition of its plot, *The Giaour* shuffles its fragments and forces the reader to pick his or her way across them like stepping-stones.[6] It seems to be singularly inefficient at arousing our desire to get to the end, leaving some readers frustrated. '*The Giaour* collects and interprets its material in an extremely circular way that seems finally unproductive of any insight at all', Marjorie Levinson writes; 'Byron's "snake of a poem" is an *ourobouros*'.[7] The poem does not channel narrative desire towards a denouement, but turns it back on itself. Although the *Quarterly Review* was troubled by the poem's 'abrupt and capricious transitions', Francis Jeffrey in the *Edinburgh Review* praised the 'fragments thus served up by a *restaurateur* of such taste as Lord Byron', saying that 'the greater part of polite readers would now no more think of sitting down to a whole Epic, than to a whole ox'.[8] The fragment form opens up in an unusually literal fashion narrative gaps or blanks of the sort theorised by Wolfgang Iser, which stimulate the reader's curiosity, desire for knowledge and active response to the text.[9] The reader is invited into the text to join in the author's meaning-making by filling the gaps. But in *The Giaour's* case, the reader's interventions after the poem's first appearance could only be temporary postulates, because new editions kept appearing with additions which filled in some of the gaps while creating more blanks of their own.

Deprived of a linear plot with the clear sense of an ending, the reader's desire to get to the end is displaced by a desire to get the whole story, to reconstruct the tale and fully possess the poem. Byron's reference in the Advertisement to 'the story, when entire' suggests an ur-narrative which a sufficiently imaginative or perspicacious reader could discern behind the 'disjointed fragments'. The fragment form and the frequency of new editions turned Byron's accretive compositional practice into a strategy for arousing and sustaining readers' desire to possess the poem completely. Complete possession meant both materially owning the latest expensive edition from Murray to display on one's table and imaginatively possessing the fullest possible details of the poem's plot and characters from those bits of text that did not appear at first. The title pages of the early editions announced continually enhanced versions of the poem. The second edition declared itself to be 'a new edition, with some additions'. This was followed by the 'Third Edition / with considerable additions', which emphasised its length by adding the marginal line numbers that would appear in all subsequent editions. The fourth edition was also 'with additions' and the fifth 'with considerable additions'. The sixth edition had no additions, and the seventh and eighth had 'some additions', after which the text stabilised, running to 14 editions in all and selling 13,500 copies by 1819.[10] These additions serially embellished the original version of 684 lines (itself expanded from a proof of 453 lines) to the received 1334 lines, without ever providing all the information that the reader desires. The fragment form makes complete possession impossible, because no matter how many fragments are added, they cannot add up to the whole story. To fill all the gaps would require the poem to be recast into a linear narrative – which would make it a different poem altogether. *The Giaour* will never provide its readers with all the answers they desire. As a result of these strategies, the publisher made a profit, the poet gained in celebrity and the readers were treated to the excitement of a protracted engagement with the narrative, an extended arousal of narrative desire that always left room to want more.

It was not formal factors alone that made complete possession impossible. It was widely believed that the tale had a concealed origin in something that had happened to Byron while he was abroad. Until the link with Lord Byron's life was made explicit, the reader's desire to possess the whole story could not be satiated. By turning to that story here, I aim not to repeat the biographical readings that characterise celebrity culture, but to uncover the Byronic strategy from which those readings took their cue. Briefly, when Byron was in Athens in 1811, he was apparently returning from bathing one day when he came across a procession bearing a young woman sewn up in a sack. She was to have been drowned for infidelity, as Leila is in the tale. Byron intervened, drawing his pistols, and forced the party to return to the Governor of Athens, where, by a mixture of threats and bribery, he secured the girl's release, on condition that she left Athens. Byron arranged for her safe passage to Thebes. Rumour had it that Byron had been the girl's lover and was indirectly the cause of the sentence.[11]

Byron arranged for Lord Sligo, who had arrived in Athens just after Byron left, to provide a letter stating the story as he had heard it. Byron circulated this letter among his acquaintance in 1813, with ten lines inked out so heavily as to have torn the paper – another tantalising narrative gap.[12] He intended to include the letter, as the 'official' version of events, in a note to the fifth or seventh edition (*CPW*, III, 424). But he never did. His vacillation reveals his complex repertoire of strategies for producing and sustaining his audience's curiosity about him, even under the guise of doing something quite different. Claiming that 'it is not requisite for me to subjoin either assent or contradiction', Byron submitted in evidence, as it were, a second-hand report of second-hand gossip (*BLJ*, XI, 186). For his circle, this went some way towards revealing the incident and its connection to the poem, and it would have done the same for a wider readership had it been published. But by allowing Sligo to speak in his place, Byron only went far enough to arouse, not to satiate the desire for the whole story. Byron himself, who could have given the definitive account, refused 'either assent or contradiction' and therefore perpetuated the uncertainty.[13]

The letter was never printed. The note that was printed in its place makes no mention of the incident, but asserts Byron's faulty memory as the reason for the fragment form:

> The story in the text is one told of a young Venetian many years ago, and now nearly forgotten. – I heard it by accident recited by one of the coffee-house story-tellers who abound in the Levant, and sing or recite their narratives. – The additions and interpolations by the translator will be easily distinguished from the rest by the want of Eastern imagery; and I regret that my memory has retained so few fragments of the original. (1334n)

Concealed somewhere in Byron's mind, the note seems to imply, are the definitive answers to the text's mysteries, the information to fill its lacunae and the truth about the link to Lord Byron's life. *The Giaour* conceals both the whole truth about the story it tells and the adventurer Byron, with his pistols, his Athenian mistress and his scrapes with the Turks. Only Byron himself has the answers. Only he could speak from a position of authority outside or behind the poem, which, until the eighth edition at least, it is always possible that he will do. Whilst the narrative of *The Giaour* creates desires, it also establishes Byron as the only person who can satisfy those desires. Only he could fill in the gaps in the story, and only he could explain the truth about the biographical incident that was understood to underlie it in a peculiarly private way. *The Giaour* seduced its readers by suggesting that Byron might at some point in its serial elaboration enable them fully to possess the story, and his own story, by a complete revelation of the elements that it had so far concealed.

But if the poem cannot achieve the desired narrative closure on its own, then the reader reaches an impasse, condemned to desire that with which he or she can never be presented. How are readers to get the answers they want from Byron if he won't step forward and explain? The poem suggests a way out that would become central to the hermeneutic of intimacy in Byron's first four tales. At the same time as it tantalisingly conceals details in its fragment form and shadowy relation to Byron's life, *The Giaour* suggests that crucial information can be gleaned by looking at bodies, especially the Giaour's body and face. The poem suggests that its narrative answers can be found inscribed on bodies, where close observers can read them. I argue, then, that Byron used the fragmentary form and multiple editions of *The Giaour* to arouse his readers' desire to possess the story completely. Since its fragments could never provide narrative closure, and it was understood to depend on a biographical incident, the text alone could not satisfy this desire. Instead, readers' desire overflowed the poem and fixed on the poet as its object. He suggested that the missing narrative information that would enable the poem's complete possession could be obtained by scrutinising the bodies of his characters and, by extrapolation, fostered a scopophilic fascination with his own body.

Childe Harold's Pilgrimage had already broached the idea that faces and bodies bore traces of hidden crimes or sorrows:

> Yet oft-times in his maddest mirthful mood
> Strange pangs would flash along Childe Harold's brow,
> As if the memory of some deadly feud
> Or disappointed passion lurk'd below[.]
>
> (1. 8)

In the tales, however, that idea became more generalised and more germane to the plot, generating a specifically scopophilic desire.[14] While *The Giaour* mimics to some extent the qualities of oral poetry, claiming to imitate Levantine 'coffee-house story-tellers' who 'sing or recite their narratives' (1334n), its effects are visual as much as aural. Whether we consider the spectator's 'gaze of wonder' (201) or the hero's 'evil eye' (196) in *The Giaour*, the 'fatal gaze' Selim casts on Zuleika as he dies in *The Bride of Abydos* (2. 565) or the 'gladiator's look' that 'rolls wide and wild' in Lara's eyes (1. 222, 228), visual tropes are essential to the tales' poetry, just as eye-witnesses are important in their plots.

The Giaour's body is inscribed with narrative meanings and concealed information that propels the story, stoking the reader's narrative desire. It is presented as a site of possible narrative answers from his first appearance:

> I know thee not, I loathe thy race,
> But in thy lineaments I trace
> What time shall strengthen, not efface;
> Though young and pale, that sallow front
> Is scath'd by fiery passion's brunt,
> Though bent on earth thine evil eye
> As meteor-like thou glidest by,
> Right well I view, and deem thee one
> Whom Othman's sons should slay or shun.
>
> (191–9)

Although he doesn't know the Giaour, the speaker can 'trace' meanings in his 'lineaments'. His character is 'scath'd' indelibly onto his face, which in turn 'impressed / A troubled memory on my breast' (204–5). Similarly, the Giaour's 'fearful brow' (231) reveals his changing emotions:

> He stood – some dread was on his face –
> Soon Hatred settled in its place –
> It rose not with the reddening flush
> Of transient Anger's hasty blush,
> But pale as marble o'er the tomb,
> Whose ghastly whiteness aids its gloom.
>
> (234–9)

Here the speaker can discern the nature and quality of the Giaour's innermost emotions by scrutinising his face. The external attribute of colour is eloquent of the unspoken emotions which it signifies.

The Giaour is marked by his past crime, like the inmate in Kafka's penal colony, in such a way that it cannot be concealed. In his confession, he says:

> She died – I dare not tell thee how,
> But look – 'tis written on my brow!
> There read of Cain the curse and crime,
> In characters unworn by time[.]
>
> (1056–9)

Unable to speak his guilt, the Giaour offers his face to the monk to be read, in the certainty that it will accurately reveal his secret. By scrutinising the Giaour's body, we can know his history, the poem suggests. 'Along with the semioticization of the body', Brooks asserts, 'goes what we might call the somatization of story: the implicit claim that the body is a key sign in narrative and a central nexus of narrative meanings.'[15] The Giaour bears narrative meanings on his face and elsewhere on his body, for instance in his long hair, which encodes his difference from the monks, his (Medusa-like) corruption and (Samson-like) strength (898–900). While the fragment form of the text leaves unanswered questions, the poem also suggests that those answers might be found on the bodies of its characters and that if our desire for narrative answers were directed, with our gaze, at those bodies, it might be satisfied. The body in the narrative reveals to the reader's gaze what is otherwise left unsaid.

The Bride of Abydos turns on the apparent transformation of its hero's body and foregrounds the ways in which gendered bodies can be read and misread. Byron depicts a regime in which the body and its performances signify all personal worth for men. The attributes of the manly body, such as strength, martial skill and horsemanship, must be proved by display in battle or competition. For this purpose, Giaffir maintains an elaborate system of spectacular military exercises.[16] He leaves his couch to 'witness many an active deed / With sabre keen, or blunt jerreed' (1. 237–8). With his 'Maugrabee' (mercenaries) and 'Delis' (cavalrymen), Giaffir performs martial arts (1. 235–6). The 'javelin-darting crowd' exhibits its prowess by 'cleav[ing] the folded felt / With sabre stroke right sharply dealt' (1. 248–50). These displays add up to a Butlerian performance of masculinity, 'a repetition and a ritual, which achieves its effects through its naturalisation in the context of a body'.[17] Judith Butler emphasises that the subject's agency in such a performance is severely circumscribed by 'the situation of duress under which gender performance always and variously occurs'.[18] Giaffir proscribes Selim from the theatre of 'mimic war', the arena where masculine roles are played out, and so underwrites his powerful inscription of Selim's body as feminine (1. 450). 'Vain were a father's hope to see / Aught that beseems a man in thee', he taunts (1. 83–4).

But when Giaffir claims to discover Selim's effeminacy, he in fact coercively constructs it from a polemical reading of Selim's bodily performance. Giaffir's powerful gaze splinters Selim's body into a substandard assemblage of arms, eyes and hands, and reads these shards as effeminate. Having excluded Selim from 'the game of mimic slaughter' that Giaffir plays with his henchmen (1. 247), he taunts him with claims that he would rather lounge about in the garden 'when thine arm should bend the bow, / And hurl the dart, and curb the steed' (1. 85–8). Selim's resentment at being excluded from these performances of masculinity boils over in Canto Two, where he complains that:

> Giaffir's fear
> Denied the courser and the spear –
> Though oft – Oh, Mahomet! how oft! –
> In full Divan the despot scoff'd,
> As if *my* weak unwilling hand
> Refused the bridle or the brand[.]
>
> (2. 323–8)

Reading Selim's body for signs of masculinity, Giaffir surveys Selim's arm and finds it wanting: 'his arm is little worth' (1. 135). His eyes likewise fail to meet Giaffir's standards of masculinity:

> Would that yon orb, whose matin glow
> Thy listless eyes so much admire,
> Would lend thee something of his fire!
>
> (1. 90–2)

Giaffir mocks Selim's body for being boyish, claiming that he would only fear him if 'thy beard had manlier length' (1. 122). And he reads femininity in his hands: 'Go – let thy less than woman's hand / Assume the distaff – not the brand' (1. 99–100). Listing the failings of Selim's 'listless' body, Giaffir enforces a standard of masculinity based on his claim that the body is inscribed with gendered signs of the individual's value.

At the tale's pivotal moment, when Selim reveals himself to be the leader of a pirate band, we are invited to look at his body in a new way. Byron presents Selim's new performance of masculinity to the reader's gaze in 20 descriptive lines (2. 131–50).[19] He is now adorned not in the luxurious vestments that become a pacha's son, but in the simple clothes of a sailor. His ornamental dagger is replaced by a brace of pistols and a sabre, and he's armoured with 'cuirass' and 'greaves' (2. 144–5). 'High command' now '[speaks] in his eye, and tone, and hand', where before Giaffir read effeminacy and worthlessness (2. 147–8). When Selim reveals his alter ego, he transforms his body in the reader's eyes from a docile site of coercion to an eloquent site of resistance. Where Giaffir previously read his eyes and hands, they now speak for themselves, as Selim performs his gender differently. Selim's body, now actively signifying, performs for Zuleika's eyes the masculine identity that it was thought to lack when Giaffir's gaze rendered it docile. This transformation cannot secure Selim's success once he leaves the confines of his cave, but he dies convinced that his true identity is now obvious to see. 'I said I was not what I seem'd; / And now thou see'st my words were true' (2. 151–2).

The tropes of somatic inscription enabled readers to think of themselves as privileged observers, possessing the cultural virtue of nice discernment. Byron suggested that somatic secrets were legible only to particularly perspicacious readers of texts or of bodies. Whilst 'In Conrad's form seems little to admire', the hero of *The Corsair*, like the Giaour, repays close scrutiny (1. 195). 'Yet, in the whole, who paused to look again, / Saw more than marks the crowd of vulgar men' (1. 199–200). The vulgar men who 'gaze and marvel' (1. 201) sense something of Conrad's charisma, but cannot probe his subjective depths. For those who have eyes to see, however, his aristocracy of spirit is written in his distinctly Byronic features:

> Sun-burnt his cheek, his forehead high and pale
> The sable curls in wild profusion veil;
> And oft perforce his rising lip reveals
> The haughtier thought it curbs, but scare conceals.
>
> (1. 203–6)

Those who know how to read 'the lip's least curl, the lightest paleness thrown / Along the governed aspect' know that these somatic traces 'speak alone / Of deeper passions' (1. 231–3). Conrad's 'secret spirit' (1. 248) can be read from the 'Flush in the cheek, or damp upon the brow' (1. 242):

> Then – Stranger! if thou canst, and tremblest not,
> Behold his soul [...]
> Mark – how that lone and blighted bosom sears
> The scathing thought of execrated years!
>
> (1. 243–6)

Those readers sophisticated and robust enough to discern and bear so cruel a knowledge are invited to trace Conrad's history and inmost thoughts, seared onto his bosom.

Similarly, if we scrutinise the chiaroscuro of the Giaour's body with the requisite attention, we are promised a revelation both of his remorse and of his aristocratic nature:

> But sadder were it still to trace
> What once were feelings in that face –
> Time hath not yet the features fixed,
> But brighter traits with evil mixed –
> And there are hues not always faded,
> Which speak a mind not all degraded
> Even by the crimes through which it waded –
> The common crowd but see the gloom
> Of wayward deeds – and fitting doom –
> The close observer can espy
> A noble soul, and lineage high.
>
> (859–69)

Although the Giaour's face betrays only the ruins of emotion, 'what once were feelings', the story of his past crimes is there if we would only look. The face is still sufficiently alive to tell its story, and its appearance 'speaks' of the mind concealed within. The speaker here invites us to scrutinise the face he conjures into our imagination, to set ourselves apart from the 'common crowd' and be the 'close observer' who can see the Giaour's noble soul.

While they suggested that discerning readers could glean narrative information from bodies, Byron's tales were also in the business of marketing mystery. Part of his heroes' fascination, and Byron's own attraction, was that they could not be completely understood, even by the most perceptive readers. The fascinating mystery at the centre of their identities ensured their continued popularity with Romantic consumers. *Lara* especially emphasises the engaging difficulty of reading its hero's face and body, foregrounding his 'chilling mystery of mien, / And seeming gladness to remain unseen' (1. 361–2). Lara's innermost nature can only be read on his body at moments of high excitement. 'In voice – mien – gesture – savage nature spoke' (2. 262). When he becomes enraged, his anger is written on his brow, which 'upon the moment grew / Almost to blackness in its demon hue' (2. 73–4). Mostly, however, the reader remains outside the intimate circle of those who could interpret Lara's body. When he's stripped and lain in his grave, his attendants find his body marked with scars which tell of his past strife (2. 542–6). But the only two people who could decipher those hieroglyphs, his devoted page Kaled and his bitter enemy Ezzelin, are dead. Lara's body is inscribed with details of his subjectivity and history, which would explain the mysterious allegations Ezzelin hinted at, but neither Byron's discerning readers 'Nor common gazers could discern the growth / Of [his] thoughts' (1. 286–7). Byron's tropes of somatic inscription thus offered readers by turns the pleasure of feeling especially perceptive or discerning, and the stimulation of probing the selfhood of a particularly mysterious and fascinating individual.

Bodies of both sexes and all races could bear the traces of hidden subjective interiority, but the narrative uses to which Byron put them were profoundly gendered. While his heroes' bodies were charged with the information which drove the narrative forward, his heroines' bodies were often exhibited to the reader's gaze in narrative hiatuses, and only appeared inscribed with significant narrative information when they transgressed the norms of female behaviour. In an orientalist manipulation of his readers' visual pleasure, Byron interrupted *The Giaour*'s narrative to exhibit Leila's body in a fragment of its own. We are invited to linger over her 'eye's dark charm', her 'fair cheek', her 'hyacinthine' hair, her white feet and 'whiter neck' and her 'high and graceful' gait (473–518). Her beauty demands a flurry of similes. Her blush is like pomegranate blossoms, her skin like mountain snow before it falls, her gait like a cygnet swimming, her neck like a swan's and her eye like a gazelle's. Leila's appearance, in Laura Mulvey's cinematic terms, is 'coded for strong visual and erotic impact so that [she] can be said to connote to-be-looked-at-ness'.[20] Byron repeated the technique for Zuleika in *The Bride of Abydos*. Her first appearance generates a narrative hiatus, marked by a shift from eight- to ten-syllable lines (1. 158–81). Byron drew attention to her 'graceful arms' and 'gently-budding breast' but substituted abstract similes for Leila's natural ones (1. 182–3). She is like an unfallen Eve, like an erotic dream or a memory of lost love, like a child's prayer or like music. Her male spectators are both aroused and unmanned, fainting 'with [their] own delight' (1. 173). In both cases, the speaker reads soulful depths in the heroine's eye, unsettling the orientalist view of Islamic orthodoxy, 'Which saith, that woman is but dust, / A soulless toy for tyrant's lust' (489–90). 'Soul beamed forth in every spark' of Leila's gaze, while Zuleika's 'eye was in itself a Soul' (477; 1. 181). Exhibited to the eroticised gaze of an implied male reader, these female bodies feed an orientalist fantasy, but are not inscribed with narrative information.

On those exceptional but pivotal occasions when female bodies *are* freighted with narrative information, they transgress feminine norms and usurp masculine prerogatives. Leila's body, writhing as it sinks in its sack, becomes a locus of key narrative significance because her transgressive sexual desire sets *The Giaour's* plot in motion. The 'hectic tint of secret care' on Kaled's cheek and her 'femininely white' hand both enable us to read her body as feminine despite her transgressive cross-dressing (1. 534, 576). Her legible body bears crucial narrative information at *Lara's* climax, when 'In baring to revive that lifeless breast', she is revealed to be a woman (2. 516). The most significant narrative inscription on a female body also marks the most fundamentally transgressive woman. When Gulnare murders her master Seyd to rescue Conrad, she rejects every assumption about female passivity, tenderness and devotion that the tales endorse. In that moment, her body is marked with the spot of blood, the 'slight but certain pledge of crime', which both Conrad and the reader effectively decipher, grasping the tale's pivotal narrative event (3. 417). In each case, the heroines annex supposedly masculine attributes: active sexual desire, male costume or violent efficacy. For Leila and Kaled, somatic inscription of narrative significance comes only with their deaths; for Gulnare, it comes with her horrified rejection by Conrad. While female bodies in Byron's tales can be exhibited in narrative hiatuses for the reader's pleasure, when they start actively to signify narrative information they transgress gendered assumptions and face the reader's censure and the plot's sanctions.

By suggesting that only the male body could be inscribed with narrative information with impunity, Byron smoothed the path for readers' gazes to move from characters in the poems to the celebrity poet who created them. Once Byron was identified as somehow lurking behind his protagonists, his invitation to gaze at them could be recognised as an invitation to gaze at Byron himself. By the curious transference that made so many of the poems' first readers certain that Byron had drawn himself in his heroes, desire for the answers that their bodies would provide became desire for Byron himself, Byron in the flesh. Although his crimes are revealed on his body, the Giaour conceals Byron beneath his skin, and the link to the biographical incident, so carefully stage-managed with Sligo's assistance, strengthened the identification. Similarly, Byron heard 'an odd report, – that *I* am the actual Conrad, the veritable Corsair, and that part of my travels are supposed to have passed in privacy [i.e. piracy]' (*BLJ*, III, 250). And one of his female admirers quoted from *The Corsair* in a fan letter, adding, 'I cannot help believing the truth of the following lines as applied to yourself.'[21] What is more, many of the poems' earliest readers were in fact in a position to gaze on Byron in person, or at least to glimpse him, since they belonged to the upper echelons of Regency society, in which Byron moved at this time. William St Clair has estimated that 20 per cent of *The Giaour's* sales, and 36 per cent of *The Corsair's*, were to families with an income of over £200 per annum, an income which he identifies as a benchmark of 'gentility' based on examples drawn from Navy pensions.[22] The tales' early editions were relatively expensive, and large numbers of them sold to people whose social geographies might intersect with Byron's, at the time when he was drawn into fashionable society as a celebrity who added lustre and often intrigue to any gathering.[23]

Byron's occasional stiffness and formality in company only encouraged the impression that his socialising was display; he was to be looked at from a distance as much as interacted with. And Byron was looking back, with a seductive '*under* look', which made Lady Mildmay's heart 'beat so violently that she could hardly answer him'.[24] Four years later, in Rome, Lady Liddell would warn her daughter, 'Don't look at him, he is dangerous to look at.'[25] Gazing on Byron, as those two ladies realised, had become charged with the potential for illicit eroticism. From the records of those readers who gazed at Byron, it is possible to recover a response that paralleled his interest in somatic inscription, but directed scopophilic attention to the poet in place of his heroes. One reader who took the chance to scrutinise Byron in society was Annabella Milbanke, who saw him for the first time on 25 March 1812 at a morning visit to Melbourne House.[26] Annabella, who had read *Childe Harold's Pilgrimage* over the previous 3 days, didn't seek an introduction, but observed Byron from a safe distance. In her diary that night, she wrote:

> His mouth continually betrays the acrimony of his spirit. I should judge him sincere and independent – sincere at least in society as far as he can be, whilst dissimulating the violence of his scorn. He very often hides his mouth with his hand while speaking. [...] It appeared to me that he tried to control his natural sarcasm and vehemence as much as he could, in order not to offend; but at times his lips thickened with disdain, and his eyes rolled impatiently. Indeed the scene was calculated to shew human absurdities.[27]

Byron's face, like the Giaour's or the Corsair's, displays his innermost nature, but only to the close observer. Annabella was convinced that, by scrutinising his face, she had discovered 'the acrimony of his spirit', which less careful observers had overlooked, 'continually betray[ed]' by his features. Characteristically, she also made this a moral judgement – she claimed to have seen what the people speaking to Byron were too preoccupied and shallow to notice. Byron's emotions leave physiological traces which Annabella reads in his lips and eyes, determined to be the 'close observer' that readers of *The Giaour* are invited to be. Much later, after they separated, Byron would charge her with having failed at that task, having been a careless reader of his body:

> Would that breast, by thee glanced over,
> Every inmost thought could show!
> Then thou would'st at last discover
> 'Twas not well to spurn it so.
>
> ('Fare Thee Well' 9–12)

Here Byron seems unsure how much information the body can bear, but in any case, Annabella has only 'glanced over' him and not read thoroughly. Both husband and wife participated in a discourse that figured Byron's body as a site of inscription where fascinating information was to be found.

Reading his poems made people want to look at Byron, in the conviction that the sight of him would in some way provide answers, solve mysteries or reveal secrets. It was not only his future wife who responded visually to Byron. Coleridge remembered his teeth as 'so many stationary smiles' and his eyes as 'open portals of the sun'.

His forehead, Coleridge continued, was 'so ample, and yet so flexible, passing from marble smoothness into a hundred wreaths and lines and dimples correspondent to the feelings and sentiments he is uttering'.[28] His readers imagined Byron's body in the same way as he imagined the Byronic hero's – as a surface on which traces of hidden subjective depth were inscribed. Whether they endorsed Coleridge's conviction that appearance was 'correspondent' to emotion or shared Annabella's belief that his face 'continually betray[ed]' his feelings, they understood Byron's subjectivity to be structured around a hidden interior that nonetheless made itself legible to close observers on the surface of his face and body. Readers passed from reading his books to reading his face with remarkable ease.

The body that fascinated them was not the natural, pre-discursive ground on which Byron's celebrity was built; when he obliquely directed attention towards it, it was only after careful preparation. Byron's body itself, and not only its representation, was shaped as part of the apparatus of celebrity. Since his youth, Byron had aspired to cut a fashionable figure with 'a tinge of Dandyism' (*BLJ*, IX, 22). Dandyism provided a discourse and a praxis which validated the slender, tastefully adorned male body and implied its plasticity. Stendhal opined that 'during at least a third part of the day, Byron was a dandy, [and] expressed a constant dread of augmenting the bulk of his outward man' (*HVSV*, p. 201). His cultivated slenderness would become central to his self-presentation. We have detailed information about Byron's weight between January 1806 and July 1811 from a ledger in the archives of the vintner Berry Brothers and Rudd. Their customers enjoyed weighing themselves on the set of scales in the shop, and ledgers record the weight of Charles James Fox, Beau Brummell and Thomas Moore, among others.[29] Byron was first weighed on 4 January 1806 (he weighed 13 stone 12 pounds). By that autumn he weighed 14 stone 6 pounds: very overweight for a man of 5 feet 8½ inches. In 1807, Byron began a regime of weight loss, writing to an acquaintance:

> I have lost 18 LB in my weight, that is one stone and four pounds since January [...] as I found myself too plump [...] my clothes have been taken in nearly *half a yard*. (*BLJ*, I, 114)

By 10 June 1809, he weighed 11 stone 5¾. He must have eaten frugally on his travels in 1809–1811, because when he returned to Berry's scales he was only 9 stone 11½: 22 pounds lighter than when he left, and 4½ stone below his heaviest recorded weight.[30] Having produced a body that was fit for his entry into public life, Byron maintained his low weight by tapping into a Romantic discourse on diet.[31] We know he bought a treatise on corpulence in 1811, and in September 1812 he instructed his publisher to 'send [him] Adair on Diet and regimen' (*BLJ*, II, 191).[32] By 1816, his library contained at least two more works on the subject.[33] In his quest for public prominence (as a peer, a dandy or a poet) Byron responded to the somatic expectations of Romantic celebrity culture. He produced, by an effort of will, a body that he conceived to be fit for the kind of public figure he aspired to become. Byron went on display in the House of Lords, in Whig society and in his portraits, inviting scrutiny of the body whose outlines he maintained with considerable effort.[34] Apparently a natural pre-textual entity, inscribed with traces of an authentic interior subjectivity, Byron's body was in fact a rigorously artful formation. His physical appearance, whether in portraits, in dandified clothes or in the flesh, was an aesthetic production: his art was also body art.

The rhetoric of somatic inscription, the scopophilic desires it aroused and the celebrity identity it helped to consolidate all implied a particular understanding of subjectivity. Whether the individual in question was Byron or one of his characters, the subject was understood, with gendered inflections, to be structured around a deep and hidden interior. That interior never remained totally concealed, however, but left its mark on the surfaces of the body, regardless of the individual's attempts to conceal it. The body's traces of subjective interiority were not easily legible and always seemed to leave some mystery. Yet spectators who possessed or had acquired the cultural virtues of discernment, and who paid close attention to the subject's face and body, could decipher fascinating information about his (or, more problematically, her) true selfhood. Both Byron's characters and Byron himself came to be understood, in a recognisably modern fashion, as paradoxically possessed of both a hidden interior and a legible exterior, as having subjective depths that nonetheless became inscribed on somatic surfaces.

That understanding of the subject is related to a physiognomic tradition stretching back to antiquity, but it also retools the old problem of reading the mind's construction in the face, making it fit for the capitalist culture of celebrity. The long eighteenth century witnessed a number of important physiognomic innovations. Charles Lebrun's *Method to Learn to Design the Passions* (1698, trans. 1734) attempted to systematise the representation of emotion and influenced Reynolds's painting and Garrick's acting with its account of how the passions distorted the features. Johann Caspar Lavater's *Essays on Physiognomy*

(1775–1778, trans. 1789–1798), which Byron owned by 1816 (*CMP*, p. 237), enjoyed enormous popularity across Europe.[35] The new science of phrenology was promoted by Johann Spurzheim, who, within six months of arriving in England in 1814, had examined Byron's head.[36] These examples reveal an eighteenth-century concern with reading bodies, but the account of somatic inscription in Byron's tales offered new elements that were especially conducive to celebrity culture. Byron radically personalised the notion of somatic inscription, so that instead of seeing the particular abstract passion which possessed the individual in the moment, as Lebrun aimed to do, or the combination of abstract traits which formed an individual's moral or national character, as Lavater claimed to make possible, the discerning spectator could read the secret and uniquely private history of a troubled and fascinatingly deep subject.

This understanding of subjective depth should be distinguished from the Wordsworthian version which has often been taken as representative in Romantic studies. By 1805, Wordsworth had already come to view deep subjective interiority as normative, and the ability to perceive it as a mark of distinction:

> When I began to inquire,
> To watch and question those I met, and held
> Familiar talk with them, the lonely roads
> Were schools to me in which I daily read
> With most delight the passions of mankind,
> There saw into the depths of human souls,
> Souls that appear to have no depth at all
> To vulgar eyes.[37]

Like Byron, Wordsworth uses the metaphors of reading and depth to describe gaining knowledge of subjectivity. But unlike Byron, Wordsworth's knowledge is based in 'question[ing]' as well as 'watch[ing]', and he sees into the depths of subjectivity as the result of an encounter in which the speaker and his subject exchange '[f]amiliar talk'. Wordsworth's ability to raise himself above the 'vulgar' relied on face-to-face encounters and conversations which, despite the leech-gatherer's difficulty in making himself understood, were at least potentially reciprocal. On the lonely roads, the pedestrian poet and the common man could get to know one another. By contrast, when Byron's tales described somatic inscription and stimulated scopophilic desires, they presented a kind of subjectivity that could be known intimately *without* a personal encounter. The relationship between poet and reader that Byron offered his admirers was asymmetrical and always mediated. If subjective information was inscribed on the surface of the body, then by gazing on a celebrity's body from a distance, seeing it reproduced in prints or reading descriptions of it (or its heroic stand-ins), Romantic consumers could come to know him without becoming known themselves.

With his tropes of somatic inscription and his careful elision of fiction and autobiography, Byron turned his verse tales into relays of desire, lenses through which his readers' gazes and desires could pass, centring, finally, on the poet's body as a locus of signification for interior subjective realities. Byron's body came to be understood as the authentic register, legible to the perceptive observer, of hidden inward depths – the canvas of his soul. Once his celebrity gained a visual dimension, a whole new industry of artists and engravers, printmakers and book illustrators, proprietors of print shops and magazine editors could turn his celebrity into their profit. Their products are studied in the next chapter. Most important of all for modern celebrity culture, Byron was understood to share with his heroes a kind of subjectivity whose depths could be read by the discerning. You no longer needed a reciprocal or unmediated relationship in order to become acquainted. With the help of poems and pictures, you could come to know him, potentially intimately, without him knowing you.

5
The Visual Discourse of Byron's Celebrity

Scrutinising a print of Byron, Caroline Lamb found herself infatuated with the sitter and infuriated with the artist:

> I marvel how a man who attends so minutely to every button and tassell should not study the hand more – and the ear: In all England I know but of two that have ears similar – and that eye [...] expresses every feeling the young Corsair has not – such as ill-humour, obstinacy, industry, instead of fire, genius, craft, spirit and incessant variety.[1]

Caroline subjected the print to the kind of scopophilic scrutiny that was typical of the eroticised visual response to Byron that he stimulated in his oriental tales, and which I traced in Chapter 4. She conflated the poet with his heroes and then expected his portrait to reveal his character (which she equated with theirs) in his eyes. She felt sure that his eyes, when seen in reality, did indeed reveal his spirit. Caroline had the opportunity to study Byron in the flesh, but the efficacy of celebrity culture was guaranteed by the fact that readers didn't need that kind of access to Byron to relate to him visually. Isabel Harvey, the 17-year-old fan who wrote to Byron under the pseudonym Zorina Stanley after he left England, had no chance of seeing him in the flesh; nonetheless, she responded to him visually. 'In Mr. Haydon's picture of the Raising of Lazarus there is a head he thinks like you,' she wrote. 'I have been twenty times to see it. They think I am absorbed in admiration of the picture, but it is only one head that engrosses my mind's eye.'[2] Visiting Benjamin Robert Haydon's painting, which was on display in the rather lowbrow 'Egyptian Hall' in Piccadilly, couldn't satisfy Zorina for long. She soon acquired her own print of Byron, 'to which I talk every day', and offered to send him a picture of herself. 'I should like you to fancy me a friend', she wrote, 'one you have known and seen.'[3] This kind of emotional investment in images of Byron was repeated all over Britain and beyond, made possible by the emergence of a secondary industry supplying pictures that circulated alongside Byron's poems. In this chapter, I contend that Byron's image was an essential element of his cultural impact and I unearth the conventions of a Byronic pictorial discourse, which shadowed his poetry and supported his public profile.

To bring the specific significance of Byron's visual celebrity into focus, compare Zorina's gaze with that of Elizabeth Bennet in *Pride and Prejudice* (1813). As Elizabeth stood in front of Darcy's portrait at Pemberley, she felt 'a more gentle sensation towards the original, than she had ever felt in the height of their acquaintance'; she 'thought of his regard with a deeper sentiment of gratitude than it had ever raised before; she remembered its warmth, and softened its impropriety of expression'.[4] *Pride and Prejudice*, as Deidre Lynch has argued, teaches its readers to look beyond surface impressions and read characters' depths, just as Elizabeth 'stood several minutes before the picture in earnest contemplation' before she felt herself softening towards Darcy.[5] His picture can only become a crux of the novel's plot, however, because Elizabeth has already met him socially and is about to encounter him again. Only one picture in Pemberley's gallery can hold Elizabeth's gaze because she knows only one sitter. The scene is a pivotal one precisely because it punctuates a relationship otherwise based on social interactions. Once Byron's celebrity had gained a visual dimension, however, his images did not supplement a social relationship, but substituted for it. For those, like Zorina, who could not hope to meet Byron in the flesh, pictures of him, and the visual tropes of his poems, enabled a kind of relationship that was always mediated through commercialised works of art.

As a result, Byron's image was engineered over time, by several artists, until it was sufficiently simple and memorable to recognise in silhouette. Through archival research, this chapter traces that process, investigating how Byron's image proliferated in a variety of media from 1806 to the 1830s. My aim is not to present a comprehensive survey, but to identify the logic according to which the visual element of Byron's celebrity operated. There were early and late attempts to produce silhouettes of Byron from life or from memory. John and Robert Leacroft were among Byron's friends at Southwell, and Robert acted with him in amateur theatricals in 1806. One of the brothers drew a silhouette in ink at around that time, which shows Byron's face in profile turned to the right.[6] Leigh Hunt's wife Marianne cut another silhouette from paper in the 1820s, showing Byron in a peaked cap and frock coat, wearing spurs and carrying a whip, as he appeared after his daily ride.[7] Both of these were executed by amateur acquaintances of Byron who had the chance to observe him closely, but neither of them would have been recognisable to a wider public during his lifetime. Within a few years of his death, however, Byron's silhouette *was* recognisable, in a version that had been modified and branded through a series of reproductions and metamorphoses that made it distinctive, but may have left it looking very little like Byron in the flesh.

Despite the many images of Byron produced in his lifetime, his critics have been reluctant to consider texts and images as part of a single field of enquiry. David Piper began his study of poets' portraits by admitting that '[t]he subject lies on the periphery of literature' and expressing his concern that it would appear 'noxiously distracting'.[8] That kind of anxiety may be the product of the post-Romantic disciplinary division of knowledge and the legacy of a 'fear of [...] visual images' that William Galperin identifies as 'endemic to romantic poetics'.[9] In recent years, however, literary critics and art historians have shown greater willingness to cross disciplinary boundaries in pursuit of phenomena that elude analysis with received methods. As literary critics become more interested in book history and art historians become more concerned with visual culture, we are learning more about why encounters between text and image are significant. W. J. T. Mitchell has promoted interdisciplinary engagements of this kind, which are, he claims, 'the result of following out the imperatives of a problem central to a single discipline'.[10] Timothy Clayton has urged us to integrate the study of printed images into accounts of print culture.[11] And Gillen D'Arcy Wood has offered a striking account of Romanticism's involvement in 'a century-long conflict between the literary elite of late Georgian England [...] and a booming recreational industry in visual media'.[12] For Wood, authors such as Wordsworth, Coleridge and Charles Lamb invested intellectually in a literary art that opposed itself to visual spectacle, while a mass audience omnivorously consumed word and image alike.

The Romantic period's new technologies of letterpress printing (described in Chapter 2) were accompanied by new methods for reproducing images (steel plate engraving, stereotypy), new levels of accomplishment in existing techniques (mezzotint, stipple engraving, aquatint) and new distribution infrastructures (macadamised roads, canals and eventually railways). As a result there were more printed texts and images in circulation, and these two kinds of print product interacted in new ways.[13] This was a period of rich cross-fertilisation between texts and images, in which books provided subjects for paintings, paintings circulated in reproductive prints and those prints often got bound into books. As William St Clair notes, in the Romantic period, 'the explosion of reading of literary texts was accompanied by an explosion in the viewing of engraved pictures'.[14] The images examined in this chapter circulated in a number of ways and therefore had different relationships with the poems that were disseminated in an overlapping infrastructure. In some cases the images appeared as part of picture books with minimal text, in some cases they formed an integral part of a letterpress book or magazine and in many cases they were published separately for individual purchase. An image that had been sold singly could later be issued as a frontispiece and vice versa. Moreover, the purchaser could put an image to a number of different uses. The same image, sold individually, could be hung on the wall by one purchaser, displayed in a portfolio by another and used by a third to extra-illustrate a book. A picture book sold in paper wrappers could be bound up in its existing format, or broken up and used as illustrations in one or more other books. These complexities make it difficult to study this material, but they also indicate the degree to which the circulation of printed images intersected with the circulation of letterpress texts within a single media ecology. For Byron's first readers, images of the poet appeared not as a troublesome distraction from properly unmediated critical engagement with his poems, but a welcome adjunct to reading them. 'Believe me', his publisher John Murray wrote in 1819, 'your portrait is engraved & painted & sold in every town throughout the Kingdom.'[15]

Byron was cannily complicit in propagating his own image. The portraits by Richard Westall and Thomas Phillips that he commissioned in 1813 set the basic terms of his visual representation. Richard Westall exhibited a preparatory drawing for his portrait of Byron at the New Gallery, Pall Mall, in 1814.[16] Like many portraits, Westall's is the result of a potentially tense collaboration between the artist and his patron, the sitter. Byron appears in half length, seated in profile facing the left of the picture, with his chin resting on his hand.[17] X-ray photography reveals that Westall altered the line of the shirt collar, which initially covered more of Byron's throat.[18] We cannot know for sure whether it was the poet or the painter who wanted Byron presented in profile, with an open neckline, creating two of his most enduring visual motifs. But we can be certain that when Byron appeared visually before his public, he had to involve others in his strategies of self-presentation. Once the Byronic image was no longer under Byron's sole control, it could begin to shift. Westall produced another version of his portrait at the same time, showing Byron in generic Renaissance costume, and later made a copy in which Byron's eyes are turned heavenward as if in a moment of inspiration.[19] While Byron could maintain a degree of negotiated control over the images he sat for and paid for, the artists he commissioned could then produce copies and variant versions over which he had little jurisdiction.

Thomas Phillips painted two portraits of Byron in 1813–1814, now known as the 'Albanian' portrait and the 'Cloak' portrait. The 'Albanian' portrait is one of the most widely known images of Byron today, but after being exhibited at the Royal Academy in 1814 it disappeared from public view for the rest of Byron's life.[20] Lady Noel, Byron's mother-in-law, stipulated in her will that it should be kept 'safely inclosed and shut up' until Byron's daughter Ada came of age in 1836, and even then shown to Ada only with her mother's consent.[21] As a result, the Albanian portrait was unknown to the wider reading public until 1841, when it was published in an engraving by William Finden. By contrast, Phillips's 'cloak' portrait became widely known through engravings.[22] Phillips worked on this portrait at the same time as the one of Byron in Albanian costume. Byron wears the same shirt, brooch and waistcoat, but he appears wrapped in a dark cloak. Phillips exhibited the picture at the Royal Academy in 1814. Once again, Byron evidently had some control over his representation in this *ad vivum* portrait, because, although he told Phillips that 'one can never tell the truth of one's own features', he asked him to retouch the nose (*BLJ*, IV, 79). But, like Westall's, this portrait exists in more than one version, including a variant which shows Byron with lighter hair and a more rounded jaw-line.[23]

These portraits by Westall and Phillips established what Suzanne K. Hyman calls the 'Byron pose', with the head turned right in profile or three-quarter view. 'This pose', she writes, 'cuts across style and convention to imprint itself on nearly every representation of the poet.'[24] Byron's visual celebrity began in commissioned paintings like these, and their many reproductions. When Murray hung a portrait of Byron above the fireplace in his drawing room in Albemarle Street, published prints of Byron as frontispieces or as singletons, and sealed his letters with a signet ring showing Byron's head, he cemented the visual to the verbal to form Byronic celebrity, extending his business into the burgeoning market for prints and fostering readers' fascination with the man behind the poems. Byron was both eager to be represented and anxious about the result, and he attempted to exert control over how his image was reproduced. In September 1812, he wrote to Murray from Cheltenham to inquire when 'the graven image' of his portrait would be ready 'to grace or disgrace some of our tardy editions' (*BLJ*, II, 191). But when Byron saw the frontispiece engraving, which was intended for the fifth edition of *Childe Harold's Pilgrimage*, he strongly objected to it and repeatedly instructed Murray to destroy it.[25] Thrust into the public eye by his poetry, Byron was kept there partly by the circulation of his image, which he felt as both a boon and a burden.[26]

But while these 'authorized' paintings and engravings lie at the root of Byron's visual celebrity, his image circulated so widely because it rapidly escaped his control. Byron permeated Romantic visual culture not just because these paintings were faithfully reproduced, but also – and I think more importantly – because their image of Byron was appropriated, altered, improved, rethought, varied or transformed. The result was a free-standing visual discourse that can account for Captain Forrester's 'great [...] astonishment' when he met Byron in 1824 and found himself facing 'a being bearing as little resemblance to the pretended fac-simile, as I do to Apollo'.[27] Being a celebrity in the Romantic period meant seeing one's images proliferate, evolving or deforming as they suffused visual culture. Byron became visible to his readers when a relatively small number of 'authorized' images were transformed in the process of reproduction. As a result, visual representations of the poet became cheaper and more widely distributed, simplified and commercially appropriated, eroticised and available to view in private. Byron's image slipped further and further out of his control. But the less Byron could control his representation, the more it could saturate Romantic visual culture, complementing the popularity of his poetry and extending his visual impact to those who could not see him in the flesh. John Gibson Lockhart comically claimed that 'every boarding-school in the empire [...] contains many devout believers in the amazing misery of the black-haired, high-browed, blue-eyed, bare-throated, Lord Byron. How melancholy [he] look[s] in the prints!'[28]

When James Asperne wanted to publish a portrait of Byron in his *European Magazine*, he wrote to the poet on 14 December 1813, asking him to sit for the popular artist Samuel Drummond. Byron declined, suggesting that Asperne should use an engraving of one of the portraits in the studios of Westall or Phillips instead. His refusal to sit for Drummond may indicate his discomfort at the proposal as well as his full diary. Flatteringly insisting that he would hate the painter's talents to be 'thrown away on a restless and impatient subject', Byron arranged for Asperne to reproduce one of the portraits he had already commissioned, restricting the circle of people who collaborated in the dissemination of his image (*BLJ*, III, 198).[29] Westall had apparently already been approached about this, and had objected. He explained, in a letter to Byron of 11 January 1814, his 'repugnance to seeing the work with which I have taken considerable pains, engraved in any other than the best manner.'[30] In the event, Asperne commissioned the engraver Thomas Blood to produce a picture that transformed Westall's portrait, but without Westall's permission (Fig. 5.1).

Blood's engraving took Byron's head from Westall's portrait and bolted it onto a completely different body.[31] He turned Westall's richly coloured oil painting into a black-and-white stipple engraving which allowed almost endless reproduction. In the process, he moved Byron's body from its three-quarter turn to a frontal view. Blood replaces the single-breasted jacket with a double-breasted coat, covers Byron's throat with a white cravat and substitutes large flamboyant collars for the small ones in the painting. Byron's hair becomes darker and his eyebrows more clearly defined, and his distinctively small ear lobes are enlarged. His neck ends up unrealistically elongated, and his body much fuller than in the original. Altering the neck makes Byron's head seem erect, where before his chin lent pensively on his hand. Where Byron was previously gazing out of the frame lost in thought, he now stares disdainfully away from the viewer. Westall's suggestions of background are left out and the image becomes a vignette. To view Westall's original, you needed to be in London and to have a shilling for the entry fee to his exhibition. Prints like Blood's made Byron's image affordable to those who could not pay the admission charge, accessible to those who lived outside London and available for viewing in private. Byron's readers could now possess their own portrait of him to look at in their own home.

Blood's engraving was only the beginning of the transformations Westall's painting underwent. Charles Turner produced an 'authorized' reproduction of Westall's painting in May 1814, but unauthorised versions continued to appear.[32] James Heath produced his own version in 1815, which seems to derive from Blood's engraving rather than from Westall's original.[33] Another version appeared anonymously as the frontispiece to the pirated *Don Juan, with a Preface by a Clergyman* (1823), and Archibald Dick engraved yet another version in 1824.[34] The portrait was still being engraved afresh in the 1830s, when Fisher's Drawing Room Scrapbook published a version. In the poem that accompanied this print, Letitia Elizabeth Landon paid tribute to Byron by echoing his own claim that poetry is 'the lava of the imagination' (*BLJ*, III, 179). 'Thrice beautiful the outward show', she wrote, 'Still the volcano is below.'[35]

Figure 5.1 *Byron*, engraved by Thomas Blood after Richard Westall, *European Magazine*, January 1814. National Portrait Gallery, London.

Thomas Phillips's 'cloak' portrait underwent a similar series of transformations, especially after Byron's death. Byron appeared in a series of portraits of philhellenes published by Adam Friedel in the 1820s. In one of Friedel's prints, published in 1825, Byron wears his Homeric helmet (Fig. 5.2)[36] The print bears the inscription 'Drawn from a Sketch in Possession of the Comte Demitrio Deladezima, in Cephalonia: corrected & Published in London, Feby 1825, by A. Friedel, Publisher of Portraits of all the principal Greek Chiefs'. This marketing puff is certainly untrue. Although Byron did have a Homeric helmet made, there is no record that he ever wore it, let alone allowed himself to be sketched in it.[37] The print clearly derives from the 'cloak' portrait, but it purports to be a new *ad vivum* portrait. Friedel apparently thought it would be in his interest to claim that this was a previously unseen image. Not only that, he subsequently published a second portrait of Byron, which also derived from the 'cloak' portrait. This time the image appeared in reverse, perhaps as a result of tracing, but the distinctive collar and the beading on the edge of the jacket show clearly that it derives from the same source. In this print the Homeric helmet sits next to Byron and the cloak has been transformed into a Scottish plaid, suggesting his upbringing in Aberdeen.[38] The artist also added a piece of paper in Byron's hand, which signifies both his literary vocation and his involvement with receiving reports and dispatching orders in Greece. William Benbow, the radical publisher and pornographer who hung an image of Byron's head above his shop, produced a similar forgery for the frontispiece to his pirated edition of *Don Juan* (1822).[39] This image purports to be an engraving by William Holl of a drawing by Holroyd of a bust of Byron. But no such bust ever existed. The drawing shows an image of Byron derived from Phillips's 'cloak' portrait, with the head and shoulders terminating in a spurious plinth, on which the word 'Byron' appears to have been engraved.

Phillips's portrait was once again appropriated to make the frontispiece for *The Duke of Mantua*, a tragedy in five acts published anonymously by John Roby in 1823 and dedicated to Lady Byron (Fig. 5.3). Roby was a banker, author of *Traditions of Lancashire* and occasional contributor to *Blackwood's* and *Fraser's* magazines. He had no connection with either Byron or his wife, apart from the fact that he lived for most of his life in Rochdale, the seat of Byron's barony.[40] *The Duke of Mantua* contains nothing relevant to Byron's life and work, but Roby thought he could attract attention to his play by associating it with the Byron family and perhaps passing it off as Byron's own. The frontispiece derives from the 'cloak' portrait, but adds a mask in Byron's hand, which

Figure 5.2 *Byron*, 'Drawn from a Sketch in Possession of the Comte Demitrio Deladezima, in Cephalonia: corrected & Published in London, Feby 1825, by A. Friedel, Publisher of Portraits of all the principal Greek Chiefs'. National Portrait Gallery, London.

THE

DUKE OF MANTUA,

A TRAGEDY.

BY

LONDON:

PRINTED BY THOMAS DAVISON,

WHITEFRIARS.

1823.

Figure 5.3 Frontispiece to [John Roby], *The Duke of Mantua* (London: Thomas Davison, 1823). The Beinecke Rare Book and Manuscript Library, Yale.

he holds so as to cover most of his face. Here Byron's image is reduced to the simplest arrangement of lines, with only his left eye visible from behind the mask, but it is still recognisably Byron. Similarly, when Henry Chorley published a picture of Byron in 1838, he seems to have been as much concerned to demonstrate a new etching technique as he was to place Byron's image before the public yet again. The medallion print was part of Chorley's book *The Authors of England,* which consisted of 14 portraits of contemporary or recently deceased authors.[41] The 'patent process' of Achille Collas was mentioned in the inscription to each print, suggesting the importance of technological advances to this book and the phenomenon of which it was part. When James Asperne borrowed Byron's image for the *European Magazine,* when Adam Friedel included it in his series of engraved portraits, when William Benbow capitalised on it to promote his piracies, when John Roby placed it on the title page of *The Duke of Mantua* and when Henry Chorley used it to show off a new etching process, they all aimed to turn Byron's visual celebrity to their own advantage, transforming his image in the process. Byron's image circulated so widely because it could be appropriated easily and could be pressed into service in a variety of commercial enterprises. Visual reference to Byron kept his star in the ascendant, while it helped to sell products over which Byron and his publisher had no control and from which they could make no profit.

These images are all recognisably portraits of Byron – not just images influenced at a distance by Byronic motifs, but visibly representations of the man himself. But they are a long way from the paintings by Westall and Phillips on which they draw. Byron's image has been simplified to make it more memorable and repeatable, focussing on a few recognisably Byronic visual signifiers. Caricatures of Byron also contribute to this process. In December 1812, the proprietors of *Town Talk* published a caricature called 'The Genius of the Times', showing a crowd of contemporary writers scrambling to get up Parnassus, in order to occupy a vacant place in the Temple of Fame.[42] Leading the race are Walter Scott, riding on the back of his publisher, and Byron, who sits astride a cask of ale being carried by several men. At the foot of the hill, a number of authors are drowning in Lethe, including Wordsworth, Coleridge and Southey. Others, including Matthew Lewis, dash in the opposite direction, following a sign to the Bank of England. At this early stage in his career, before Westall and Phillips were commissioned to paint his portrait, Byron had not yet achieved a distinct visual identity. He is only recognisable in this caricature because of the labels attached: he has *Childe Harold's Pilgrimage* in his pocket, his Drury Lane address is in his hand, and there is a legend at the bottom of the picture which identifies some of the figures.

By contrast, Isaac Robert Cruikshank's caricatures from 1815 to 1816 show how, by that time, Byron had developed a more distinctive visual identity. 'The Separation, a Sketch from the Private Life of Lord Iron' shows Byron in the act of abandoning his wife and child, supposedly to run off with the well-known actress Charlotte Mardyn. 'Lobby Loungers' shows Byron ogling the improbably buxom actresses or courtesans in the foyer of the Theatre Royal, Drury Lane.[43] In both of these examples, Byron is easy to spot in wide trousers (worn to cover his malformed leg) and a double-breasted, militaristic jacket. These caricatures draw some of their elements from the portraits by Westall and Phillips: Byron is shown in profile, but looking the other way, and Cruikshank gives him an exaggerated curling forelock, which recalls Westall. But neither the jacket nor the trousers are taken directly from an *ad vivum* portrait of Byron. Rather, they are features observed from Byron's appearance in Regency society and made into visual motifs. Cruikshank's caricatures of Byron draw upon elements observed both from life and from Byron's portraits to create an image of Byron made up of certain simple trademark features that are easily recognised.

This process was extended and accelerated by those illustrations that made Byron's heroes look like portraits of the poet, encouraging his readers to identify the two with each other. A well-known illustration to *Childe Harold* elides Byron with his hero and places him in a gothic and erotic version of the 'caritas Romana' episode from Canto Three of the poem. Mingling elements from different visual sources, it reproduces Byron's profile from Westall's painting, but seems indebted to Phillips's portrait for the cloak.[44] George Cruikshank (Isaac Robert Cruikshank's brother) rushed out a set of woodcuts in 1825, just after Byron's death, including an image with the legend 'Juan opposing the entrance to the Spirit-room' (Fig. 5.4).[45] This illustration to *Don Juan* also draws on Westall's portrait, depicting Juan with a considerably simplified version of Byron's profile. Cruikshank eroticises some elements of the image, exaggerating the open-necked shirt to reveal a chest whose chiselled muscles are well defined by the simple lines of the woodcut. Byron appears as Juan, caught in a moment of heroic action.

Instances of Byron's celebrity visibility were sufficiently widespread to be made fun of in several graphic satires which cannot strictly be called 'caricatures'. Two anonymous prints appeared around 1825, titled 'Anecdotes of Byron – or a touch of the Marvellous'.[46] They satirise the posthumous rush to publish memoirs of Byron. In this case the target

Juan opposing the Entrance to the Spirit Room.

Figure 5.4 'Juan opposing the entrance to the Spirit-room' from George Cruikshank, *Forty Illustrations of Lord Byron* (London: James Robins and Co. [1825]). Private collection.

is *Anecdotes of Lord Byron, from Authentic Sources,* written by Alexander Kilgour and published anonymously in 1825.[47] This was a cheap book, in duodecimo format, containing a series of anecdotes about Byron, with no attempt to link them into a continuous narrative. The satirist apparently found some of the anecdotes rather unremarkable, and drew these pictures to poke fun. The first image is called 'Weather Wise' (Fig. 5.5) and bears the following inscription:

> One Day on a voyage to Athens, a dark cloud appeared to windward, his Lordship regarded it steadily for some time, untill [*sic*] at length feeling a few drops of rain fall, he called to Fletcher to bring him Cloak [*sic*] so certain he was of an approaching shower.

This cheap, low quality print relies on the standard white collar, trousers and profile presentation to make Byron recognisable. If Byron's meteorological discernment was no more than ordinary, his gastronomic discrimination impressed the satirist even less. The second print's

Figure 5.5 'Anecdotes of Byron – or a touch of the Marvellous', anonymous, circa 1825. The British Museum.

inscription reports that 'nothing could induce him to partake of fish which had been caught more than ten days, indeed he had a singular dislike even to the smell'.[48] There's nothing very 'singular' about such a dislike, nor about this print. It picks up the profile depiction of Byron and the trademark white collar from earlier representations, and includes the exaggerated forelock from Cruikshank's caricatures.

Another graphic satire, titled 'Specimen Illustrations for a New Edition of Lord Byron's Works', appeared in *McLean's Monthly Sheet of Caricatures* in 1832. It mocks the fashion for illustrating Byron's works, and makes its point with three quite dreadful puns: a gentleman with matted and uncontrollable hair is 'The Coarse-Hair' (*The Corsair*); a Bride taking a quick fortifying drink before leaving for her wedding (or perhaps her wedding night) is 'The Bride of A-Bye-Dose' (*The Bride of Abydos*); and a pair of drunkenly singing tramps disturb Scottish guardsmen inspecting their troops in 'English Bards and Scotch Reviewers'. The picture of 'The Coarse-Hair' (Fig. 5.6) obliquely satirises the habit of presenting Byron as his heroes, picking up the 'Byron

Figure 5.6 'The Coarse Hair', from 'Specimen Illustrations for a New Edition of Lord Byron's Works', in *McLean's Monthly Sheet of Caricatures* (1832). The British Museum.

pose' from the Westall portrait. These graphic satires suggest that visual representations of Byron were important not only because they helped to foster a visual element of his celebrity, to stoke scopophilic responses to the poet or to propagate the identification of Byron with his heroes; images also played a part in *satirizing* those phenomena, poking fun at Byron and the growing industry that surrounded him. But even these oppositional images are distant descendants of the authorised images of Byron with which I began: another twist in the tangled trajectories Byron's image followed once it had slipped out of his control.

The transformations Byron's image underwent produced a visual discourse of Byronic celebrity, which made Byron recognisable as an assemblage of disjunct signifiers: a bare throat, a white collar, a curling forelock, a receding hairline, a characteristic pose. For a celebrity in the age before photography, gaining cultural ubiquity meant having your image adjusted, simplified and branded until visual recognition became immediate. My final images are an index of the extent to which this is true of Byron. In the early nineteenth century there was a vogue for puzzle prints, which depended on visual puns for their effect.[49] Figures or profiles were often concealed in the pictures, and Napoleon was a

Figure 5.7 'The Spirit of Byron at Newstead Abbey', designed on stone by A. Picker; published by W. Day, lithographer to the King, Gate Street, London, circa 1830. Private collection.

common subject. In a number of prints the spirit of Napoleon, outlined among trees in the landscape, returns to brood over his grave. It was also quite common for the profiles of Napoleon, his wife and child to appear hidden in bouquets of flowers. In these images, Napoleon's *hat* is an indispensable emblem, a visual trademark signifying Buonaparte's identity. Byron featured in at least three puzzle pictures of this kind. In one (unusually, octagonal) watercolour, Byron's spirit returns to Newstead Abbey, where his profile appears sketched out in the trees and clouds, and surrounded by the hidden profiles of those closest to him (Fig. 5.7).[50] Dark storm clouds double for Byron's hair, while an unrealistically bright patch of sky forms his open white collar. The picture unites Byron in spirit with his devoted lover Theresa Guiccioli and his legitimate daughter Ada at his ancestral home. Intriguingly, in this picture Theresa Guiccioli displaces Lady Byron as the presiding spirit in an image of the bourgeois nuclear family Byron never had. In the print 'The Spirit of Byron', his profile appears in the clouds over the sea (Fig. 5.8). *Childe Harold's Pilgrimage* lies on the shore, as his legacy. His

Figure 5.8 'The Spirit of Byron', designed and engraved by E. Brookes; London; published Feby 1st, 1832 for the Engraver; by J. B. Brookes, Book & Print Publisher, 2 New Bond Street. Copyright ©2006 Hordern-Dalgety Collection. http://puzzlemuseum.com

Figure 5.9 'The Spirit of Byron in the Isles of Greece', designed on stone by H. Burn; printed by Engelmann and Co.; published by R. Ackermann, 96 Strand, London, circa 1830. Private collection.

face is lit up by the setting sun, but in its whiteness also appears as a new sun rising, perhaps, over a free Greece. His image is immediately recognisable, but its representation is extremely economical. Byron has been reduced to a white collar, a distinctive hairline and a characteristic left profile.[51]

Rudolph Ackermann issued another Byronic puzzle print from his shop in the strand around 1830, entitled 'The Spirit of Byron in the Isles of Greece' (Fig. 5.9).[52] Here a diminutive Byron, in a pose that reverses the Westall portrait and with his conventional white trousers, is bathed in a patch of sunlight, lost in contemplation of the landscape. The view he looks out on is full of Byronic elements: cliffs, ocean and a fast flowing stream to the bottom right. The landscape is dominated by the left-of-centre tree which, for the fraction-of-a-second first glance, seems to be the feature around which the print is composed. It stretches up, towering over Byron and dominating the top half of the picture. Then the penny drops. Byron's noble profile is repeated in the rocks and stones and trees, looking back on the figure that looks out at them. This spirit Byron is sketched out from the Byronic signifiers of his high forehead, the hair receding from the temples, and his characteristic open white collar, which seems to serve no purpose here as a feature of the landscape. There is a subtle criticism of Byron contained here. Looking on nature's works for inspiration, Byron sees only himself writ large. It's a critique of the viewer too, of course, who had learned to view Europe's sublime landscapes through Byronic lenses with the aid of the guidebooks Murray published after Byron's death. But by this time, Byron *was* writ large in the visual culture of the nineteenth century. His face looked out from frontispieces and books of illustrations, caricatures and engraved prints, dinner services and Toby jugs. In an image consisting of almost no lines at all, he was now recognisable in silhouette. The visual discourse of Byronic celebrity had developed to such an extent that it had a fully functioning set of conventions that operated with reference to earlier depictions of Byron, not to Byron's actual appearance in reality. Byron's celebrity produced its visual impact through an extraordinary proliferation of images that played variations on a set of visual motifs. By the time this print was published, the portraits that Byron had had painted in 1813 had been reproduced so many times, and passed through such an extensive series of modifications and simplifications, that he could be represented by just a few conventional markers, and yet still be unmistakable.

6
The Handling of *Hebrew Melodies*

By the end of 1814, when *Childe Harold's Pilgrimage* was in its ninth edition and his verse tales numbered four, Byron was a poet with a number of problems. He had mined his experiences of exotic travels almost to exhaustion – he had some unpublished scraps of Oriental poetry, but seemed incapable of turning them into a fifth verse tale. The sheen had worn off his celebrity, making fame a fact of life which was rapidly becoming routine. Worse still, his series of four Turkish Tales was increasingly being charged with that most unByronic of qualities: predictability. Lord Byron, it was whispered, had written himself out, and what was to come promised only paler and paler imitations of his former glories. Where once Byron's poetry had made him a celebrity, it now seemed that his poetry would be read only because he was a celebrity. George Daniel, in *The Modern Dunciad* (1814), put the complaint into Popeian couplets:

> The town is pleas'd when BYRON will rehearse,
> And finds a thousand beauties in his verse;
> So fix'd his fame – that write whate'er he will,
> The patient public must admire it still;
> Yes, – though bereft of half his force and fire,
> They still must read, – and, dozing, must admire[.][1]

But while Byron was heading for an impasse and in need of a new direction, Murray was becoming aware that the profitable celebrity he and Byron had collaboratively created was not a limitless source of reputation and income.

Byron's meteoric rise to fame was a business success story to make any entrepreneur proud. His relationship with his publisher, as I have indicated, was an important element of his celebrity. It also made an impact on Byron's writing in ways that studying his celebrity can bring into focus.[2] Technological advances in printing and the expansion of commercial publishing meant that, in the Romantic period, poets were increasingly forced to engage with their publishers in new ways, while often theorising poetry as something apart from, and untouchable by, commercial interests. In Byron's case, that engagement was often highly collaborative, but always subject to strain. Poet and publisher differed in their politics, but Murray's political conservatism was less of a problem for Byron than his business caution. Murray had urged Byron to alter the freethinking stanzas of *Childe Harold's Pilgrimage* not because he objected to their content, but in case they should 'deprive [him] of some customers amongst the Orthodox'.[3] An astute businessman, Murray hedged his bets and reduced his risks to a minimum. As well as Byron's poems, he published the Tory *Quarterly Review* and the wildly successful *Domestic Cookery* by Mrs Rundell. Byron quipped, in a parody of John Clare, 'Along thy sprucest bookshelves shine / The works thou deemest most divine – / The 'Art of Cookery,' and mine, / My Murray.'[4]

These different ventures clearly didn't cohere into a list with a single strong flavour, and so it was important that each element had a distinctive individual identity in the marketplace. Murray had invested heavily in the image of Byron as an aristocrat, traveller and object of desire with just the right degree of thrillingly heterodox charm. With his purse and his reputation swelled by Byron's success, Murray moved from Fleet Street to the more stylish West End in 1813. He bought the Albemarle Street premises of his old rival William Miller, who had turned down *Childe Harold's Pilgrimage*. Murray wrote to a relative:

> I have lately ventured on the bold step of quitting the old establishment to which I have been so long attached, and have moved to one of the best, in every respect, that is known in my business, where I have succeeded in a manner the most complete and flattering.[5]

The step was indeed bold: Murray had taken on a mortgage that he would not pay off until 1821 and, according to his biographer, 'the step which Murray had taken was so momentous and the responsibility so great, that at times he was driven almost to the verge of despondency'.[6] Murray must have watched his star poet's writing and its reception with some anxiety. After *Lara's* publication, Byron was unable or reluctant to extend the sequence of tales any further, and lacked the impetus to return to *Childe Harold*. He needed to find a new direction. But Murray wanted yet more of the poetry which had made Byron's name and was making his publisher's fortune. While Byron needed new subjects and new styles so as not to atrophy, Murray needed more of the same to sustain his income.

In this chapter, I want to tell a story of conflict between the celebrated product identity that Byron and Murray had collaboratively created and the poet who had begun to find that identity constraining. Borrowing Michel de Certeau's terms, I regard the business practices of the Tory publisher as a 'strategy', and the artistic practices of the oppositional poet grappling with his own celebrity as 'tactics'.[7] When discussing this phase of Byron's career, it is not meaningful to speak of Byron and Murray collaborating on a strategy for presenting Byron to the public through his poems, but only of what Certeau would call the 'tactics' Byron engages in, given the fact of his publicity. Those tactics are sometimes in tune with Murray's strategy and sometimes in conflict with it. *Hebrew Melodies* has proved difficult for critics to accommodate in smooth narratives of Byron's career, and the collection has too often been seen as either a sop or a fillip to the pious Annabella Milbanke.[8] I suggest that its tactical importance lies precisely in this difficulty and that its strangeness can be accounted for if we understand the tension between Byron's tactical attempt to write a reformed and newly satisfying poetry and Murray's subsequent strategy which attempted to contain the lyrics within familiar Byronic parameters. *Hebrew Melodies* is Byron's first attempt to resist the logic of his celebrity, and it would prove to be unsuccessful. When critics marginalise the collection, they repeat Murray's strategy of containment. In this chapter, then, I am concerned with Byron's creative urge to write a different kind of poetry to that which sustained his fame, and Murray's business imperative to make sure that this poetry could still be read as recognisably Byronic, that it was still part of the Byronic sequence which was, and must remain, closely associated with the house of Murray. I use Certeau's terms to help locate Byron as a creative individual within both generic constraints and a promotional apparatus that increasingly seemed to impose someone else's agenda on him.

Before he began *Hebrew Melodies*, there were complaints that all Byron's poems were the same, that he was wasting his talent and that his scepticism was a danger to public morality. The *British Review* could 'scarcely criticise as fast as Lord Byron can write'; but fortunately it was spared the need to review every new poem 'by the uniformity of his lordship's productions'.[9] The *Critical Review* accused Byron of squandering his talents on trash: 'we regret to see powers that can unlock the springs of terror and pity with such fearful effect, wasted upon garish and incompatible fiction'.[10] And Byron was everywhere urged to reform, to take the lessons of Christianity to heart and further to ennoble his poetry by directing it to virtuous ends.[11] One reader signing himself 'H. S. B.' was so delighted by *The Bride of Abydos* and so distressed by Byron's scepticism that he penned some poetry of his own for the *Gentleman's Magazine*, including the following lines:

> If from that feeling heart, that radiant mind
> Religion beam'd, enshrining and enshrin'd;
> How would the holy Minstrels, who rejoice
> O'er triumphs far less brilliant, wake a strain,
> That e'en thy lay might emulate in vain,
> With all their hallow'd fire and pure angelic voice! [12]

These critical strands came together, in a thoroughly over-determined fashion, in the *Christian Observer*'s review of *The Corsair*.[13] The anonymous reviewer mourns Byron's decision to withdraw from writing (stated in *The Corsair*'s dedicatory letter to Thomas Moore), and ventures to hope that his leisure will now be spent in improving ways. He hopes that Byron will one day resume the Spenserian stanza, perhaps taking as his hero 'a seventh knight, to whom we could assign the patronage of one of the choicest Christian Virtues', and builds a peroration in which Byron is castigated for not expressing properly Christian sentiments.[14] Finally, the reviewer claims that he will give up reading all this degraded modern literature 'till Christians shall begin to talk as Christians', and hopes to read Byron again only when the poet has reformed himself: 'how should we then rejoice to meet our renovated friend!'.[15]

Byron could have ignored these criticisms if they hadn't chimed with a more personal dissatisfaction. In the two years between his first and second proposal to Annabella Milbanke, Byron had been in search of sensation: 'in my pursuit of strong emotions & mental *drams* I found them to be sure and intoxicated myself accordingly – but now I am sobered my head aches & my heart too' (*BLJ*, IV, 217). The heartache was caused by his affair with his half-sister Augusta, which emotionally fascinated and morally alarmed Byron. His moral hangover worsened when Annabella accepted his second proposal, leaving him 'quite horrified in casting up my *moral* accounts of the two intervening years' (*BLJ*, IV, 179). She assured him that throughout their strange and cautious courtship, 'I honored you for that pure sense of moral rectitude, which could not be perverted, though perhaps tried by the practice of Vice',[16] but Byron still affirmed that there was 'nothing I would see altered in *you* – but so much in myself' (*BLJ*, IV, 208). During the previous two years he had corresponded with Annabella about religion, discussed theological questions with Francis Hodgson and the future Bishop Kaye at Cambridge and become fascinated by Joanna Southcott.[17] Southcott had announced in 1813 (aged 63) that she was miraculously pregnant with the child of Christ, who would prepare the way for His Second Coming. Byron was understandably inclined to debunk, and insisted that he longed to know who the earthly father was and how he had managed such a feat 'for I am sure the common materials would not answer so pious a purpose'.[18] But he was also 'afraid seriously – that these matters will lend a sad handle to your profane Scoffers and give loose to much damnable laughter' (*BLJ*, IV, 167). His concern about the sceptical scoffers – among whom he was so often numbered – is underlined by the Biblical reference signalled by the capital 'S': 'there shall come in the last days scoffers, walking after their own lusts' (II Peter 3.3). By the end of 1814, Byron was growing tired of walking after his own lusts, and as his marriage drew closer, he promised anyone who would listen that he would reform, using that word 'seriously' again and again. To Lady Melbourne:

> In course I mean to reform most thoroughly & become 'a good man and true' in all the various senses of those respective and respectable appellations – seriously[.] (*BLJ*, IV, 172)

To Thomas Moore:

> I must, of course, reform thoroughly; and, seriously, if I can contribute to her happiness, I shall secure my own. She is so good a person, that – that – in short, I wish I was a better. (*BLJ*, IV, 178)

And to Lady Jersey:

> Pray forgive me for scribbling all this nonsense – you know I must be serious all the rest of my life – and this is a parting piece of buffoonery which I write with tears in my eyes expecting to be agitated. (*BLJ*, IV, 196)

Marriage to the supremely moral Annabella would keep him away from Augusta and encourage him to leave behind the dissipations of the last few years.[19] 'A wife would be my salvation', he wrote in his journal

(*BLJ*, III, 241).[20] Doubtless the salvation he was looking for was as much financial as spiritual, but his mercenary motives, and the disastrous outcome of his marriage, should not blind us to the serious thought that he gave to reforming during his engagement.

Byron was not immediately enthusiastic about the *Hebrew Melodies* project when Douglas Kinnaird interceded on behalf of the composer, Isaac Nathan. But he came to see the project, I suggest, as an opportunity to write his way out of the poetic and moral problems in which he felt himself mired. Writing himself out of dissipation and into marriage, he asked Annabella to make fair copies of some of the lyrics during their engagement and honeymoon, and while visiting his future parents-in-law, he used the Milbanke family Bible, working from the book in which his marriage to Annabella would shortly be recorded.[21] *Hebrew Melodies* provided a chance to write a new kind of poetry, whose content would be part of Byron's reformation and whose form was an innovation in his career. With the help of his unlikely collaborator, Isaac Nathan, and his first amanuensis, Annabella Milbanke, Byron would answer his newly strident critics and his newly awakened conscience at once.

In *Hebrew Melodies*, typically Byronic concerns modulate into deeper keys. I will cite three cases. First, the theme of (self-imposed) exile from a homeland – such as Harold's nonchalant search for new pleasures after those found in England pall, or the Giaour's lonely wanderings from Venice when he becomes 'apostate from his own vile faith' (616) – turns into a meditation on Jewish Diaspora. The forced exile from Israel of the whole race and the Jews' longing to return to their homeland replace the self-motivated exiles who wander because they never want to go home:

> But we must wander witheringly,
> In other lands to die;
> And where our fathers' ashes be,
> Our own may never lie:
> Our temple hath not left a stone,
> And Mockery sits on Salem's throne.[22]

The idea of exile, through its connection with the Diaspora, becomes in turn a metaphor for mortality as exile from God's presence. Judah is 'where their God hath dwelt', but believers can now only return to His presence, their true homeland, after death, 'The wild-dove hath her nest, the fox his cave, / Mankind their Country – Israel but the grave!'[23]

Secondly, Childe Harold's urbane cynicism, ennui and satiety return transformed into the religious themes of *contemptus mundi* and *vanitas vanitatum*. For example, in 'All is Vanity, Saith the Preacher', the first stanza recalls Childe Harold's revelry. While Harold's 'goblets brimmed with every costly wine' (1. 11), this speaker's 'goblets blushed from every wine', and Harold's 'laughing dames in whom he did delight' (1. 11) become the 'lovely forms' who caress the speaker of 'All is Vanity' (4). But this is no longer the sneer of the youthful Harold 'who ne in virtue's ways did take delight' (1. 11); it is rather a quasi-ascetic rejection of worldly goods. While Harold's worldly pleasures lose their savour through long indulgence, this speaker's are always embittered by the taint of sin:

> There rose no day, there rolled no hour
> Of pleasure unembittered;
> And not a trapping deck'd my power
> That gall'd not while it glittered.[24]

In the final stanza, the image of the tortured mind as a scorpion girt by fire from *The Giaour* appears transformed by contact with Genesis. Scorpion-mind becomes serpent-heart, and the mental anguish of remorse becomes the moral torment of sinfulness that 'stings for evermore / The soul that must endure it' (23–4).

Finally, the scepticism about revealed religion with which Byron had been charged in the light of his earlier poetry becomes, in the mouths of his new speakers, a painful registering of the terrible silence of God in the face of injustice. In 'On Jordan's Banks' the speaker asks how God, who appeared on Sinai and is both loving and jealous, can allow His own land to be overrun and His chosen people to be exiled and dispersed, without intervening with compassion for His people and a terrible vengeance for His enemies:

> On Jordan's banks the Arabs' camels stray,
> On Sion's hill the False One's votaries pray,
> The Baal-adorer bows on Sinai's steep –
> Yet there – even there – Oh God! thy thunders sleep:
>
> There – where thy finger scorch'd the tablet stone!
> There – where thy shadow to thy people shone!
> Thy glory shrouded in its garb of fire:
> Thyself – none living see and not expire!

Oh! in the lightning let thy glance appear!
Sweep from his shiver'd hand the oppressor's spear:
How long by tyrants shall thy land be trod?
How long thy temple worshipless, Oh God?

(*CPW*, III, 293)

God remains silent in the face of the speaker's urgent rhetorical demand that He speak. Byron had been labelled a sceptic, but in this carefully patterned poem he gives his speaker a plea for certainty and a complaint that the ways of God are inscrutable.[25] These examples suggest that Byron was moving established themes in new directions in *Hebrew Melodies* and attempting to depart from popular formulae.

But Byron's attempt to use *Hebrew Melodies* to move his poetry in the direction of a new moral and theological seriousness was compromised both by the literary marketplace in which he took up his position and by Murray's handling of the collection's physical production. When Isaac Nathan advertised, in the *Gentleman's Magazine* for May 1813, that he was 'about to publish "Hebrew Melodies" all of them upwards of 1000 years old and some of them performed by the Antient Hebrews before the destruction of the Temple', he was planning to move into a crowded but lucrative market.[26] Romantic-period readers were enthusiastic for the antiquarianism of Macpherson's Ossian and Chatterton's Rowley, and there was a growing vogue for national melodies, embodied by Moore's *Irish Melodies*, which came out serially throughout the period. A publication which combined the two attractions, such as Scott's *Minstrelsy of the Scottish Border*, was almost guaranteed success. Nor was Nathan the first to approach Byron to provide lyrics for a national melodies project.[27] When Byron wrote *Hebrew Melodies*, he wove in a variety of Hebraisms and names of scriptural places and people.[28] Importing Hebraic words to *Hebrew Melodies* reprised Byron's technique of deploying Oriental words in his tales, and archaisms in *Childe Harold's Pilgrimage*.[29] To some eyes, the diction of *Hebrew Melodies* was the same old thing played out against a new backcloth, with Scottish, Spenserian or Turkish cycloramas replaced by picturesque views of Sinai. Turning to the Old Testament instead of the Koran, and Josephus instead of the *Bibliothèque Orientale*, Byron found ripe new poaching grounds for his magpie muse, and studded his verses with stolen linguistic gems. The scattering of Hebraisms, for some reviewers, was the outward form of Christian observance without the inward devotion.[30] It seemed as though, with their arrival in the Holy Land, Byron's language and themes had been translated, but not transformed.

The *British Review*'s comments suggest why Byron's attempt to produce a newly reformed seriousness through a shift into Judaic diction was compromised before it began. The reviewer provided a recipe for cooking up national melodies:

> The way to proceed is first to prepare your melodies, and then you have the whole world lying between the polar circles, north and south, wherein to choose for them a proper designation and origin. One thing only will remain, which is to sprinkle the composition over with a few names of places and persons belonging to its adopted country.[31]

Given the numbers in which national melodies collections were produced, the reviewer may well have felt swamped. Joseph Slater records books of *Scottish Airs, Irish Melodies, Welsh Melodies, Scottish Melodies, Indian Melodies* and *Welsh Airs*,[32] and the reviewer asserts that:

> If we should now see the melodies of Kamtschatka, or of Madagascar, or of the Hottentots, advertised, we should not only not be surprised, but we should know what to expect[.] [33]

The reviewer describes a self-enfolded discourse in which ersatz markers of national authenticity were attached to generic lyrics in an utterly tendentious and endlessly transferable fashion, manufacturing kitsch to feed the public appetite for 'authentic' specimens of antique national song. So long as the resulting confections were dusted with foreign words, as though with icing sugar, the public found them palatable.

The national melodies genre, as the *British Review* described it, was a Baudrillardian closed circuit of simulacra, talking to itself in its own terms, but making no contact with the realities of national identity or religious belief. Once religious and national identity, so closely imbricated in Judaism, could be simulated with a sprinkle of words, *any* authenticity was imperilled. All national identities were up for grabs to all writers of melodies, and therefore none could be authentically expressed. Once authenticity becomes a choice amongst other choices, Baudrillard claims, it returns as a simulacrum of itself.[34] If Hebraism is understood to be one among many possible options for the writer of melodies, it can no longer be seen as the privileged vehicle of a reformed poetry, what Byron called 'the sacred model' (*BLJ*, IV, 220). Rex Butler has urged us to see Baudrillard's theory not as it is often perceived, as a gleefully intoxicated abandonment of the real in favour of surfing the postmodern waves of hyperreality, but rather as a defence of the real, a nostalgia for the real or a series of interventions which aim to point to the vanishing real and, with increasing desperation, to search for the conditions in which it would again be possible to experience it. '[H]is problem', Butler writes, 'is how to think the real when all is simulation'.[35] Being serious about reform required a 'real' or 'authentic' expression of religious themes, where 'Christians shall begin to talk as Christians', in contrast to the 'degraded' poetry on which Byron's celebrity rested and with which other authors flooded the market. But choosing the national melodies genre (as described by the *British Review*) made it all but impossible for Byron to write a reformed poetry. Because the Hebraisms of *Hebrew Melodies* could be read as interchangeable both with the foreign words which signified the nationality of other melodies from Ireland to India and with the foreign words that spiced Byron's tales, Byron's attempt to write a 'reformed' poetry fell at the first fence, failing to differentiate itself either from the rest of the market or from his previous productions.

While some saw it as a step towards Christian faith, Byron's Jewishness was generally seen as just another costume for the poet to try on. In a poem called 'The Universal Believer; By Lord Byr*n, In Imitation of his Friend Tommy M**re'[36] the anonymous author ventriloquised Byron giving Lady Jersey an account of his career so far:

> 'Come, tell me,' says J*RS*Y, one midnight at whist,
> And she trump'd me the moment she spoke,
> 'Come riddle my riddle, come tell me the list
> 'Of the creeds you have sworn to and broke.'
> 'Believe me, my syren,' I bowing reply'd,
> 'Truth and title but seldom agree;
> 'But I'll try and remember how often I've ly'd,
> 'And my *lying* shall finish with thee.'
>
> (1–8)

'Byron' recounts that 'first philosophy touch'd me' (9) and that he was an enthusiast for 'rascals in France' (12), but that, 'sicken'd of Frenchmen, to Turkey I flew' (17). There he learnt a variety of sybaritic Oriental ways, but finally these too palled:

> 'Then of freaks sadly tired, and lost in a fog
> 'Of systems, old, middle, and new,
> 'I turn'd my loose legs to the first synagogue,

'And at present I'm fix'd in - the Jew!
'So of critics and scissars no longer in dread,
'Thou thy BYR*N a Rabbi shalt see,
'By libel and psalmody earning my bread,
'And rhyming for NATHAN and thee!'

(25–32)

For the author of these lines, Judaism is not the route to reform, but simply another twist in the tale of Byron's reprobate career.

The second factor that compromised Byron's attempt to move in a new direction, away from the staples of his celebrity, is involved with the physical appearance of these poems in several books in 1815. The collection was a departure not only from popular formulae, but also from familiar formats, and the book that Isaac Nathan would produce was contentious even before it appeared. Nathan reported that one evening when he was at Douglas Kinnaird's house, Kinnaird said:

> Mr. Nathan, I expect a – a – that – a – you bring out these Melodies in good style – a – a – and bear in mind, that – a – a – his Lordship's name does not suffer from scantiness – a – a – in their publication. (*HVSV*, p. 85)

Byron apparently visited Nathan the following day, saying 'Nathan, do not suffer that capricious fool to lead you into more expense than is absolutely necessary; bring out the work to your own taste' (*HVSV*, p. 85). Nathan's taste, in fact, was for a handsome and expensive volume. When *A Selection of Hebrew Melodies, Ancient and Modern with appropriate Symphonies & accompaniments* came out in April 1815, it was in crown folio (measuring approximately 36 × 24 cm) with an ornate, engraved title page and dedication to Princess Charlotte. It sold for one guinea. This volume contained 12 melodies, with each lyric printed once under the music and once separately.[37] It was quite unlike anything Byron had published before: a larger format, more expensive and with a different publisher and collaborators. This singularity was a problem for Murray not simply because he could not make money from books that other people published, but because it interrupted the previously unblemished association between publisher and celebrity poet. Murray would produce a multifaceted strategy to repossess *Hebrew Melodies*, to contain its strangeness and rehabilitate it to the trajectory of Byron's collaboration with him. This strategy is subsequently extrapolated by Romanticists who anthologise 'She Walks in Beauty' and forget the rest, masking the character of *Hebrew Melodies* by reducing the collection to its most uncharacteristic poem. I shift focus here from the words Byron wrote to the books Murray published, from the poet's tactical insistence on going his own way to the strategy which contains his tactics and reconnects his writing both to a linear narrative of poetic development and to a homogenising set of Byronic traits.

Murray first brought out an edition of *Hebrew Melodies*, which went into direct competition with Nathan's edition. Immediately after this he embedded the poems in the first collected editions of Byron's works.[38] The overall aim was to repossess Byron from Nathan by representing the melodies as part of Byron's works and Byron's works as part of Murray's list. As early as January 1815, Murray asked, 'does your Lordship wish or not to incorporate the Melodies in your collected works[?]'[39] This put Byron in rather a difficult position, since he had already given the copyright to Nathan.[40] He wrote to ask if Nathan would allow Murray 'the privilege' of including *Hebrew Melodies* in the forthcoming 'complete edition of my *poetical effusions* [...] without considering it as an infringement of your copyright' (*BLJ*, IV, 249). Byron wrote to Murray on 6 January, 'Mr Kinnaird will I dare say have the goodness to furnish copies of the Melodies if you state my wish upon the subject – you may have them if you think them worth inserting' (*BLJ*, IV, 250). But Nathan was understandably reluctant to let the lyrics out of his hands, and Murray wrote to Byron on 11 January:

> I was not <out> wrong in suspecting that Mr Kinnaird would not allow us to have the Melodies – but Mr Hobhouse thinks it unreasonable that they should not be included in the edition of your Lordships [*sic*] works collected
>
> – We had agreed that they should not be printed separately – nor even *announced* as contained in the works – but those who had the works would find them there with a note stating that they had been set to music very beautifully by so & so – which we supposed might operate as an advantageous announcement of the Music – & they would just have filled up our rather meagre Vol 4 –[41]

As I will show, all the promises in this letter were disingenuous. Byron was irritated, and exploded to Hobhouse on 26 January, '"The Melodies" – damn the melodies – I have other tunes – or rather tones – to think of – but – Murray *can't* have them, or shan't – or I shall have

Kin[nair]d and Braham upon me' (*BLJ*, IV, 260).[42] The matter was still unresolved on 17 February, when Murray wrote to Byron:

> I am delaying the publication of our edition in four volumes only until you find a leisure moment to strike off the dedication to your friend Mr. Hobhouse, who still thinks that it is not precisely the same thing to have music made to one's poems, and to write poetry for music; and I advise you most conscientiously to abide by the determination of Mr. Hobhouse's good sense.[43]

This correspondence was all about the projected four-volume collected edition, but before that Murray published *Hebrew Melodies* in May 1815. This book was in demy octavo, cost 5 s. 6 d., and contained 24 melodies, plus 'On the Death of Sir Peter Parker, Bart'. It contained twice as many poems as Nathan's volume, at a fraction of the price and, importantly, it was uniform with Byron's other works.[44] With this volume, Murray went into direct competition with Nathan's book and detached the lyrics from the music for the first time. His ledgers show no record of any payment to Nathan for copyright.[45] Bringing out *Hebrew Melodies* in a format that matched the rest of Byron's publications helped to accommodate it in Byron's oeuvre, and this process was furthered by Murray's plans for collected editions.

Murray's *Hebrew Melodies* came with title pages and half-titles for Byron's collected works bound into the back, enabling and encouraging readers to bind up their own collected edition in two octavo volumes. These title pages invited readers to consolidate their Byron purchases into two volumes, buying those poems they hadn't got.[46] Those readers who did not want to bind up their own collected edition in two volumes could wait for the projected four-volume edition in small octavo, 'including *Hebrew Melodies*' which was advertised in the back of Murray's edition of the melodies.[47] When this collected edition appeared, the melodies were in the fourth volume, along with 36 lyrics which had previously been appended to successive editions of *Childe Harold's Pilgrimage*. This gave the impression that *Hebrew Melodies* was of a piece with Byron's other lyrics rather than, as I have argued above, a significant development of Byron's poetic concerns in a new direction.[48] Murray went on adding volumes to this edition as Byron continued writing, producing a set of eight uniform volumes by 1818. Each of these three artefacts – Murray's edition of *Hebrew Melodies*, the two-volume 'do-it-yourself' collected works and the four-volume collected works – contributed to the assimilation of *Hebrew Melodies* within Byron's oeuvre. Together they formed the mainstays of Murray's strategy for repossessing the poems, minimising their strangeness and making them seem like Byronic business as usual.

In addition, Murray used the poem 'On the Death of Sir Peter Parker, Bart' as a thread to stitch the *Hebrew Melodies* into Byron's oeuvre. The poem first appeared anonymously in the *Morning Chronicle* on 7 October 1814. Murray reprinted it in the tenth edition of *Childe Harold's Pilgrimage*, again in his edition of *Hebrew Melodies* and yet again in the fourth volume of the collected edition, where it is the last of the short poems printed before *Hebrew Melodies*. In this way, Murray ensured that when readers of *Childe Harold* turned to *Hebrew Melodies*, they easily recognised Byron's work because not only were the volumes uniform, but they were linked by this poem. The collected edition further consolidated the impression. The reviews indicate the success of Murray's strategy for establishing his edition of *Hebrew Melodies* as the definitive one and for rehabilitating the decidedly different poems to the reassuring uniformity of Byron's works. Of the twelve journals whose notices of the melodies are collected by Donald Reiman, seven reviewed Murray's book, four reviewed Nathan's and one, the *Gentleman's Magazine*, noticed both.[49] The dominance of his edition among the reviews may reflect Murray's well-established connections among journalists and the fact that he could afford to send out more review copies of his much cheaper book. He also spent £48 on 'advertising &c'.[50] The reviewers continued the work Murray had started, making his book the version of *Hebrew Melodies* that mattered. Murray sold six thousand copies of his edition, and his ledgers show a profit of £836 5 s.[51] No reliable figures are available for Nathan's edition, but soon after its publication he was forced to leave London to avoid his creditors.[52]

And so Byron returned, somewhat uneasily, to the verse tale. *The Siege of Corinth* and *Parisina* marked a return to the form that sustained Byron's celebrity and to material that he thought he had abandoned. Both poems were assembled from fragments intended for a single tale, which Byron had been working on since as early as 1812.[53] Byron had been tinkering with these fragments throughout his celebrity, but he couldn't make them cohere into a poem. The fact that he gave the lines which later became the opening of *Parisina* to Nathan to publish in *Hebrew Melodies* as 'It is the Hour' suggests that, while he was working on the melodies, he may have thought that these materials would never become a narrative poem.[54] Had *Hebrew Melodies* been greeted as a new direction for Byron, refuting the charge of sameness and heralding his reform, he might well have abandoned these materials altogether. As it was, with Murray's publishing strategy stressing the uniformity of *Hebrew Melodies* and Byron's other poetry, he returned to the fragments yet again. Having decided around January 1815 that they should become not one but two poems, he worked up the fragments to produce two verse tales in his popular style.

Murray must have been delighted with Byron's return to familiar ground. But the adventure of *Hebrew Melodies* left its mark. *The Seige of Corinth* could be read as Byron's rejection of religious themes as a route to reformed poetry. It disrespectfully refers to the infant Christ as 'the boy-God' (910) – an 'irreverent compound invented by Lord B.' according to the *Augustan Review*[55] – and culminates in an explosion which destroys a cathedral and leaves dead Christians indistinguishable from dead Muslims (996). Byron's fascination with religious ideas remains visible, however, in *Parisina's* very unByronic concentration on judgement and repentance. After Hugo's speech to Azo, accusing him of crimes at least as great as Hugo's own crime of sleeping with his stepmother (234–317), he ceases to be a Byronic hero in the mould of the Giaour or Corsair. He deviates from their defiant unrepentance in the face of their crimes, and we see him 'Kneeling at the Friar's knee' (397). Byron makes much of Hugo's remorse, confession and prayers. In complete contrast to the Giaour, who refused to be shriven, Hugo seeks a way of holy dying:

> As his last confession pouring
> To the monk, his doom deploring
> In penitential holiness,
> He bends to hear his accents bless
> With absolution such as may
> Wipe our mortal stains away.
>
> (412–8)

'[P]enitential holiness' had no place in the tales that preceded *Hebrew Melodies*. When he came to write Hugo's death, Byron characteristically directed attention to his eyes, which Hugo insists should not be blindfolded. But those eyes were left uncovered not so that they could stare fiercely out at their accusers, but so that they could be turned to heaven:

> He died, as erring men should die,
> Without display, without parade;

> Meekly had he bowed and prayed,
> As not disdaining priestly aid,
> Nor desperate of all hope on high.
> And while before the Prior kneeling,
> His heart was weaned from earthly feeling[.]
>
> (462–8)

Hugo dies with 'No thought but heaven – no word but prayer' (472). The theological seriousness and eschatological focus of his repentance and death are the last trace of Byron's attempt to write a reformed poetry.

These features went unnoticed by the reviews. They complained that 'the subject was every way ineligible',[56] and many of them restricted themselves to criticising *The Siege of Corinth* and refused to discuss *Parisina* at all. The *British Critic* scrupled that 'the story of the second poem is of a nature which must prevent us from entering into an analysis of its merits', while the *British Review* felt called upon to 'solemnly proscribe this poem from the English fireside, and summon all that religion, morality, and policy enjoin, to give authority to the interdict'.[57] Blind to the themes of judgement and repentance, the reviewers once again complained that '[t]his sameness of character begins to grow insufferably wearisome, and is indeed one of the chief faults of Lord Byron's poetry'.[58] *The Champion* produced an indictment:

> Our charge against Lord Byron is, that, in a temper of restless and indecent disdain, he presumes on his popularity to become a downright scribbler, – trying the public to what extent they will receive what he does not think it worth his while to prepare.[59]

Hebrew Melodies was Byron's attempt *not* to become a downright scribbler and *not* to presume on his popularity by giving his readers more of what they were familiar with and recognised as Byronic. Ironically, the result of Murray's strategy was that once again people asked whether Byron had written himself out, whether he still justified his celebrity and whether his celebrity was itself the problem.

The tensions between the celebrity poet and the enterprising publisher who made celebrity his business show their strained interdependence. Byron's need to challenge himself with new poetic forms and styles in a protean saga of self-fashioning and refashioning was a headache for the businessman Murray, trying to create a recognisably branded Byron who would answer the demands of a large readership with minimum commercial risk. Byron's return to the genre which characterised his celebrity suggests the extent to which business concerns feed back, influencing the kind of poetry that gets written. His risky tactical unpredictability succumbed to Murray's profit-motivated strategy of containment. To account for current criticism's comparative neglect of *Hebrew Melodies*, we need to recognise that Byron and Murray were pursuing conflicting objectives when the collection first appeared, and acknowledge that the ways in which Byron's poems were first marketed may still affect our focal points within his corpus.

7
Childe Harold Canto Three: Rewriting Reading

In 1816, everything seemed to slide into crisis. With the breakdown of his marriage, his ostracism from polite society and his departure from England, never to return, Byron seemed to have become what he called 'The careful pilot of my proper woe'.[1] But it wasn't a crisis in quite the way we tend to think. For a start, Byron's celebrity was not truly imperilled by the scandalous rumours that flared around him. Scandal is not a crisis for celebrity, but another part of the apparatus; transgressions can be almost instantly reclaimed and made to function in its service. It was a crisis because Byron no longer felt able to use some of the rhetorical strategies on which he had come to rely. In the aftermath of his departure from England, Byron returned to the poem that had made him famous in the first place, but not in an effort to placate his erstwhile admirers. He was trying to rethink his position in the apparatus of individual, industry and audience that structured Romantic celebrity culture. In *Childe Harold* Canto Three, I argue, this effort took two forms: firstly, he re-imagined his relationship with the audience by experimenting with possible shifts in his hermeneutic paradigm; secondly, he renegotiated his relationship with the industry by changing his compositional and commercial practices. Neither of these efforts was entirely successful: Byron's reviewers declined to endorse the new paradigms of reading he imagined, and his publisher found ways to circumvent his wishes. To understand the nature of this crisis, I begin by considering Byron's separation from his wife in terms of the rhetorical strategies they each deployed. I'm not interested in what happened during the year of Byron's marriage (whether incest, sodomy, adultery or violence), but in how people talked and wrote about what happened.

The acrimonious breakdown of Byron's marriage produced an enormous amount of text at the time, and has continued to do so ever since.[2] Moreover, the participants understood themselves to be engaged in producing texts. They appreciated that the separation would be defined by the texts in which it was recorded and that the arguments they engaged in were arguments over what sort of texts would be produced, authored by whom and open to what kinds of reading. This was especially important given the almost total absence of orality in the procedures of the ecclesiastical courts, which handled separation cases.[3] The courts required Lady Byron's lawyers (technically acting on behalf of her father, since a wife could not act in law independently of her husband) to submit a document called a 'libel', which stated clearly the charges against Byron. Such a document was actually drawn up, but it was never served, and was destroyed.[4] The court did not call witnesses in public, but collected written statements. A court officer twice examined witnesses in private, first to make their depositions and secondly to answer written questions submitted by the other side. A notary wrote down their answers, and no cross-questioning took place.[5] Through these protocols, the courts aimed to produce texts devoid of equivocation or ambiguity, where hidden crimes would be brought to light in documents that resisted misreading and conveyed determinate meanings.

Lady Byron was placed in a very weak legal position by the court's reluctance to grant separations and the high standards of proof demanded, combined with the impossibility of acting for herself, and the laws which gave a husband control over his wife's property and automatic custody of his children.[6] It was therefore in her interests to draw up a private separation agreement. Lady Byron wrote that her husband 'pique[d] himself' on his equivocations and feared that 'this ambiguity of Language will avail him in the Law'.[7] But she needn't have worried; ambiguity was more powerful outside the courts and, in the event, came to her aid not that of her husband. Drawing up a deed of separation and the legalistic correspondence that surrounded it meant a wrangle over textual interpretation. Both parties kept each other's letters with a view to producing them in court if necessary, and the mass of correspondence that the separation generated was always potentially subject to public exegesis. Every letter was a possible legal weapon. Byron added a thorny postscript to one of his letters expressing his frustration at the possibility of uncontrollable readings:

> P.S. – As I do not write with a lawyer at my elbow – I must request a fair construction of what I have written. (*BLJ*, V,47)

The separation alerted Byron to the impossibility of guaranteeing a 'fair construction', even while his postscript acknowledged that meanings must be construed as well as intended. For Lady Byron, the problem was equally acute, and later became chronic as she amassed an enormous archive designed to vindicate her.[8] For both husband and wife, drawing up the deed of separation meant trying to maintain maximum control over the possible construction placed on their words.

In her adviser Stephen Lushington, Annabella found a master of legal writing who could take account of both generous and malicious readings and deploy ambiguity and equivocation in his client's favour. On 22 February 1816, she revealed to Lushington a secret grievance so unspeakable that we still don't know what it was.[9] Lushington understood that power lies in controlling the circulation of knowledge as much as simply possessing it, and he refused to reveal either what Lady Byron said to him or what charges would be brought against Byron if the case went to court. Byron complained bitterly to his wife:

> On the charges preferred against me – I have *twice* been refused any information by your father & his advisers: – it is now a fortnight – which has been passed in suspense – in humiliation – in obloquy – exposed to the most black and biting calumnies of every kind: – without even the power of contradicting conjecture & vulgar assertion as to the accusations – because I am denied the knowledge of all and any particulars, from the only quarter that can afford them – in the mean time I hope your ears are gratified by the general rumours. (*BLJ*, V, 27)

By indicating that they knew Byron to be guilty of scandalous crimes, the nature of which they declined to make explicit, Lady Byron and her advisers triggered endless speculation, which she would neither confirm nor deny. Instead, she stated that 'the various reports injurious to Lord Byron's character [...] have certainly not originated with or been spread by those most nearly connected with her'.[10] That was entirely beside the point – not only did they not need to spread the rumours, it was precisely because they remained silent in public that the rumours flourished and multiplied. They were, as Byron said Augusta was not, 'mute, that the world might belie'.[11]

In pursuing this legal strategy, Lushington appropriated a key technique of the hermeneutic of intimacy. Hints about concealed crimes were a recognisable motif of the Byronic hero, already visible in *Childe Harold's Pilgrimage*, employed in *The Giaour* and *The Corsair* and most fully developed (before *Manfred*) in *Lara*. Creating morally ambiguous characters with secretive subjective depths – characters who could be read as surrogates for the celebrated author – was one of Byron's most successful textual strategies for arousing his reader's fascination with the man behind the poems. It provided a thrilling whiff of transgression, but always stopped short of provoking actual moral outrage among the majority of Byron's readers. It relied on a favourable construction of his texts, in which hints about Byron's own transgressions were either discounted as fictional or excused as youthful footling in foreign climes. Some readers, however, insisted on putting an unfavourable construction on Byron's words. By 1816, these included Lady Byron. 'Lord Byron has never *expressly* declared himself guilty of any *specific* crime' she wrote, 'but his insinuations to that effect have been much more convincing than the most direct assertion'.[12] When Lushington appropriated Byron's rhetoric and turned it against him in the separation proceedings, he deprived Byron of two key elements in his *modus operandi*: first, his reliance on the trope of concealed crimes and, second, his confidence that his readers would put a favourable construction on his words. Once the hidden crime trope was in the hands of his enemies, Byron could no longer use it to structure his relationship with his readers. Having become embroiled in the separation, he could no longer rely on 'a fair construction of what I have written'. He returned to *Childe Harold* in 1816, in part, because it was in that poem and its paratexts that he had first elaborated the hermeneutic of intimacy. Forced by the rhetorical strategies of the separation to re-examine his hermeneutic paradigm, Byron experimented with alternatives in *Childe Harold* Canto Three.

Byron tried two solutions to this problem, neither of which proved to be entirely satisfactory. First, he tried to write his readers out of the poem altogether, claiming that its reception was an extraneous and unimportant adjunct. Rejecting fame as 'the thirst of youth', Byron asserts that he is not 'so young as to regard men's frown or smile, / As loss or guerdon of a glorious lot' (3. 112). Turning his back on society, he claims to value his poem not as a medium of communication, but as an experience for the poet; not as a public engagement, but as a private event. What is important about the poem is not the effect it has on the reader, but the effect it had on the poet. He asserts this conviction in the famous sixth stanza:

> 'Tis to create, and in creating live
> A being more intense, that we endow

With form our fancy, gaining as we give
The life we image, even as I do now.

(3. 6)

These lines evacuate all moments but the moment of creation, the 'now' of the poet's pen on the page in the fourth line, they discard all effects the poem produces that are not effects on the poet and they value above all the poem's ability to produce intensity. Byron cancelled the words 'better' and 'brighter' before he hit on 'intense', rejecting both a moral judgement and a metaphorically visible effect in favour of a fiercely personal concentration of experience (*CPW*, II, 78). He returned to that word again in stanza 89 to describe a mystic moment of stillness:

All heaven and earth are still: From the high host
Of stars, to the lull'd lake and mountain coast,
All is concentered in a life intense,
Where not a beam, nor air, nor leaf is lost,
But hath a part of being, and a sense
Of that which is of all Creator and defence.

(3. 89)

Here the speaker becomes hypersensitive to perceptions; at the centre of his own universe, he gains an expanded consciousness and a numinous clarity, which he expresses with traces of Wordsworthian 'one-life' panentheism and Christian orthodoxy.[13] But such epiphanic intensity is experienced 'in solitude, when we are *least* alone', and the reader has no place here (3. 90). The first person plural in stanza six excludes the reader from the poet's experience even as it suggests that that experience is not unique. Either it means 'each of us severally and individually' or it means 'we poets (but not you readers)'. In *Childe Harold* Canto Three, Byron denies that readers complete poems. Rather, he asserts, poems need encounter no one except the poet, whose ecstatic experiences of intensity they both enable and record.

This new poetic pose operates partly as a defence against Byron's sense of self-belatedness, his fear that his best work is behind him and that he cannot possibly live up to expectations:

Since my young days of passion – joy, or pain,
Perchance my heart and harp have lost a string,

> And both may jar: it may be, that in vain
> I would essay as I have sung to sing.
>
> (3. 4)

'To feel / We are not what we have been, and to deem / We are not what we should be', he comments later, 'is a stern task of soul' (3. 111). But it doesn't matter if the poem 'jar[s]' with the public, he claims, because it is not intended for them. Instead, Byron presents it as a palliative, a refuge and a Tennysonian narcotic:

> Yet, though a dreary strain, to this I cling;
> So that it wean me from the weary dream
> Of selfish grief or gladness – so it fling
> Forgetfulness around me – it shall seem
> To me, though to none else, a not ungrateful theme.
>
> (3. 4)

Even if no one else but Byron benefits from this 'dreary' poem, he will still value it for the emotional effects it produces in him. He signals this stance right from the epigraph, 'Afin que cette application vous forçât à penser à autre chose' [So that this effort will force you to think about something else], where the poem is seen as primarily a diversion from the pain of the separation – a trauma that is too well known to be named.

While Byron validates the creative individual, he denigrates the consuming crowd. To support his claim that the poet creates for himself alone, he produces his most sustained description of society as a 'peopled desart' (3. 73). The 'hum / Of human cities [is] torture' to the poet (3. 72), and he imagines all society as systemically malicious, constraining and coercive, in what the *Christian Observer* called 'a long and unmerciful philippic against all social converse with his species'.[14] Walter Scott expressed concern that this 'desperate degree of misanthropy' would 'end either in actual insanity or something equally frightful'.[15] To 'join the crushing crowd' is for Byron to be 'doom'd to inflict or bear' (3. 71). All social relations are here reduced to the exchange of wrong for wrong, and the worst way of all to engage society is as a writer, as Byron punningly asserts, 'mingling with the herd had penn'd me in their fold' (3. 68). Society demands that Childe Harold 'yield dominion of his mind / To spirits against whom his own rebell'd', but instead of submitting, Harold finds a way to 'breathe without mankind' (3. 12).

This is what Byron claims to do with his new canto: to find a way to go on without the audience who had celebrated him.

The fact that the poem was published at all indicates that Byron was able to handle this moment of crisis by transforming it into the performance of crisis, employing what Sheila Emerson calls a 'typically Byronic desperation measure: that is, [...] Byron's carefully measured use of desperation'.[16] This was a calculated move within the apparatus of celebrity, not an exit from it. Byron did not actually learn to manage without the public in 1816, despite publicly stating his desire to do so. In fact, the poem was eagerly awaited and commercially successful, and Murray was able to report to Byron in December 1816 that he had sold seven thousand copies at a bookseller's dinner.[17] Faced with the need to re-imagine his relationship with his readers, Byron tried to imagine a kind of poetry that had no investment in how it was received, but his rejection of reading was still widely read.

In such a conception of poetry, the only role left for the reader is to be a passive consumer, spectating at the poet's experience of intensity. Byron attempted to enforce his readers' passivity by imagining the reader being completely overcome by the poet's forceful self-expression. In a stanza added late in the poem's composition, he fantasises about a kind of self-expression so powerful that it would entirely negate the reader's subjectivity and force the writer's meaning upon him or her with the elemental power of lightning:

> Could I embody and unbosom now
> That which is most within me, – could I wreak
> My thoughts upon expression, and thus throw
> Soul, heart, mind, passions, feelings, strong or weak,
> All that I would have sought, and all I seek,
> Bear, know, feel, and yet breathe – into *one* word,
> And that one word were Lightning, I would speak;
> But as it is, I live and die unheard,
> With a most voiceless thought, sheathing it as a sword.
>
> (3. 97)

This laments Byron's failure to produce a poem concentrated into a single word so loaded with force and meaning that it would compel understanding. The reader would not be able to resist the poet's intended meaning. This stanza picks up from 'Kubla Khan', which Byron had urged Coleridge to publish, the Romantic topos of an imaginable but regrettably unwritable poem whose extraordinary descriptive or expressive power would assert its author's preternatural or vatic attributes.[18] Describing the failure to write such a poem is understood to provide hints of its brilliance and to leave the failing poet with the trace of the powers he is unable to actualise.[19] In this stanza, Byron does not need to rely on his readers putting a favourable construction on his words, because his stormy self-expression overcomes them entirely. This is a model of the writer/reader nexus as a site of struggle in which the writer aspires to dominate the reader by the force of his subjectivity, expressed with symbolic violence, and to claim exclusive control over the poem's meanings. 'Wreak' suggests aggression and incorporates its archaic meaning, 'to avenge'.[20] The lightning metaphor images a poetry that produces instantaneous illumination in the reader, with no hermeneutic lag, no need for the reader actively to construct or reconstruct the poem's meaning. The elemental double-edged force of electricity, both destructive and creative, would power such poetry. Electricity was still mysterious in the Romantic period, associated with both revolution and the primal life-force and featured in spectacular demonstrations as part of Humphry Davy's fashionable lectures.[21] This stanza conjures the possibility of a poetry that not only describes the natural sublime, but harnesses sublime power to enforce its signification. What Byron has to express, but cannot, is a 'sword' sheathed instead of used. This figures the self-expression that Byron can't achieve as an assault on the reader's consciousness, and even – given the patently phallic image – a rape.

The reviewers – usually the spikiest of readers – bore witness to the power of this fantasy of domination. The *Belle Assemblé* was completely overcome, and reduced to writing that Byron's poetry 'bids defiance to criticism, and all comments on his works, the merit of which speaks for them, would be vain and useless'.[22] The *Portfolio* noted that 'Lord Byron seeks to gain an ascendancy over the judgement of the public.'[23] And John Wilson, surveying Byron's career while reviewing the final canto for the *Edinburgh Review*, observed:

> So that he command [his readers'] feelings and passions, he cares not for their censure or their praise, – for his fame is more than mere literary fame; and he aims in poetry, like the fallen chief whose image is so often before him, at universal dominion, we had almost said, universal tyranny, over the minds of men.[24]

Byron's first solution to the problem of guaranteeing 'a fair construction of what I have written' was aggressively to imagine that his poetry didn't need to be construed at all, since it was valuable chiefly for the effect it produced on its author, and to fantasise about a kind of poetry that could not be misconstrued because it struck the reader's consciousness like lightning.

That was Byron's first, aggressive attempt to rethink the hermeneutic paradigm that structured his celebrity; but he also entertained another, gentler solution to the problem in *Childe Harold* Canto Three. This was to imagine his daughter Ada as an ideal reader who, because of her uniquely intimate relationship with Byron, would place a fair construction on his words. The thought that Ada would read *Childe Harold* Canto Three in the future reinstated the idea of the poem as a medium of communication and stretched it out in time, extending it from the moment of writing to the moment of reading, rather than concentrating it into an imagined instant of composition. The first stanza – fractured on the page by the break inserted in the middle of the fifth line – mimics Byron's separation from Ada and establishes the poem not as inward-turned and self-centred but as outward-looking and interpersonal. Rather than being concentrated into one word or one moment, the poem preserves words through time to be reanimated by reading at a later date. He figures his poem as a gift and a message from father to daughter:

> Albeit my brow thou never should'st behold,
> My voice shall with thy future visions blend,
> And reach into thy heart, – when mine is cold, –
> A token and a tone, even from thy father's mould.
>
> (3. 115)

Although Byron's relationship with Ada is a 'broken claim', he makes the poem his legacy to her and makes her the only reader who matters (3. 117). Her reading 'blends' the 'voice' of her father, preserved on the page, with the alliterated 'visions' of her own imagination, producing a complete poem through a collaborative effort. She draws Byron out of his self-absorption and absorbs all his attention herself: 'I see thee not, – I hear thee not, – but none / Can be so wrapt in thee' (3. 115).

But presenting the poem as a message from father to daughter did not make it a private communiqué. Any message Byron sent to Ada had to go through the public domain whether he liked it or not, because Lady Byron's antipathy ensured that all other channels were closed. His name was 'shut from thee, as a spell still fraught / With desolation' (3. 117), and no message could be sent via Augusta, since Lady Byron was still nurturing what she described as 'an insurmountable repugnance to Ada's being in [Augusta's] company' in November 1818.[25] Given his financial situation, his separation from her and her close supervision by Lady Byron, the only legacy Byron was in a position to leave Ada was his poem. Doing so meant producing a text that could be called 'writerly', but not in the sense that Roland Barthes would recognise. Opening his text to one uniquely sympathetic individual, Byron is prepared to relinquish full control over his significations only if he can guarantee a fair construction. Ada is not a reader born at the cost of the death of the author, but, literally and metaphorically, the author's 'child of love' (3. 118). Like the rest of Byron's readers, she would have to use his texts as a way to relate to him.

Addressing (usually lyric) poems to particular (often female) readers was, of course, common in the Romantic period. What made Ada different was the context in which her reading was imagined. Byron had previously used Ianthe to enable large sections of his readership to project themselves into an imaginary intimacy with him. He made that projection possible by rendering the particular addressee (Lady Charlotte Harley) into a generic figure (Ianthe): a subject position that many readers could imagine themselves occupying. When Ada replaced Ianthe as the imagined ideal reader of *Childe Harold*, she closed off that possibility. Ada was a specific figure, with a subject position that no one else could project themselves into. She represented both an intensification of the hermeneutic of intimacy and its failure. It intensified because it became concentrated on a single figure with an unassailable claim to intimacy with Byron. It failed because that imagined relationship could no longer serve as a pattern for other readers.

Imagining Ada's reading meant indulging a second fantasy of perfect communication, but this time it was a fantasy of compassion. Ada appears as a reader so genuine and generous that there is no chance of misreading. Whilst on the one hand he dismisses 'the world', as his claim to poetic self-sufficiency demands, on the other hand Byron keeps hold of the dream of a perfect reader:

> I have not loved the world, nor the world me, –
> But let us part fair foes; I do believe,
> Though I have found them not, that there may be
> Words which are things, – hopes which will not deceive,
> And virtues which are merciful, nor weave

> Snares for the failing: I would also deem
> O'er other's griefs that some sincerely grieve;
> That two, or one, are almost what they seem, –
> That goodness is no name, and happiness no dream.
>
> (3. 114)

This is a credo of embattled optimism linked to an ideal of reading. L. E. Marshall describes it as 'a declaration of faith in the identity of idealising words and actual things'.[26] It imagines a reading so sympathetic and perfectly attuned to the poet's meanings that words pass between poet and reader as 'things'; tokens exchanged without loss, like the 'token' that Byron imagines his poem will be for Ada in the next stanza. Byron would return to the idea that 'words are things' with more confidence in *Don Juan* (*DJ*, 3. 88), but here it is a hard-won consolation, as the extremely circumspect diction suggests ('some', 'two, or one', 'almost'). Whereas Byron had previously imagined a kind of self-expression so forceful that it would guarantee understanding, he now imagined a reader so keenly responsive and a language so perfectly referential that a message could be transmitted with no interference, no noise. In this ideal there is a perfect fit between the writer's intention and the reader's construction. They both grasp the words in exactly the same way as a result of the reader's generosity and emotional sympathy. This is made possible by a language imagined as reliably referential. Goodness is 'no name' because the word is not detached from its referent, but can be consistently applied to reality.[27] Although Byron has not yet found such a reading, Ada's future encounter with the poem underwrites the dream of perfect communication. This dream is all the more remarkable because Byron maintained it in the face of his anxieties about how his words would be construed. Ada's generous reading is defined against Lady Byron's refusal to put a fair construction on Byron's writing. While he idealises Ada, he anathematises his wife by implication. Reprising the passive-aggressive manoeuvre of 'Fare Thee Well' within this larger context, Byron's wistful optimism and apparent magnanimity works by tacitly delineating Lady Byron's faults. She is understood to be so mercilessly self-righteous that her 'virtues' are 'snares' which wait to trap and condemn others, in whose 'griefs' she takes a hypocritical delight. The discourse of proscriptive virtue that shapes Lady Byron has no connection with the reality of goodness as Byron experiences it. He looks forward to a future vindication when Ada will recognise Lady Byron's viciousness and Byron's generosity of spirit.

Byron's attempts to reposition himself in Romantic celebrity culture extended beyond the text of his poem to his compositional method and his handling of the work's copyright. Broadly speaking, Byron's characteristic compositional method prior to *Childe Harold* Canto Three was to write the first draft of a poem very rapidly and, after making minor changes, to send it to Murray. He then bombarded Murray with additions and corrections, in a series of letters. Murray incorporated all this material, on Byron's instructions, into proofs, when Byron would make further alterations and embellishments. After publication, the process of accretion would often extend through subsequent editions, most obviously in the case of *The Giaour*, a 'snake of a poem' which 'lengthen[ed] its rattles each month' (*BLJ*, III, 100). This practice meant that Byron relied on Murray to help bring his poems to their published versions, and the first time Byron saw his poems as artefacts with any material integrity was often in the first printed edition. For both practical and conceptual reasons, these habits were inappropriate for *Childe Harold* Canto Three. The postal service between Switzerland and England was uncertain, especially through France, where 'letters are rather more carefully investigated than delivered' (*BLJ*, V, 78), which made it impractical to send corrections by letter, or to correct proofs and revises. More importantly, Byron changed his habits in an effort to renegotiate his relationship with the industry of celebrity. He supported his claim that he had written a poem which required no readers, or only one, by the extent to which he turned his manuscript into a finished artefact *before* he sent it to Murray.

Having composed his first draft on single sheets of paper, Byron then made a fair copy in a red morocco-bound notebook. This was the first time in his mature career that he had used a notebook in this way. The book had initially been used for keeping accounts, but once Byron had copied his poem into it, he cut all the other pages out. After he began using the book, Byron wrote two more short sequences of stanzas on separate sheets, and had them sewn into the notebook. He numbered the pages that contained the text of his poem from one to one hundred. He then made a few additions, sometimes written crosswise, and the poem was complete. In a departure from his former method, Byron made no more additions or corrections before publication. As a result, the poem became embodied as an artefact with its own discreet integrity, before Murray's intervention, to an extent unprecedented in Byron's oeuvre. Byron's practice is certainly less extreme than, say, Blake's artisanal productions or Emily Dickinson's fascicles, but the impetus behind it is comparable. By cutting out some pages and sewing in others, Byron tried to make the poem appear complete and free-standing before sending it to the publisher. Unlike any of Byron's previous mature poems, *Childe Harold* Canto Three existed in a pre-publication state as a craftwork before it appeared as an industrial product. In this way, he concretised his claims that the poem's achievement was complete before it reached the eyes of the public and that it was primarily a personal gift and not a public performance.

Byron was 'very anxious that it should be published with as few errata as possible', but his efforts to ensure the textual integrity of the poem before it left his hands did not protect it from the interventions of others (*BLJ*, V, 90). Byron gave his notebook to Scrope Berdmore Davies to take back to England, but first he arranged for two copies to be made, to guard against loss.[28] One copy was made by Mary Shelley and stayed in Switzerland, the other was made by Claire Clairmont and given to Percy Shelley to take to England. In the event, Shelley arrived in England first, and his copy became the printer's copy (*CPW*, II, 297–8). Shelley understood that Byron had authorised him to correct the proofs, but Murray was wary of Shelley's politics and he wanted William Gifford to see the poem through the press instead. Murray contrived to marginalise Shelley and give Gifford free reign to amend the poem. Byron had long relied on Gifford's judgement, and he gradually came to accept Gifford as an editor. As McGann notes, 'Murray and Gifford carefully excised all the more radical political content in the notes, something which they knew Shelley would not have permitted' (*CPW*, II, 299). Thus Byron's effort to create a more autonomous compositional practice by turning his poem into an artefact before it left his hands had only limited success.

The same concern to renegotiate his relationship with his publisher and his readers also affected his sale of the poem's copyright. Whereas Byron had previously refused payment for his poems, presenting them as lordly gifts to his readers, he drove a hard bargain for the copyright of *Childe Harold* Canto Three.[29] Murray offered fifteen hundred guineas for the poem in September 1816. Douglas Kinnaird, acting on Byron's behalf, declined this offer and pressed for two thousand, which Murray agreed to.[30] Murray flattered Byron, saying, 'The poem [. . .] is so much beyond anything in modern days that I may be out in my calculation: it requires an ethereal mind, like its author's, to cope with it.'[31] But he also protected himself against piracy and drove home the point that he, and not Byron, now owned the poem, writing, 'Remember I do stipulate for all the original MSS., copies or scraps.'[32] Murray and Byron agreed that the final five hundred guineas should only be paid after Murray had sold an agreed number of poems, and in December and January Byron twice asked Kinnaird to chase Murray for payment: 'give him a hint – & exact performance' (*BLJ*, V, 139).[33] This was the first time that Byron had entered into negotiations over the sale of copyright, and it marks an important shift in the way he viewed his poems.[34] Initially seen as gifts to his publisher and through him to his readers, they now became the objects of a transaction, a commodity for which the public, through their representative Murray, must pay. Beginning with *Childe Harold* Canto Three, as Caroline Franklin notes, 'Byron drove hard bargains with his long-suffering publisher, as he now not only accepted but threw himself with gusto into the role of paid professional.'[35] As Marcel Mauss suggests in his classic anthropological study, gifts can entwine both giver and receiver in a complex reciprocity with social implications and temporal extension, which may involve a competitive element.[36] By transacting the copyright of *Childe Harold* Canto Three, Byron attempted to reduce the reader/writer nexus to the cash nexus, removing from it any trace of a gift economy and making it an exchange which was imagined to be immediately complete, and to require no further contact between the parties.[37] This new attitude underwrites both of Byron's attempts to remodel the reader/writer nexus in the poem. On the one hand, since the poem's value lies in the moment of composition, Byron knows its worth and can bargain accordingly, rather than leaving it up to the reader to gauge its merit. On the other, because he declines to make a gift of the poem to the public, he reserves the possibility of making a gift of it to Ada. Taking care to distinguish gifts from transactions, Byron quarantines one against pollution by the other in order to redefine his relationship with the industry and the audience that constituted his celebrity.[38]

For a celebrity in the Romantic period, however, it was not so easy to renegotiate one's position in the cultural apparatus. The reviewer for the *British Critic*, for example, resisted Byron's attempt to rethink his celebrity. 'The noble Lord', the reviewer complained, 'is ever informing us how vastly superior both he and his genius are [...] we now begin to call for proof, and all the proof we can find is in his own assertion.'[39] In an effort to debunk Byron's new hermeneutic paradigms of titanic self-sufficiency or emotional investment in a single ideal reader, the critic applied the discourse of political economy to Byron's celebrity career:

> The man who sends out into the world a single poem, the labour perhaps of years, may affect, with some pretence of probability, to scorn the voice of public censure or approbation, but he who, at intervals of only a few months, shall continue to court the expectations

> of the world with the successive fruits of his poetic talent, not only exists a pensioner upon public fame, but lives even from hand to mouth upon popular applause.[40]

According to this reviewer, Byron is not at liberty to renounce his readers; rather, he is 'a pensioner upon public fame', indentured to the celebrity apparatus. Figuring the celebrity apparatus as a subsistence economy of recognition, this critic represents Byron as a commodity producer in a high-volume, low-value business. Having become embedded in industrial culture, Byron could not easily replace the hermeneutic of intimacy with the kind of self-sufficiency or self-determination that he imagined in *Childe Harold* Canto Three.

From its first publication, *Childe Harold* Canto Three has been read as a canto of crisis: a crisis in Byron's personal life as he faced the aftermath of the separation; a crisis in his poetics as he reread Wordsworth more sympathetically at the urging of Shelley; a crisis in his politics as he contemplated the defeat of Napoleon and the restoration of the Bourbons. Now we can see that it was also a crisis in his celebrity. Faced with Lushington's appropriation of his rhetorical techniques and his readers' refusal to construe his writings favourably, Byron was compelled to rethink his place in the celebrity apparatus that had shaped his career. In an effort to do so, he imagined alternative ways of understanding how poetry worked, modified the way he composed his poems and adjusted his dealings with his publisher. These responses may have helped Byron to reconceptualise his position within Romantic celebrity culture, but they did not transform that culture. The apparatus of celebrity was too tenacious, too firmly entrenched, to be shifted by Byron's tactics. At the same time, Byron's ability to stage his moment of crisis suggests that he was not yet ready to renounce his celebrity, despite his dissatisfaction with it. *Childe Harold* Canto Three shows Byron moving from collaborating in his own celebrity to criticising celebrity as a whole. But not until *Don Juan* would he embark on a more profound critique of some of the fundamental assumptions sponsored by celebrity culture.

8
Don Juan: Celebrity and the Subject of Modernity

Don Juan presents subjectivity in stubbornly un-modern ways during the historical period when the emergent celebrity culture was helping to normalise modern ideas about subjectivity. In this final chapter, I will suggest that celebrity culture relied on elements of a distinctively modern understanding of subjectivity and therefore sponsored its normalisation, shutting down a variety of earlier possibilities in the process. The new understanding of subjectivity that emerged was linked to a new moral culture, elements of which *Don Juan* set out to resist. My reading of its moments of dissent reveals *Don Juan*'s attempt to think outside the moral prescriptions of modern subjectivity at the last historical moments before their universality became unquestionable.

Today, we commonly speak of a revolution in understandings of the self at the end of the eighteenth century in the West. Michel Foucault pioneered its study, Charles Taylor placed it in a long perspective of philosophical and moral thinking, and Dror Wahrman examined it in historical detail.[1] Literature played a part in this revolution as both commentator and agent, as authors (in Nancy Armstrong's words) 'sought to formulate a kind of subject that had not yet existed in writing'.[2] The changes were far-reaching and surprisingly rapid; as a result, people looking back at the end of the century found the attitudes of a generation or two before eccentric, ridiculous or inexplicable. For Wahrman, the shift from an '*ancien regime* of identity' to a 'modern regime of selfhood' involved a rapid hardening of identity categories such as those of gender, race and class.[3] The modern subject who emerged from this revolution was deep, unique, expressive, self-regulating and mentally equipped for the bourgeois, imperial world of the nineteenth century. As I suggested in Chapter 1, elements of this modern understanding of subjectivity were crucial to the success of

Byron's celebrity career. Two aspects of the modern subject were particularly problematic for Byron: its capacity for development and its supposedly legible depths. This chapter will explore his opposition to these two facets of modern selfhood.

As Charles Taylor makes clear, models of selfhood invariably underpin moral judgements; Taylor calls this 'moral ontology'. The concept of subjectivity that became normative at the end of the eighteenth century produced what Taylor describes as 'a new moral culture'.[4] This new understanding of morality entailed a new moral discourse – Byron's 'cant' – which *Don Juan* resists by deploying a counter-normative conception of the subject. Byron was not alone in resisting elements of modern subjectivity; as Andrea Henderson has shown, a variety of possible identities persisted throughout the Romantic period.[5] But his dissent was distinctive for its moral dimension and its self-consciously oppositional character. In *Don Juan*, Byron considered the costs involved when the identity play of the *ancien regime* was shut down in favour of rigid identity categories and a new moral discourse, and he performed a strategic reversal of the new desiderata for writing about subjectivity. I will show how he presented non-developmental, inconsistent and illegible characters, refused to probe hidden depths and satirised the tendency to do so, and insisted on the irreducible contradictions and mobility of himself and of the world.[6]

These priorities baffled his contemporaries more and more, including those, such as Hobhouse and Gifford, on whose judgement he had previously relied. Increasingly indifferent to the opinions of others, Byron was determined to follow a path which seemed to them to be worryingly idiosyncratic. T. G. Steffan notes that 'Byron ordered Murray to send him no more ephemerae, periodicals, and poetic trash. Praise and censure interrupted the current of his mind. [...] He returned to Murray a *Quarterly Review* unopened.'[7] William Blake, for whom being out of step with prevailing opinion held no fear, acknowledged this tendency when he dedicated *The Ghost of Abel* 'To LORD BYRON in the Wilderness'.[8] The wilderness was a place for outcasts, but it was also, Biblically, a place to overcome temptation and prepare for a great endeavour. In the wilderness, Byron found a space of possibilities in which he could play with counter-normative ideas about subjectivity, unsettling his contemporaries by subjecting their commonsensical conceptions of the subject to a *verfremdung* effect.[9]

In his effort to think beyond modern norms, Byron drew on a wide variety of writers who had thought about identity and morality in earlier periods; but none was more important to him, I think, than

Montaigne. Byron refers to Montaigne by name only once in *Don Juan*, where he cites Montaigne's authority in an important stanza on scepticism ('"Que sçais-je?" was the motto of Montaigne' (9. 17)). But he read Montaigne's *Essays* extensively, and he may have felt some affinity with the earlier writer. Both were aristocrats living in different sorts of retirement from a power centre that nonetheless passionately concerned them.[10] Both mourned a like-minded friend: Etienne de la Boëtie in Montaigne's case, Percy Shelley in Byron's. Both wrote wide-ranging and self-reflexive books in a conversational style, and both made the most of parenthetical comments. While Philip Davis notes that 'so many big things in the verse of *Don Juan* pass inside little brackets', André Tournon asserts that in the *Essays* 'all incidental interventions, remarks and comments should not be considered accessory, treated as if they were in parenthesis or outside the dialectic of the text'. On the contrary, '[t]hese interventions are a part of the text, and they play an essential role in its organisation'.[11] Byron himself acknowledged the *Essays* as a model for *Don Juan* when he wrote, 'I mean it for a poetical T[ristram] Shandy – or Montaigne's Essays with a story for a hinge' (*BLJ*, X, 150).

Byron appears to have used four copies of Montaigne's essays at different times. Two copies appeared in the sale catalogue when Byron sold his library in 1816.[12] Leigh Hunt lent him a copy of the *Essays* in Charles Cotton's translation between July and September 1822, and observed that 'the only writer of past times whom he read with avowed satisfaction, was Montaigne'.[13] And James Hamilton Browne recorded that Byron read another copy on the boat to Cephalonia, between the end of June and the beginning of August 1823:

> He made it a constant rule to peruse every day one or more of the Essays of Montaigne. This practice, he said, he had pursued for a long time; adding his decided conviction, that more useful general knowledge and varied information were to be derived by an intimate acquaintance with the writings of that diverting author, than by a long and continuous course of study. (*HVSV*, p. 387)

In 1827, Leigh Hunt published an article in the *New Monthly Magazine*, indicating which page-corners Byron had turned down in his copy of Montaigne,[14] and informing his readers that:

> Lord Byron had a peculiar way of marking the pages that pleased him. He usually made a double dog's-ear, of a very tight, and, as it

> were, irritable description; folding the corner twice, and drawing his nail with a sort of violence over it, as if to hinder 'the dog's' escape from him.[15]

Richard Kirkland used this article to identify the essays in which Byron marked passages.[16] In what follows, I will refer chiefly to these essays, in order to argue that Byron turned to Montaigne for support when thinking about morality and modern subjectivity. In doing so, I am engaging in a form of source or influence study which, while it remains at times necessarily impressionistic, takes its cue from the material traces left by Byron's interaction with a particular physical text.

1. The developmental subject

The first feature of the modern subject that concerned Byron was its capacity for development. The modern subject's life is usually understood as a developmental narrative, in which he or she makes rational choices in order to surmount obstacles and progressively approach self-realisation. The adjective 'developmental' distinguishes what concerns me here from a separate philosophical debate about whether a sense of life as a narrative is essential, either for subjectivity *per se* or for living morally. Charles Taylor, Alasdair MacIntyre and Daniel Dennett all espouse a version of this view.[17] What concerns me here, however, is the specifically modern, developmental form of that narrative (which emerges alongside what Taylor calls 'the affirmation of ordinary life'), in which events accumulate into a progressive story of self-fulfilment or *Bildung*. Clifford Siskin calls this 'the Romantic redefinition of the self as a mind that grows', and defines development as 'an all-encompassing formal strategy underpinning middle-class culture'.[18]

Subjective development relies on the individual's ability to narrate his or her life in a particular way, subsuming failures, transgressions and setbacks into a narrative arc of progressive self-realisation. Paradoxically, the events in these developmental narratives both produce the modern subject and yet also reveal his or her latent nature. Although you are shaped by events, you become more and more fully the self that you have 'truly' been all along.[19] The capacity to narrate one's life in this particular way points forward to the emergence of the bourgeois career. 'This mode of life-narration', Taylor notes, 'is the quintessentially modern one.'[20] As it becomes normative, it produces the kind of subjectivity that Anthony Giddens labels 'a reflexive project, for which the individual is responsible' and which, he claims, 'forms a trajectory of development'.[21]

That trajectory held together the sequence of poems that branded Byron's identity, in which each new publication had to be distinctly different but recognisably the same. If the new book were to be marketed successfully, devoted readers had to be convinced that it would offer similar gratifications to the last volume they had bought and enjoyed. If it deviated too far from the established ingredients of his celebrity, readers would be likely to reject it and to regret that Byron had lost his touch. But readers also had to be convinced that the new volume would offer a new pleasure; a satisfaction they could not get by rereading the last volume they had bought, a diversion they had not already enjoyed. Otherwise, why should they pay for an experience they had already bought and could repeat as often as they chose? The idea of a developmentally narrativised subject enabled Byron and Murray to walk this marketing tightrope. Byron's celebrity career required that each publication should be different while at the same time being connected to the last by a developmental narrative. Each time Murray issued another uniform volume of his ongoing collected edition of Byron's works, that narrative was consolidated. This was not *The Prelude*'s kind of development, which justified ceaseless revision and repeatedly deferred publication, but development expressed in a series of published poems marketed as cumulative instalments in the ongoing story of their author's fascinating life.

Normalising the modern subject meant assuming that all life stories were developmental narratives like this and allowing highly visible examples of developmental selves, like Byron's, to become models for thinking about subjectivity. Development could then become an evaluative category: well-regulated individuals developed on their own, deviant ones did not. *Don Juan* highlights the limits of this assumption. As the modern subject became normalised in the Romantic period, the capacity for development became the sign of being fully human. But in *Don Juan*, self-determining development is a feature not of human nature but of cultural power. While some people get to forge their own path, those less fortunate are constrained to run on tracks (or on treadmills) made by others. The subject of modernity can autonomously subsume minor setbacks into a larger success story, making sense of local failures by connecting them to a developmental narrative. But Byron directs attention to those marginalised individuals who are subjected to censure, who have their setbacks condemned and their stories told for them. Some people get to reform: others are disciplined.

One example of this is the significantly nameless country girl, whose premarital pregnancy brings her to the attention of Lord Henry Amundeville in Canto Sixteen. Lord Henry's version of development is continually to improve his house and its contents, cultivating his sensibilities through consumption. He covets 'A special Titian, warranted original', which a picture dealer has brought to show him (16. 56), and commissions improvements to Norman Abbey, which will display its owner's well-developed taste for 'Gothic daring shown in English money' (16. 59). While Lord Henry makes his mark in the county, the scarlet cloak she's forced to wear marks out the shamed country girl. When Lord Henry gets round to his duties as a justice of the peace, she's lined up with 'two poachers caught in a steel trap' and forced to submit with 'patient tribulation' to a legal framework that polices morality with the same instrumental rationality that it uses to govern land economy (16. 61, 65):

> Now Justices of Peace must judge all pieces
>   Of mischief of all kinds, and keep the game
> And morals of the country from caprices
>   Of those who have not a license for the same;
> And of all things, excepting tithes and leases,
>   Perhaps these are most difficult to tame:
> Preserving partridges and pretty wenches
> Are puzzles to the most precautious benches.
>
> (16. 63)

In this octave masterclass in enjambment and zeugma, Byron explains the operation of the steel trap that has caught the 'espiegle' girl (16. 65). Lacking the license for her moral caprice that might be granted to an upper-class man, she is subject to the kind of justice dispensed by Lord Henry. In the coarse pun that the enjambment points, she becomes a 'piece' to be administered along with the estate; the magistrate provides a judicial solution to a moral question. The woman's sexuality and the county's game are both subject to acts of enclosure; 'tame[d]' by judicial power, they are yoked together by Lord Henry's disciplinary bench and Lord Byron's satirical zeugmas.

When she becomes subject to the law, the pregnant country girl is denied the possibility of repenting and therefore of developing. Since repentance requires a free choice, when the constable detains the woman 'beneath a warrant's banner', her evidences of repentance become at once compulsory and irrelevant (16. 62). Following the practice of *amende honorable*, by which public displays of contrition could be legally required, she is obliged to wear a scarlet cloak which ostensibly displays her shame. But her legal punishment reveals nothing about her moral condition; while it purports to signify her repentance, in fact her cloak signifies only her subjection. Repentance cannot, by definition, be enforced. Instead of being allowed to repent, atone and reform, she is arrested, found guilty and punished. This violates the moral imperative that goes along with a developmental understanding of selfhood, 'the demand', in Taylor's words, 'that we give people the freedom to develop their personality in their own way'.[22] Excluded from the precincts of pristine morality by her runaway sexuality and from the beau monde of fashion by her class, the girl blanches with terror instead of blushing with embarrassment (16. 64).

When Byron read Montaigne's condemnation of such attempts to enforce contrition, in the essay 'Of Repentance', he dog-eared the essay's final page. Montaigne asserts that repentance must be autonomous and that it takes place beyond the reach of any social apparatus. Although Montaigne 'seldom repent[s] of any thing', when he does he rejects the kind of outward show that is imposed on the girl in the scarlet cloak.[23] 'I have no notion of a repentance that is superficial, moderate, or ceremonious', he writes, '[i]t must sting me throughout before I can give it that name, and it must pierce my heart as deeply and universally as God sees into me' (III, 14). Repentance at the instigation of others or for their benefit is not worthy of the name; 'our consciences must amend of themselves' (III, 18). Although he welcomes his friends' assessments of his moral health, he insists that true virtue comes from within. 'We [...] ought to have a tribunal established in our breasts, whereby to try our actions', he writes, 'I have my laws and my court of justice to judge myself by, and apply myself to those more than to any other rules' (III, 5). Contrary to the assumptions that place Lord Henry in judgement over the girl in the scarlet cloak, virtue cannot be administered. It does not flow from teacher to pupil, institution to individual, government to population, or magistrate to miscreant.[24]

Permanently shamed by the loss of her virtue, the pregnant country girl is denied the chance to write her fall into a narrative of development in which it becomes a minor setback in a march of progress. As a result, her selfhood cannot become Giddens's 'reflexive project, for which the individual is responsible'. Byron had previously warned Caroline Lamb, 'woman once fallen forever must fall', and elsewhere in *Don Juan* he generalised this complaint to apply to women of all classes, who 'if there's an eclât [...] lose their caste at once, as do the Parias' (12. 78).[25] If they are detected, 'Society, that china without flaw, / (The hypocrite!) will banish them like Marius' (12. 78). While claiming to leave the matter well alone, the narrator makes his opinion felt:

> Perhaps this is as it should be; – it is
>   A comment on the Gospel's 'Sin no more,
> And be thy sins forgiven:' – but upon this
>   I leave the saints to settle their own score.
> Abroad, though doubtless they do much amiss,
>   An erring woman finds an opener door
> For her return to Virtue – as they call
> That Lady who should be at home to all.
>
> (12. 79)

Society's rush to judgement leaves no space for grace, no possibility of freely chosen repentance and therefore no chance of becoming the developmental subject of modernity. By foreclosing the opportunity to reclaim particular falls as part of a narrative of general progress, such 'uneasy Virtue' undermines its supposed intent and 'leads / People some ten times less in fact to mind it, / and care but for discoveries and not deeds' (12. 80). Or as Montaigne puts it, in an essay Byron marked, they 'reform seeming vices; but as for real vices they leave them as they were, if they do not augment them' (III, 10).[26] For those caught in their steel traps, these moral laws 'aggravate the crime [they] have not prevented, / By rendering desperate those who had else repented' (12. 80). With the advent of modernity, the capacity to understand your life as a developmental narrative becomes a 'natural' attribute of subjectivity; something that everyone is assumed to have. But this normalisation means overlooking those nameless individuals, such as the pregnant country girl, who are not allowed to develop and who do not get to tell their own stories. The cost of normalising the developmental subject was that, while some lives could be written up as narratives of progressive self-realisation, other lives had to be written off as irredeemably perverse or crooked, and subjected to disciplinary intervention.

Suspicious of claims for development's universality, Byron foregrounds the non-developmental and contradictory nature of Juan and the narrator. In the world of *Don Juan*, change is rarely developmental, and stability is unknown – Byron only uses the word 'perpetual' twice, and on both occasions it comes before the word 'motion'.[27] The poem can be seen as an anti-*Bildungsroman*, and Juan as a character who stubbornly refuses to develop as a 'modern' character in a realist novel might be expected to.[28] He 'lacks the ability to organise and schematize life' according to Alvin Kernan, and he 'lacks [the] mental function [of] memory' on which the modern subject relies to construct a developmental narrative of his or her life.[29] 'Whether his progress can be classified as a *Bildungsroman* and he can be said to develop as a result of experience', writes Timothy Webb, 'is highly debatable.'[30] Bernard Blackstone concludes that '[h]e can be corrupted, but he has small possibility for growth. He learns nothing from his experiences, except as an insect might learn, in the laboratory'.[31]

Juan does not build on the past in order to grow or to cultivate his feelings. 'There was the purest platonism at bottom / Of all his feelings – only he forgot 'em' (10. 54). Instead, he forgets the past while all the time forgetting himself with another woman. Despite the narrator's protest, he forgets Julia as soon as Haidee appears on the scene. ('But Juan! had he quite forgotten Julia? / And should he have forgotten her so soon?' (2. 208).) He remembers Haidee long enough to resist the soprano's attractions in Canto Four, but even this, the longest of his love affairs, evaporates when he comes to his senses (probably) with Dudu.[32] The only subjective development Byron planned for Juan was 'to have displayed him gradually *gaté* and *blasé* as he grew older' (*BLJ*, VIII, 78). By Canto Twelve 'his heart had got a tougher rind', but his story was not a developmental one, and Byron's varied plans for him indicate that, despite the just deserts that the Juan of legend receives, this Juan is by no means on a teleological course (12. 81).[33] Moreover, Don Juan cannot develop progressively over time, because time in *Don Juan* is non-linear. The poem, as several critics have noted, unfolds in three different time frames at once. The historical action of the plot can be precisely fixed around the siege of Ismail in 1790; most of the details, especially in the English cantos, are remembered from the height of Byron's celebrity, 1812–1816; and the narrator's interventions in the poem refer to the period of composition, 1819–1824. The poem shifts rapidly between these time frames and blurs their boundaries. This layered chronology implies that *Don Juan*'s time is non-linear and therefore not conducive to progressive subjective development.

The narrator does not develop in the poem any more than Juan does. ' "The time is out of joint", – and so am I' he comments (9. 41). Always kept on his toes by the ottava rima stanza, the narrator insists on his own inconstancy, mobility and resistance to developmental explanations:

> Temperate I am – yet never had a temper;
>   Modest I am – yet with some slight assurance;
> Changeable too – yet somehow '*Idem Semper*':
>   Patient – but not enamoured of endurance;
> Cheerful – but, sometimes, rather apt to whimper:
>   Mild – but at times a sort of '*Hercules furens*':
> So that I almost think that the same skin
> For one without – has two or three within.
>
> (17. 11)

No statement about him can be allowed to pass unqualified – not even that he is changeable. Held together only by his skin, this narrator resists narration; his subjectivity refuses to conform to a developmental narrative.

Like Juan, the narrator routinely sloughs off the past in favour of trying something new. For instance, when the eunuch Baba is leading Juan through the seraglio, the characteristically Byronic narrator refuses to be tempted into oriental descriptions, not because he has outgrown them, but because everyone else has grown into them. The party passes 'orange bowers, and jasmine and so forth':

> (Of which I might have a good deal to say,
>   There being no such profusion in the North
> Of oriental plants, 'et cetera,'
>   But that of late your scribblers think it worth
> Their while to rear whole hotbeds in *their* works
> Because one poet travell'd 'mongst the Turks;)
>
> (5. 42)

Even though 'description is my forte', the narrator declines to describe, because 'every fool describes in these bright days / His wond'rous journey to some foreign court' (5. 52). To stay ahead of the game in the literary marketplace, the narrator does not polish up his forte but abandons it: he does not develop, he simply changes. And his lack of development does not destabilise his identity. The fact that the narrator can apparently watch himself changing enables him to know that there is something in him which is unchanging, something whose continuity is assured precisely because it registers the subject's shifts.

Ten cantos later, the narrator flirts with the idea that he is developing from error to truth, reforming his opinions as he goes. But he undercuts this comforting notion by suggesting that even opposite ideas are 'twin', and in its place he introduces the possibility of an ongoing succession of contradictory ideas with no point of reference outside the sequence by which to reckon their worth:

> Also observe, that like the great Lord Coke,
>   (See Littleton) whene'er I have expressed
> Opinions two, which at first sight may look
>   Twin opposites, the second is the best.
> Perhaps I have third too in a nook,
>   Or none at all – which seems a sorry jest[.]
>
> (15. 87)

Such a narrator, with such a hero on his hands, produces not a *Bildungs-roman* but a poem as 'chequered' as 'your world' (8. 89), a 'non-descript and ever varying rhyme, / A versified Aurora Borealis' (7. 2).

Like *Don Juan*'s narrator, Montaigne had no confidence that he was developing towards truth or virtue. He continually modified and elaborated his essays, but he emphasised that he was not necessarily improving: 'I add, but I correct not' (III, 222). His mind, he insisted, in an essay that Byron marked, was no more developmental than his book:

> [M]y understanding does not always go forward, it goes backward too. I do not much less suspect my fancies for being the second or third, than for being the first, either present or past; we oft correct ourselves as foolishly as we do others. I am grown older by a great many years since my first publications, which were in the year 1580: but I very much doubt whether I am grown an inch the wiser. I now, and I anon, are two several persons; but whether the better, now or anon, I am not able to determine. It were a fine thing to be old, if we only travelled towards improvement; but it is a drunken, stumbling, reeling, ill-favoured motion[.] (III, 222–3)

Rejecting any notion that life is progress or development, Montaigne stumbles and reels along, presenting a selfhood as contradictory and inconsistent as that of *Don Juan*'s narrator. '[U]neasiness and irresolution', for Montaigne as for the narrator, 'are our governing and predominant qualities' (III, 257). This belief leads Montaigne at times to posit a radical lack of subjective integration, writing that '[a]ll we perform is no other than patch-work' and that '[w]e are all such a rude medley of compounds, and those of so various a contexture, that every piece plays every moment its own game; and we are as different from our own selves as we are from each other' (I, 436, 437). Similarly, Montaigne rejects the conventional piety that reform leads developmentally to virtue in old age. He 'hate[s] that accidental repentance which old age brings with it' (III, 16), affirming that the flesh's infirmity should not be mistaken for the soul's temperance. 'We ought to love temperance for its own sake, and in respect to God, who has commanded both that and chastity', he argues. 'What we derive from catarrhs, and what I am obliged for to my cholic, is neither chastity nor temperance' (III, 18). Just because Montaigne's ageing flesh is less libidinous does not mean he loves chastity any more fervently. For all his concern with moral self-knowledge and self-improvement, Montaigne declines to link changes in his opinions and conduct to a meliorist narrative.[34]

From the beginning of the poem, *Don Juan*'s narrator suggests that his changes are unlike the fall from grace suffered by the fallen women. While they 'lose their caste at once', are 'banish[ed]' and 'render[ed] desperate' (12. 78–80), when he falls he always recovers himself (a bit like an ottava rima stanza, which is continually getting its rhymes in a tangle and then triumphantly untangling them, only to start over again). His good intentions are never dented by his failure to live up to them:

> I make a resolution every spring
> 　Of reformation, ere the year run out,
> But, somehow, this my vestal vow takes wing,
> 　Yet still, I trust, it may be kept throughout:
> I'm very sorry, very much ashamed,
> And mean, next winter, to be quite reclaim'd.
>
> (1. 119)

The narrator's mobility here appears as inevitable moral backsliding combined with its twin opposite, the unimpaired possibility of reform. The purity of his 'vestal vow' is as fragile as the virginity of the 'pretty wenches' from Canto Sixteen, but unlike them, the narrator gets a second, and a third, chance to reform.

What Montaigne essays, Byron hinges to a story. For the narrator, every fall from grace can become the occasion for a new reformation, as predictably as the change of season. Development, and its twin opposite disciplinary intervention, is edged out of *Don Juan* by non-developmental mobility and self-contradiction. These alternative, chaotic narratives of the self allow space for freely chosen repentance that escapes the steely disciplinary traps set for 'poacher[s] upon Nature's manor' (16. 62). Byron may have drawn on his reading of Montaigne when presenting the counter-normative, non-developmental characters of Juan and the narrator, and when he wrote into *Don Juan* features which resisted the iron law of morality imposed on the subject from outside by a disciplinary apparatus that, paradoxically, made repentance impossible by trying to enforce it.

2. The legible subject

The second thing that concerned Byron about the modern subject was its legibility. Throughout the Romantic period, as many critics have noted, identity was increasingly thought of in terms of subjective depth. A person's authentic nature resided deep within him or her, but it nonetheless made itself legible in such surface phenomena as speech, gesture, facial expression and bodily appearance. Wahrman describes how, by the end of the eighteenth century, '[t]he inward mind [...] irrepressibly and ineradicably marked the face'.[35] In Chapter 4, I called this 'somatic inscription': the process by which subjective depths were understood to be inscribed on bodily surfaces.

The hermeneutic of intimacy assumed and endorsed this paradoxical sense of deep selfhood as both hidden and yet legible. For reading in industrial culture to be presented as a relationship of intimacy, the author's true character had to appear hidden from most people in order to sustain the sense of intimacy, yet legible to some in order to enable the relationship. The celebrity's authentic truth, according to the hermeneutic of intimacy, had retreated to a deep inner space where it lurked in secret, hidden from observers. And yet at the same time it continually poured out in writing, in conversation, on the surface of the body and its adornments, where it was made legible for those who knew how to look.

Byron resisted this sense that the subjective interior was legible in *Don Juan*, but the terms of the debate may seem unfamiliar at first glance. The implicit controversy is not concerned with whether the subject's hidden interior exists, nor with whether selfhood is innate or constructed.[36] Byron does not seem to doubt human inwardness – his narrator has an 'internal spirit' which 'cut[s] a caper', and Juan has an 'internal ghost' which steels him for his encounter with the external one (10. 3; 16. 118). Byron, therefore, was in tune with his Romantic contemporaries when he accepted some crucial elements in the modern regime of selfhood. But he differed from them when he disputed the extent to which the interior was legible to onlookers and the claim that being able to read it was a sign of cultural superiority. What is at stake is not the opposition of depth and surface, but the opposition of legible and illegible subjectivity.

Like other aspects of modern subjectivity, this one was linked to a new moral concern. Tied to the conception of the legible self was the idea that motivations are more important for morality than actions. Taylor traces this view in Kant, for whom '[m]orality is not to be defined in terms of any specific outcomes. The moral action is not marked as such by its outcome, but rather by the motive for which it was undertaken.' In fact, on this view, '[t]he moral person may lead the same external life as the non-moral one, but it is inwardly transformed by a different spirit. It is animated by a different end.'[37] Acting morally therefore means paying close attention to your own motives; policing morality, on the other hand, means scrutinising the motives of others. Byron opposes this on the grounds that because the deep subject is not legible to onlookers, other people's motivations cannot be reliably assayed.

This new moral concern with motivations is part of what Byron calls 'cant'. People who cant deploy a rhetoric of sincerity that depends on their understanding of the subject as hidden yet legible. They valorise statements and actions which are understood to come from the subject's hidden interior and to gain authority and authenticity from it. They therefore think, with Kant, that the appropriate object of moral judgement is not action but intention. At many points in his *Essays*, Montaigne appears to share this view, asserting that '[i]t is not in the sphere of the maturest understanding to judge us simply by our external actions; it must fathom the very soul, and find out the springs that give it motion'. But he goes on to emphasise the difficulty of knowing our own motives, let alone those of others, writing 'as this is a dangerous and sublime undertaking, I wish that fewer persons would attempt it' (I, 438). In practice, this 'sublime undertaking' often rests on faulty logic, because the merit of an action (including an act of writing such as a poem) is judged by reference to an interior state for which the only evidence is the action itself. You know an action is good by the intention that produced it: you know an intention is good by the action it produced. The hidden interior to which such rhetoric appeals can only be known in so far as it apparently makes itself legible in its epiphenomena, closing the logical circle. This rhetoric of sincerity is part of what Byron calls 'cant': dubious jargon, unreflectively employed, which refuses to engage with those who do not use its terms and mystifies what it claims to illuminate.

When things go wrong, the canters' last line of defence is to refer to their legible subjective interior by claiming that at least their intentions were good:

> [W]hat we call 'the best
> Intentions' [. . .] form all mankind's *trump card*,
> To be produced when brought up to the test.
> The statesman, hero, harlot, lawyer – ward
> Off each attack, when people are in quest
> Of their designs, by saying they *meant well*;
> 'Tis pity 'that such meaning should pave Hell.'
>
> (8. 25)

When someone comes 'in quest / Of their designs', intending to probe the hidden subjective interior where motives lurk, the canters head off the attack by claiming to bare their souls. But the road to Hell is paved with good intentions, and Byron refuses to allow good motives to be an excuse for bad outcomes. He notes satirically how producing your best intentions when you have 'a visit from the brother [. . .] to demand / What "your intentions are?" ' makes all the difference between a dalliance and a courtship (12. 60). Lady Adeline, when she takes an interest in Juan, 'might flatter / Herself that her intentions were the best' in order to keep her conscience clear, but the narrator warns, 'Intense intentions are a dangerous matter' (14. 88). Appealing to your good intentions means making your subjective interior legible to observers. But for Byron it is actions, and not motivations, that should be the objects of moral judgements.

The rhetoric of sincerity that appealed to good intentions was also used to attack bad intentions. *Blackwood's Magazine* blasted Byron's bad intentions in *Don Juan*, claiming that he:

> [Laid] bare to the eye of man and of *woman* all the hidden convulsions of a wicked spirit – thoughts too abominable, we would hope, to have been imagined by any but him that has expressed them – and [did] all this without one symptom of pain, contrition, remorse, or hesitation, with a calm careless ferociousness of contented and satisfied depravity[.][38]

Blackwood's was convinced that Byron had made his hidden interior legible in *Don Juan*, and it elided the poem with its author in order to damn both at once. Byron feigned shock that 'They accuse me – *Me* – the present writer of / The present poem – of – I know not what' (7. 3). *Blackwood's* also made its critique retroactive, recoiling from its earlier seduction by the hermeneutic of intimacy. Asserting that a man who had now revealed his hidden interior in such a way could never have been sincere before, the journal was disgusted by 'the insulting deceit which has been practised upon us':

> We look back with a mixture of wrath and scorn to the delight with which we suffered ourselves to be filled by one who, all the while he was furnishing us with delight must, we cannot doubt it, have been mocking us with a cruel mockery[.][39]

The rhetoric of sincerity was here reversed to condemn Byron for having been insincere. The critic traced Byron's secretly malignant intentions: 'the great genius of the man seems to have been throughout exerted to its utmost strength, in devising every possible method of pouring scorn upon every element of good or noble nature in the hearts of his readers'.[40]

Cant, then, is the rhetoric of people who think of themselves and others as structured around a hidden, but legible, interior. They legitimise their jargon by referring it to interior intentions and claim to be able to discern the hidden intentions of others, using this supposed knowledge to justify disciplinary measures. To oppose such a discourse would seem to call for 'some Columbus of the moral seas' who, searching out the real motives of the canters, 'Would show mankind their souls' Antipodes' (14. 101):

> What 'Antres vast and desarts idle,' then
> Would be discover'd in the human soul!
> What Icebergs in the hearts of mighty men,
> With Self-love in the centre as their Pole!
> What Anthropophagi in nine of ten
> Of those who hold the kingdoms in controul!
> Were things but only called by their right name,
> Caesar himself would be ashamed of fame.
>
> (14. 102)

Playing a set of variations upon a speech from *Othello*, in the final stanza of Canto Fourteen, Byron imagines how such a moral adventurer would map the hidden interior of the modern subject, rendering it genuinely legible and revealing the dissonance between the canters' public statements and private motives. When cant evoked the hidden but legible subject, a moral Columbus might arbitrate by discovering everyone's hidden motives and judging all public utterances accordingly. But, having provided the job description, Byron tells us – as I will show – that he is not the man for the job.

Byron frequently presents existence as a riddle in *Don Juan*, relishing the impossibility of solving 'this unriddled wonder, / The World' (11. 3). His poem is itself a riddle concealing 'mystic diapasons' and 'much which could not be appreciated / In any manner by the uninitiated' (14. 22). He is not much good at solving riddles, 'I'm not Oedipus, and life's a Sphinx' (13. 12), but in Canto Nine he writes a riddle that is easy to solve:

> Oh, thou 'teterrima Causa' of all 'belli' –
>   Thou gate of Life and Death – thou nondescript!
> Whence is our exit and our entrance, – well I
>   May pause in pondering how all Souls are dipt
> In thy perennial fountain: – how man *fell*, I
>   Know not, since Knowledge saw her branches stript
> Of her first fruit, but how he falls and rises
> *Since, thou* hast settled beyond all surmises.
>
> Some call thee 'the worst Cause of war,' but I
>   Maintain thou art the *best*: for after all
> From thee we come, to thee we go, and why
>   To get at thee not batter down a wall,
> Or waste a world? Since no one can deny
>   Thou dost replenish worlds both great and small:
> With, or without thee, all things at a stand
> Are, or would be, thou Sea of Life's dry Land!
>
> (9. 55–6)

Here the written words conceal behind their multiple *entendres* and Horatian tag an unwritten truth, which is apparently the answer to everything. Its unwriteability requires us to penetrate the surface games of the text to get to the riddle's scarcely hidden solution, which is mockingly presented as the solution to all life's riddles and the utmost profundity the text has to offer. The incomplete quotation from Horace, 'cunnus taeterrima belli / Causa', supplies the missing word and reveals a gentlemanly disregard for accuracy.[41] But you don't need the benefits of a classical education to solve the riddle. What holds for the modern subject and enables the controversy surrounding *Don Juan* holds for this text too: the hidden key is everywhere legible on the surface.

The concealed word that answers this riddle is the key to Byron's counterblast to cant and reverses his earlier gloomy diagnosis of the age in an 1819 letter to Douglas Kinnaird:

> I have written about a hundred stanzas of a third Canto – but it is damned modest – the outcry has frightened me. – I had such projects for the Don – but the *Cant* is so much stronger than *Cunt* – now a days, – that the benefit of experience in a man who had well weighed the worth of both monosyllables – must be lost to despairing posterity. (*BLJ*, VI, 232)

With his apostrophe to the 'cunt' – a thing as non-descript as his 'non-descript and ever varying rhyme' (7. 2) – Byron reverses the terms of his earlier complaint and sets out to make 'cunt' stronger than 'cant'. The joke is on those canting readers who were on the lookout for traces of Byron's hidden subjective interior. Their fascination with the intimate and concealed interior of the psychologised subject, expressed in the hermeneutic of intimacy, reappears here metamorphosed. Their refined concern is corporealised into a carnal prurience. While searching for hidden meanings in Byron's poetry they find a pudendum and are brought face to face with the unwriteable word. The satire is extended two stanzas later, where a pun makes clear what had previously been, along with so much else, implicit. Catherine, who has been moment-arily distracted by Juan's good looks, recovers herself and is described as a 'great whole' (9. 58). The lacuna in the text which arouses the reader's desire for meanings and which Byron crudely identifies with, or as, the cunt, is figured as a vacancy, a blank, a (w)hole.[42] To cant means to pour forth a jargon which no one can understand but everyone feels they have to speak, with the possibility of turning it into a tool for coercion like Castlereagh's 'parts of speech [...] Which none divine and every one obeys' (9. 49). To resist cant means changing a vowel and withholding a word which everyone can understand but no one must speak, which is comically portrayed as all-powerful but which coerces no one but the put-upon Juan, conscripted into service as Catherine's Imperial Favourite. To cant means making appeals to the hidden parts of the psyche. To resist cant means deflating its rhetoric by referring it to the hidden parts of the body. To cant means sharing an understanding of the subject as structured around a deep, hidden interior that incessantly makes itself legible. To resist cant, as this somatic riddle suggests and as I will go on to show, can involve resisting that view.

That resistance becomes apparent in the English cantos, where Byron works against the modern understanding of the subject as legible by insisting on the illegibility of his characters. These cantos are usually thought of as the most novelistic in the poem, where Byron slows the pace of narration, includes more detail, and moves towards more realistic characterisation. Some of the characters in the English cantos are given inner depths, and these 'round' characters are set off against other 'flat' characters.[43] But Byron also dissents from a 'novelistic' understanding of subjectivity in significant ways. When the Amundevilles open their house to the public in the hope of winning votes for Lord Henry in the forthcoming election, Adeline performs her part with aplomb. But when Juan 'cast[s] a glance / On Adeline while playing her grand role', the variety of partial surface impressions he receives never adds up to a rounded whole. Acting 'all and every part / By turns', Adeline's 'vivacious versatility' is too exuberant to allow Juan to get the measure of her selfhood (16. 97). The partial impressions do not cohere, leaving her illegible subjectivity ungrasped.[44] Adeline has what Dror Wahrman would call (following Sarah Knott) a 'socially turned self', one which is primarily outward looking and relationally derived from a matrix of overlapping and mutable investments in particular identity categories.[45] Hers is an identity more at home in the *ancien regime* of identity than the modern regime of selfhood.

Once again, Byron's thinking may have been informed by his concurrent reading of Montaigne, who insists on the privacy of the interior. '[W]e must reserve a back-room, wholly our own, and entirely free, wherein to fix our liberty, our principal retreat and solitude', he writes, suggesting that here 'we have converse with ourselves, and so privately, that no knowledge or communication of any foreign concern, be admitted' (I, 290). Adeline's protean role-playing is 'merely what is called mobility' (16. 97). Rather than pointing inwards towards a legible interior selfhood, Adeline's continually changing demeanour points outwards to those around her, as she is 'strongly acted on by what is nearest' (16. 97). Characters possessing mobility cannot easily be read according to realist conventions that require a consistent subject with a hidden yet legible identity. Unable to pin her down, Juan 'began to feel / Some doubt how much of Adeline was *real*' (16. 96).

Although Adeline's appearances seem disintegrated, there's no doubt that there's a 'soul' behind them. In one of those big things that pass inside little brackets, Juan sees her '(Betraying only now and then her soul / By a look scarce perceptibly askance / Of weariness or scorn)' (16. 96). Adeline's appearances may be mobile, but they do conceal a soul, a hidden interiority which can be spotted now and then. What Byron chooses to emphasise, however, is the difficulty of catching a glimpse of her soul, the fact that it is 'scarce[ly] perceptibl[e]'. In a page Byron marked 'with a *triple* dog's-ear', Montaigne similarly asserted the extreme difficulty of trying to read inner subjective depths.[46] It is 'a ticklish subject', he says, 'to follow so rambling a path as that of the mind, to penetrate the dark profundities of its intricate windings, to choose and lay hold of the many minute quavers of its agitations'(I, 491).

Reading the soul in the face is far from being a mark of cultural superiority in *Don Juan*. Only 'docile esquires' (16. 101) imagine that they can read Adeline:

> Some praised her beauty; others her great grace;
> The warmth of her politeness, whose sincerity
> Was obvious in each feature of her face,
> Whose traits were radiant with the rays of verity.
>
> (16. 102)

Duped by their own cant, the foolish folk take Adeline to be legible, believing that her hidden interior radiates forth in perfectly ingenuous appearances. In the essay 'Of Repentance', Montaigne gently mocked those who would connect interior reality to exterior appearance, asking 'who does not give Tamerlane large eye-brows, wide nostrils, a dreadful face, and a stature beyond measure, according to the conception he has formed from the report of his name?' (III, 9).[47] Byron, contrary to novelistic convention, does not suggest that a more discerning class of readers could penetrate the secrets of Adeline's subjective interior more reliably. Instead, he argues that discernment lies in acknowledging the interior's illegibility.

When the narrator turned his attention to Adeline three cantos previously, he described her in very different terms from those employed by the 'docile esquires'. The narrator rejects the normative 'common place' image of a volcano which 'beneath the snow [...] holds the lava'. He breaks off in the middle of the stock image, because 'I hate to hunt down a tired metaphor' and goes on to produce an alternative (13. 36). In his commentary, McGann writes that this is 'a good example of the kind of stylistic renovation Byron was trying to bring about with *Beppo* and *D[on] J[uan]*' (*CPW*, V, 756). But, as George Ridenour has shown, the style of *Don Juan* 'become[s] a world view and a way of life'; and Byron's half-serious claim that 'I now deduce [...] moral lessons' suggests how much is at stake in this passage (13. 38).[48] When Byron rejected the volcano image he rejected his own previous image of himself as a man whose poetry was 'the lava of the imagination whose eruption prevents an earth-quake' (*BLJ*, III, 179).[49] He had imagined poetry as the product of a subject whose hidden depths continually poured out over the surface, saving him from insanity. The new metaphor he conjures up rewrites assumptions about subjectivity:

> I'll have another figure in a trice: –
>   What say you to a bottle of champagne?
> Frozen into a very vinous ice,
>   Which leaves few drops of that immortal rain,
> Yet in the very centre, past all price,
>   About a liquid glassful will remain;
> And this is stronger than the strongest grape
> Could e'er express in its expanded shape:
>
> 'Tis the whole spirit brought to a quintessence;
>   And thus the chilliest aspects may concentre
> A hidden nectar under a cold presence.
>   And such are many – though I only meant her,
> From whom I now deduce these moral lessons,
>   On which the Muse has always sought to enter: –
> And your cold people are beyond all price,
> When once you have broken their confounded ice.
>
> (13. 37–8)

Byron substitutes for the volcano metaphor an image that emphasises the difficulty of getting to subjective interiority. The unfacetious Biblical allusion and the significant Byronic word 'concentre' signal the importance of this passage.[50] With a pun on 'spirit', Byron suggests that the truth of Adeline's subjectivity may be frozen inside her, inaccessible to onlookers and illegible to would-be readers. He praises this concealed centre as 'hidden nectar', but he doesn't claim to know anything about it. The ice confounds his attempts to know Adeline, and he suggests that this is an accurate description of 'many' people.[51] While Adeline's subjective interior remains unknown to man, it seems that Aurora's may be known only to God.[52] She 'kept her heart serene within its zone', where 'Her spirit seemed as seated on a throne / Apart from the surrounding world' (15. 47). Her depths are not easily read:

> The worlds beyond this world's perplexing waste
> Had more of her existence, for in her
> There was a depth of feeling to embrace
> Thoughts, boundless, deep, but silent too as Space.
>
> (16. 48)

Fitz-Fulke acts as the foil to these two, emphasising by contrast the difficulty of reading their inner depths. Unlike Adeline and Aurora, she is a character 'whose mind, / If she had any, was upon her face' (16. 49).

In his portrayal of the three central female characters in the English cantos, then, Byron accepted the assumption, shared by celebrity culture and the novel, that the most interesting people are those with hidden depths. But he resisted the idea that such depths are legible. While cant worked by claiming to be able to read other people's intentions and by ceaselessly referring to its own impeccable motives, Byron's narrator professed to 'hate a motive like a lingering bottle' (14. 58). While celebrity culture relied on the revelation of deep selfhood in celebrity texts, Byron's narrator refused to penetrate subjectivity and probe those depths.[53] He asserted that:

> 'Tis sad to hack into the roots of things,
> They are so much intertwisted with the earth:
> So that the branch a goodly verdure flings,
> I reck not if an acorn gave it birth.
> To trace all actions to their secret springs
> Would make indeed some melancholy mirth;
> But that is not at present my concern[.]
>
> (14. 59)

Rather than probing for concealed motives, the narrator prefers to judge outcomes. 'I say, in my slight way I may proceed / To play upon the surface of Humanity' (15. 60). On that same triple-dog-eared page mentioned above, Montaigne expressed a moment of self-doubt about his project of self-examination, describing it as 'a new and extraordinary amusement that takes us off from the common, yea, and the most commendable, employments of the world' (I, 491). In *Don Juan*, Byron also questioned the usefulness of tracing the knotty pathways of motivation. He refused to become the Columbus of the moral seas because that would mean playing into cant's hands by accepting its premise that intention, not action, should be the object of moral judgement.

When Murray wanted to go to court for an injunction against pirated editions of *Don Juan*, Byron thought the action would fail because the court would rule that, as a blasphemous or seditious work, the poem was not entitled to the protection of copyright. '[T]he cry is up – and cant is up' he noted wryly; 'I have not the patience [...] to contend with the fellows in their own slang' (*BLJ*, VI, 256–7). Insisting that even to engage the canters on their own terms required an effort of translation that he was not prepared to make, Byron rejected the premises of the debate. While cant assumed that the subject's interior was legible in order to argue about whether an individual's motives were good or bad, Byron rejected that assumption and chose instead to satirise the search for interior truth in his riddling bawdry, to foreground the illegibility of his most interesting characters and to refuse the task of trying to probe subjects in search of motives.

Byron's turn away from subjective legibility led him to turn away from his earlier enthusiasm for Rousseau and towards Montaigne. Byron had read Rousseau with Shelley in Switzerland, and that shared enthusiasm had left its mark on *Childe Harold* Canto Three. Rousseau set himself in opposition to Montaigne, claiming that the sincerity of his *Confessions* was much franker than that of Montaigne's *Essays*. Rousseau wrote that he 'had always laughed at the false naïveté of Montaigne who, while making a pretence of admitting his flaws, takes great care to give himself only amiable ones'.[54] While Rousseau is mentioned in *Don Juan* more often than Montaigne, he is never treated with the enthusiasm Byron had expressed in *Childe Harold* Canto Three.[55] Rousseau's confessional outpourings, in which the self ceaselessly made itself legible, had been displaced by Montaigne's judicious scepticism, which stressed the difficulty of self-exploration and the illegibility of the interior. It is my contention that Byron's turns from Rousseau to Montaigne, from volcanoes to frozen champagne and from legible bodies like the Giaour's to illegible souls like Aurora's are part of the same intellectual, poetic and moral project. They constitute a turn away from the modern ways of thinking about subjectivity on which celebrity relied and which it helped to promote.

This may seem to be an anachronistic or idiosyncratic attempt to revive outdated ideas, and in a way it is. It is what Jerome Christensen calls a '*hopeful* anachronism', a politically charged decision to employ ideas from the past in order to trouble the existing or emergent moral order.[56] Celebrity culture played a vital role in making that new moral order normative, because the apparatus of celebrity connected discursive conventions and material conditions in new ways. Celebrity linked a new understanding of subjectivity to an industry of textual production and dissemination that enabled it to reach a massive, socially diverse and widely distributed audience. Once this cultural apparatus began to function, celebrities such as Byron provided a spectacle of subjectivity, offering models of developmental, legible, modern selves that helped to shape their audience's understanding of individuality. The result was a normative concept of subjectivity that remains operative today.

As part of the celebrity apparatus, Byron's poetry helped to normalise that concept, but in *Don Juan* he introduced counter-normative ideas about subjectivity that resisted the new moral culture, made emergent norms seem strange once again and disrupted the functioning of the celebrity apparatus from within. If those tactics of resistance seem anachronistic, it is because they finally succumbed to the strategies of the celebrity apparatus. As celebrity extended its reach, it became an ever more powerful cultural force because its fundamental assumptions became embedded in the mundane experience of those people who fed it with their labour, sustained it in their leisure and welcomed it into their imaginations. We cannot know what role the apparatus of celebrity will play in shaping our culture in the future, but we will be better equipped to grasp its ongoing metastases if we understand the role it has played in our past.

Envoi

> 'Go, little book, from this my solitude!
>   I cast thee on the waters, go thy ways!
> And if, as I believe, thy vein be good,
>   The world will find thee after many days.'
>
> (*Don Juan*, 1. 222)

The epigraph is Southey's every line; for God's sake, reader, take it not for mine. When the lines appear transplanted in *Don Juan*, they point to the difference celebrity makes. Southey's poet has retreated from the world to a contemplative solitude. He appears as a vatic, God-like figure ('The voice of the Lord is upon the waters', Ps 29.3) whose power over his readers is partly a function of his separation from them. Not caring for the world's opinion, he is free to tell the world eternal truths in poetry of lasting merit. He casts his book upon the waters like a message in a bottle to be found washed up in another time and place. His audience, he imagines, knows nothing of the poet, but his readers recognise the value of the poem and the vein of truth it contains. Between the poet and 'the world' lies the ocean – a black box that conveys the poem to its audience through mysterious and inscrutable channels. To send a poem out into the world, Southey suggests, is to bid it farewell in the confidence that – somewhere, somehow – discerning readers will find it. True worth will receive its due in the end.

When Byron drafted the lines into *Don Juan*, as part of his 'claim to praise', he revealed the extent of their defensive mystification (1. 222). In *Don Juan*, their rhetorical *diminutio* sounds like false modesty and studied self-promotion. Their embrace of vatic solitude sounds like an affectation disguising Southey's assiduous attention to the demands of the literary marketplace. Their appeal to posterity sounds as if it were designed to protect the poet from the fear that his book would not float to the top of the sea of new publications, but drown in it. Southey's lines in Byron's book create a text that we might think of as celebrity degree zero: a controlled experiment in isolating the effects of the celebrity apparatus. The words themselves are identical, but Byron's celebrity makes all the difference in the way we read them. Byron knew this, of course, and used the borrowed words to point ironically to the celebrity culture that would structure his own poem's production, circulation and reception.

Even without having read his attack on the provincialism of the Lake School in the Dedication to *Don Juan*, few if any of Byron's readers could have imagined him occupying the kind of self-authorising solitude Southey envisaged. Instead, Byron's self-imposed exile was the result of scandal, and his leave-taking (in 'Fare Thee Well', 'Epistle to Augusta', and *Childe Harold* Canto Three) had become part of his celebrity identity. Rather than being the anonymous, vatic poet that Southey envisaged, Byron was a celebrity whose poetic career and private life, and the rumours that surrounded them, were sufficiently well known to be invoked to heighten interest in *Manfred* or raise laughter in *Beppo*. Byron did not cast his book on the waters to find its own way to the reader by some mystified or inscrutable process. He submitted it to the apparatus of celebrity culture, which structured every aspect of its production, promotion, distribution, circulation, reception, appropriation and redeployment – from the editorial interventions into the text of the poem, designed to make it more saleable, to the piracies, parodies and unauthorised continuations that ensured its enormous cultural resonance. Byron's appropriation of Southey's lines ironically thematises the celebrity culture of which he is part, indicating the impossibility for Byron of calling on the same kind of rhetoric that Southey employs, and demonstrating that celebrity cannot be regarded as extrinsic to literary texts. Thanks to Byron's celebrity, the lines have, for almost two hundred years, been immeasurably more famous in his redaction than in Southey's original.

When Byron borrowed Southey's lines, he made celebrity his subject. In making his celebrity my subject, I have tried to develop a new approach to studying Byron's writing and its cultural impact, I have identified Byron as one case study in a still-unwritten history of celebrity culture, and I have offered a theoretical framework for further studies of the celebrity apparatus. This framework is based on an historical account of the problems of information overload and alienation created by industrial culture. These problems, I have argued, were addressed – sometimes palliated, never solved – by the emergence of a celebrity culture which used the new industrial technologies to brand an individual's identity. At the same time, it concealed its use of those industrial technologies by fostering a hermeneutic of intimacy which figured celebrity texts as conduits through which to relate to a remarkable person, rather than as mass-produced standardised products. It was beyond the control of any individual and included a variety of texts, typically in several media, which ranged from the celebrity's own work, to texts which promoted a sympathetic image, to those which attacked or satirised the celebrity (while further contributing to his or her cultural ubiquity).

I have suggested that, having identified some pioneering individuals in the eighteenth century, a cultural history of celebrity should begin in earnest in the Romantic period. It should understand celebrity as a cultural apparatus constructed not only from ideas, attitudes and discourse, but also from material conditions and technological innovations. It should be able to note substantive distinctions between the kinds of public profile available to individuals of different races, classes and genders at different historical periods; and, by specifying the features of modern celebrity, it should be able to describe its emergence and subsequent metamorphoses. It should be as interdisciplinary as the phenomenon of celebrity itself, which features in theatre and literature, music and visual culture, fashion and boxing. Historians of celebrity culture need to attend to individual celebrities, without mystifying the extent of their agency, to the industry that promotes them, without imagining that its promotional strategies can be separated from the celebrity's work, and to the celebrity's audience, without presenting them as passive ideological dupes.

This study has focussed on Lord Byron, but I have also invoked a variety of other individuals whose place in the celebrity apparatus deserves further consideration. David Garrick, Laurence Sterne, Sarah Siddons, Edmund Kean, Letitia Landon, Mary Robinson, Anne Yearsley, Thomas Moore, Leigh Hunt and Walter Scott, among many others in the Romantic period and later, participated in a celebrity culture that operated even on those who – like Robert Southey – claimed to reject it. But studies of celebrity will only reiterate the assumptions of the celebrity apparatus unless they also move beyond individual celebrities to pay attention to the genres, media and discourses that enabled celebrity culture. Genres such as the gossip column, the book review, the personal essay and later the interview; media such as the theatrical portrait, the steel plate engraving and later the photograph; and discourses that identified literary 'lions', musical 'virtuosi' and theatrical 'stars' are as important for the study of celebrity culture as remarkable individuals.

We also need studies of how celebrity culture relates to its 'others': public service, sporting prowess, literary genius, intellectual endeavour and other such 'serious' undertakings. Understanding these relationships is the key to resisting the assumption that celebrity is a debased cultural phenomenon, unworthy of serious study.

Finally, we need to know more about how the borders between celebrity and canonicity can be crossed. By understanding the infrastructure of citation, appropriation and redeployment that can turn celebrities from earlier ages into canonical figures for later ages, we can grasp how their original celebrity becomes obscured, and with it the long history of celebrity culture, which seems perpetually to be a recent invention. In Byron's case this process was highly contentious. Memoirs by his acquaintances attacked journalists' speculations, expensive scholarly editions of his poetry fought off cheap piracies, and Thomas Moore's 'authorized' biography did battle with a phalanx of unauthorised accounts. While Byron was memorialised in stained glass at the University of Glasgow and in statues in London, Cambridge, Athens and Aberdeen, he was also commodified in engraved portraits, illustrated editions, Byron chinaware and affordable busts for bourgeois homes. As the century went on, memories of reading Byron were recounted in autobiographies; he appeared as a character in novels and his works featured in school anthologies; he was invoked as a shining example in political tracts and as an awful warning in revivalist sermons.[1] A nearly naked woman on horseback turned his poem *Mazeppa* into a titillating circus act, while an interpolated ballet made his play *Manfred* suitable for the Victorian stage.[2] Moreover, the verbal and visual texts that structured Byron's reception became in turn the subject of second-order texts, for example when Letitia Landon wrote a poem 'On the Portrait of Byron at Newstead Abbey'; when Charles Tennyson Turner, elder brother of the more famous Tennyson, wrote a double sonnet 'On the Statue of Lord Byron, By Thorwaldsen, in Trinity College Library, Cambridge'; and when John Cam Hobhouse wrote a pamphlet entitled 'Remarks on the Exclusion of Lord Byron's Monument from Westminster Abbey'.[3] Through a complex, varied and internally conflicted infrastructure of reception, Byron came to feature in the nineteenth-century imagination as both popular celebrity and canonical poet.

This study began in fascination and frustration. I began writing because I wanted to understand why I found everything about Byron fascinating and because I was frustrated that the discourse of literary criticism, as conventionally constituted, could not admit that fascination as a legitimate object of enquiry. I ended up writing about an apparatus of fascination – a vast cultural assemblage of industrial technologies, driving ambitions and private pleasures that coalesced at a moment in the past, no less distinct for being distant, and that continues to structure the work of some and the pleasure of many in the present. As that apparatus colonises new areas of endeavour and pleasure, including literature and its study, it should no longer be possible to remain blind to its history, nor to dismiss it as a cheapened and debased form of recognition. In a culture that remains fascinated by celebrity, we should recognise that the modern celebrity apparatus took shape in the Romantic period, and understand Byron as one of its earliest examples and most astute critics.

Notes

Preface

1. Andrew Anthony, 'Celebrity is Nothing New', *The Observer, Life Magazine*, 27 January 2002, p. 8.
2. 'I never in my life *read* a composition, save to Hodgson, as he pays me in kind.' *BLJ*, III, 206.
3. In Michel Foucault's terms, celebrity is one of the 'threads' of modernity, which he describes as a 'structure that has not yet been unravelled; we are only just beginning to disentangle a few of the threads, which are still so unknown to us that we immediately assume them to be either marvellously new or absolutely archaic'. Michel Foucault, *The Birth of the Clinic: An Archaeology of Medical Perception*, trans. by A. M. Sheridan Smith (New York: Vintage Books, 1975), p. 199.
4. Samuel Johnson, *The Rambler*, ed. Alex Chalmers, 4 vols (Philadelphia PA: E. Earle, 1812), IV, 42.
5. Dinah Mulock Craik, *The Ogilvies* (New York and London: Harper and Brothers, 1878), p. 25.
6. [Maria Jane Jewsbury], *Phantasmagoria: Or, Sketches of Life and Literature*, 2 vols (London: Hurst, Robinson and Co., 1825), I, 2.
7. Hester Thrale to Samuel Johnson, 4 July 1784, in *Letters of Samuel Johnson LL.D.*, ed. George Birbeck Hill, 2 vols (Oxford: Clarendon Press, 1892), II, 406.
8. William Hazlitt, 'On the Living Poets' (1818), in William Hazlitt, *The Complete Works of William Hazlitt*, ed. P. P. Howe, 21 vols (London: J. M. Dent and Sons, 1930), V, 143–4. Andrew Bennett has analysed the other half of this distinction, showing how Romantic poets linked poetic achievement to posthumous recognition. Andrew Bennett, *Romantic Poets and the Culture of Posterity* (Cambridge: Cambridge University Press, 1999). Claire Brock has offered an alternative reading of Hazlitt's understanding of fame and popularity, arguing that '[w]hile Hazlitt appeared to value posterity over contemporary celebrity here, he was more than suspicious of a renown that must be received only posthumously in most of his writings'. Claire Brock, *The Feminization of Fame, 1750–1830* (Basingstoke: Palgrave, 2006), p. 189.
9. John Hamilton Reynolds, 'Popular Poetry' (1816), in *Selected Prose of John Hamilton Reynolds*, ed. Leonidas M. Jones (Cambridge, MA: Harvard University Press, 1966), pp. 70–6 (p. 71).
10. Samuel Taylor Coleridge, *Biographia Literaria* (1817), ed. James Engell and Walter Jackson Bate, 2 vols (Princeton, NJ: Princeton University Press, 1985), p. 224.
11. Thomas Macaulay, 'Review of Thomas Moore, *Letters and Journals of Lord Byron: With Notices of his Life*', in *The Edinburgh Review*, 53 (June 1831), 544–72 (p. 552).

12. Matthew Arnold, 'Byron' (1881), in *Essays in Criticism, Second Series* (1888), ed. S. R. Littlewood (London: Macmillan, 1960), pp. 97–120 (p. 102).
13. Jorge Luis Borges, 'Pierre Menard, Author of the *Quixote*' (1944), in *Labyrinths* (London: Penguin, 2000), p. 70.

1 Romantic celebrity

1. '*Childe Harold's Pilgrimage, Canto III*', *Portfolio*, 23 November 1816, p. 73.
2. The *OED* cites the *Monthly Review* using 'autobiography' in 1797, and Robert Southey in the *Quarterly* in 1809.
3. These include papermaking by hand or machine, printing by hand or steam, engraving or etching on copper or steel plates, newspaper, magazine or review publication, publishers' catalogues and advertisement leaves, and the infrastructure of distribution via road and, by the end of the period, rail or canal.
4. Daniel J. Boorstin, *The Image, or, What Happened to the American Dream* (London: Weidenfeld and Nicolson, 1961).
5. Richard Dyer, *Stars* (London: British Film Institute, 1980; 1998).
6. Joshua Gamson, *Claims to Fame: Celebrity in Contemporary America* (Berkeley: University of California Press, 1994).
7. Tyler Cowen, *What Price Fame?* (Cambridge, MA: Harvard University Press, 1999).
8. P. David Marshall, *Celebrity and Power: Fame in Contemporary Culture* (Minneapolis, MN: University of Minnesota Press, 1997), pp. 36–7.
9. Graeme Turner, *Understanding Celebrity* (London: Sage, 2004).
10. Marshall, *Celebrity and Power*, p. 49; Gamson, *Claims to Fame*, p. 11; Joe Moran, *Star Authors: Literary Celebrity in America* (London: Pluto Press, 2000), p. 6. Moran employs Bourdieu's terms to argue that the celebrity author in contemporary America 'represents both cultural capital and a marketable commodity' and exists 'between the restricted and extended subfields' of cultural production (p. 6).
11. See Ghislaine McDayter, 'Conjuring Byron: Byromania, Literary Commodification and the Birth of Celebrity', in *Byromania: Portraits of the Artist in Nineteenth- and Twentieth-Century Culture*, ed. Frances Wilson (London: Macmillan, 1999), pp. 43–62. Andrew Elfenbein similarly notes that 'Byron the celebrity was a peculiar commodity because the "thing" that gave value to his products was his subjectivity'. Andrew Elfenbein, *Byron and the Victorians* (Cambridge: Cambridge University Press, 1995), p. 48.
12. Jürgen Habermas, *The Structural Transformation of the Public Sphere: An Inquiry into a Category of Bourgeois Society*, trans. by Thomas Burger with the assistance of Frederick Lawrence (Cambridge: Polity Press, 1989), especially pp. 141–80.
13. Habermas has been widely criticised for idealising and over-simplifying the concept of the public sphere. Two important collections of essays that engage with these issues are Craig Calhoun, ed., *Habermas and the Public Sphere* (Cambridge, MA: MIT Press, 1992), and Bruce Robbins, ed., *The Phantom Public Sphere* (Minneapolis, MN: University of Minnesota Press, 1993).

14. Anne Mellor argues that, through political writing, drama, literary criticism and the novel, women were in fact able to participate in the Habermasian public sphere. Anne K. Mellor, *Mothers of the Nation: Women's Political Writing in England 1780–1830* (Bloomington, IN: Indiana University Press, 2000). Linda Colley and Eve Tavor Bannet, in different ways, have shown how women participated in the public life of the nation via the analogy of domestic economy with political economy. Linda Colley, *Britons: Forging the Nation, 1707–1837* (London: Vintage, 1992; 1996), pp. 286–96. Eve Tavor Bannet, *The Domestic Revolution: Enlightenment Feminisms and the Novel* (Baltimore, MD: Johns Hopkins University Press, 2000).
15. Richard Sennett argues that private life has overtaken the public sphere in *The Fall of Public Man* (London: Faber and Faber, 1977; 1986). The concept of a liminal space between public and private appears in Paula R. Backscheider, 'Introduction', *Prose Studies*, 18, no. 3 *The Intersections of the Public and Private Spheres in Early Modern England*, ed. Paula R. Backscheider and Timothy Dykstal (1995), 1–21.
16. Marshall, Gamson, Turner, Cowen and Moran are all concerned with contemporary culture, and their sketches of celebrity's history are necessarily brief and provisional. Michael Newbury observes that Marshall performs 'the crucial service of taking the idea of celebrity seriously. It now remains to understand the historicity of that idea.' Michael Newbury, 'Celebrity Watching', *American Literary History*, 12, no. 1–2 (2000), 272–83 (p. 283).
17. '[B]y imagining that they have got hold of an apparatus which in fact has got hold of them [musicians, writers and critics] are supporting an apparatus which is out of their control, which is no longer (as they believe) a means of furthering output but has become an obstacle to output, and specifically to their own output as soon as it follows a new and original course which the apparatus finds awkward or opposed to its own aims.' Bertolt Brecht, *Brecht on Theatre: The Development of an Aesthetic*, trans. by John Willett (New York: Hill and Wang; London: Eyre Methuen, 1964; 1978), p. 34.
18. Michel Foucault, *Power/Knowledge*, ed. Colin Gordon (Brighton: Harvester, 1980), p. 194.
19. Ibid., p. 195.
20. Leo Braudy, *The Frenzy of Renown: Fame and its History* (New York: Vintage Books, 1986; 1997), p. vii.
21. Chris Rojek, *Celebrity* (London: Reaktion, 2001), pp. 13, 16. Italics in original.
22. See Alexander Walker, *Stardom: The Hollywood Phenomenon* (London: Michael Joseph, 1970), pp. 31–9; Dyer, *Stars*, pp. 9–10; Janet Staiger, 'Seeing Stars', in *Stardom: Industry of Desire*, ed. Christine Gledhill (London: Routledge, 1991), pp. 3–16.
23. Neal Gabler, *Winchell: Gossip, Power, and the Culture of Celebrity* (New York: Knopf, 1994); Charles L. Ponce de Leon, *Self-Exposure: Human-Interest Journalism and the Emergence of Celebrity in America, 1890–1940* (Chapel Hill: University of North Carolina Press, 2002).
24. Richard Schickel, *Intimate Strangers: The Culture of Celebrity in America* (New York: Doubleday, 1985; Chicago: Ivan R. Dee, 2000), p. 23.
25. Richard Salmon, 'Signs of Intimacy: The Literary Celebrity in the "Age of Interviewing" ', *Victorian Literature and Culture*, 25, no. 1 (1997), 159–77.

26. Carol Ockman, Kenneth E. Silver, Janis Bergman-Carton and Karen Levitov, *Sarah Bernhardt: The Art of High Drama* (New Haven, CT: Yale University Press, 2005).
27. Lenard R. Berlanstein, 'Historicizing and Gendering Celebrity Culture: Famous Women in Nineteenth-Century France', *Journal of Women's History*, 16, no. 4 (2004), 65–91; Claire Brock, *The Feminization of Fame, 1750–1830* (Basingstoke: Palgrave Macmillan, 2006).
28. Martin Postle, ed., *Joshua Reynolds: The Creation of Celebrity* (London: Tate Publishing, 2005).
29. Frank Donoghue, *The Fame Machine: Book Reviewing and Eighteenth-Century Literary Careers* (Stanford, CA: Stanford University Press, 1996); David Higgins, *Romantic Genius and the Literary Magazine: Biography, Celebrity, Politics*, Routledge Studies in Romanticism (London: Routledge, 2005).
30. Mary Luckhurst and Jane Moody, eds, *Theatre and Celebrity in Britain, 1660–2000* (Basingstoke: Palgrave Macmillan, 2005).
31. Ian Kelly, *Cooking for Kings: The Life of Antonin Careme, the First Celebrity Chef* (London: Walker, 2004).
32. David Garrick to Peter Garrick, 6 November 1762, *The Letters of David Garrick*, ed. David M. Little and George M. Kahrl, 3 vols (London: Oxford University Press, 1963), I, 367. For a discussion of Garrick's acting style, see George Winchester Stone and George M. Kahrl, *David Garrick: A Critical Biography* (Carbondale, IL: Southern Illinois University Press, 1979), pp. 26–50.
33. On the importance of facial expression to Garrick's style, see *The Revels History of Drama in English: Vol. 4, 1750–1880*, ed. Michael R. Booth (London: Methuen, 1975), pp. 96–9, and Allardyce Nicoll and Sybil Rosenfeld, *The Garrick Stage: Theatres and Audience in the Eighteenth Century* (Manchester: Manchester University Press, 1980), pp. 9–14. Lebrun's guide for artists was translated in 1701 and 1734, see Charles Lebrun, *A Method to Learn to Design the Passions*, trans. by John Williams, Augustan Reprint Society, Introduction by Alan T. Mackenzie (Los Angeles: William Andrews Clark Memorial Library, University of California, 1980). Jennifer Montagu provides a modern translation and sets Lebrun in the historical context of artistic thinking about facial representation. Jennifer Montagu, *The Expression of the Passions: The Origins and Influence of Charles Le Brun's 'Conférence Sur L'expression Générale Et Particulière'* (New Haven, CT: Yale University Press, 1994).
34. Michael S. Wilson suggests ways in which Garrick's acting and his portraits borrowed from and informed history painting, which helped to legitimate the theatre as a school of national virtue. Michael S. Wilson, 'Garrick, Iconic Acting, and the Ideologies of Theatrical Portraiture', *Word and Image*, 6 (1990), 368–94.
35. See Desmond Shawe Taylor and Rosie Broadley, *Every Look Speaks: Portraits of David Garrick*. An Exhibition at the Holburne Museum of Art, Bath (Bath: Holburne Museum of Art, 2003) and Shelley M. Bennett, Robyn Asleson, Mark Leonard, and Shearer West, *A Passion for Performance: Sarah Siddons and Her Portraitists* (Los Angeles, CA: J. Paul Getty Museum, 1999).
36. Ian Campbell Ross, *Laurence Sterne: A Life* (Oxford: Oxford University Press, 2001; 2002), pp. 213–14. The letter is reprinted in *Sterne: The Critical*

Heritage, ed. Alan B. Howes (London: Routledge and Kegan Paul, 1974), pp. 45–6.

37. Cited in Howes, *Sterne*, p. 73.
38. Ibid., p. 74.
39. Peter M. Briggs, 'Laurence Sterne and Literary Celebrity in 1760', *The Age of Johnson: A Scholarly Annual*, 4 (1991), 251–80 (p. 263).
40. David Garrick to George Garrick, 20 November 1764, *Letters*, ed. Little and Kahrl, II, 433.
41. Cited in Taylor and Broadley, *Every Look Speaks*, p. 46.
42. For a reading of Sterne's career as caught between paradigms of patronage and commerce, which largely supports my argument here, see Donoghue, *The Fame Machine*, pp. 56–85.
43. Ross, *Laurence Sterne*, pp. 245, 321.
44. Walter Scott, '*Childe Harold's Pilgrimage, The Prisoner of Chillon, a Dream*, and other Poems', *Quarterly Review*, XVI (October 1816), 172–208 (p. 175).
45. James Raven has studied the figures for the eighteenth century in detail. He writes, '[t]he impressive growth-rates of the second half of the century are clear [...] What is also clear is the watershed of the early 1780s.' James Raven, *Judging New Wealth: Popular Publishing and Responses to Commerce in England, 1750–1800* (Oxford: Clarendon Press, 1992), p. 35. Raven provides a graph of his ESTC statistics on p. 32. Lee Erickson notes that 'Having risen gradually from roughly 1,800 printed items of all kinds in 1740 to around 3,000 items in 1780, English publications suddenly double to 6,000 by 1792.' He observes, 'the take-off pattern of an exponential growth curve is evident.' Lee Erickson, *The Economy of Literary Form: English Literature and the Industrialisation of Publishing, 1800–1850* (Baltimore, MD: Johns Hopkins University Press, 1996), p. 7 and note. William St Clair disputes these interpretations, suggesting that, when rising population and economic growth are taken into account, the slow and steady rise in the output of print during the first three quarters of the century may represent a fall in real terms. Instead of a slow rise followed by an exponential take-off, St Clair reads these statistics as indicating a long stagnation followed by an explosion of the reprint market following Donaldson v. Beckett. William St Clair, *The Reading Nation in the Romantic Period* (Cambridge: Cambridge University Press, 2004), esp. pp. 88–91, 103–21 and appendix 1.
46. Isaac D'Israeli, Preface to *An Essay on the Manners and Genius of the Literary Character* (London: T. Cadell and W. Davies, 1795), xvii–xix.
47. See Marilyn Butler, 'Culture's Medium: The Role of the Review', in *The Cambridge Companion to British Romanticism*, ed. Stuart Curran (Cambridge: Cambridge University Press, 1993), pp. 120–47 and Derek Roper, *Reviewing Before the Edinburgh: 1788–1802* (London: Methuen, 1978).
48. The reasons for this increase in the percentage anonymity of novels are beyond the scope of this book, but may include a rise in female authorship of novels, if women were more likely to preserve a decorous anonymity; what Peter Garside calls a male 'cult of anonymity in the 1820s', influenced by the anonymous successes of Walter Scott; and, since some publishers appear to have encouraged anonymity while others discouraged it, a shift in market share between publishers with different policies. See Peter Garside, 'The English Novel in the Romantic Era: Consolidation and Dispersal', in

Peter Garside, James Raven and Rainer Schöwerling, eds, *The English Novel 1770–1829: A Bibliographical Survey of Prose Fiction Published in the British Isles*, 2 vols (Oxford: Oxford University Press, 2000), II, 15–103, especially pp. 66–7.

49. Mary Robinson, 'January, 1795' (33–6) in *Mary Robinson, Selected Poems*, ed. Judith Pascoe (Peterborough, ON: Broadview, 2000), pp. 356–8.
50. James Granger, *Biographical History of England*, Suppl. 1769–74, 3rd ed., 4 vols (London: J. Rivington et al., 1779).
51. Ibid.
52. See Robert A. Shaddy, 'Grangerizing: "One of the Unfortunate Stages of Bibliomania"', *Book Collector*, 49, no. 4 (2000), 535–46. Granger set out to produce a catalogue of portrait engravings, but extended his plan to include biographical sketches for each entry.
53. Colley, *Britons*, p. 173.
54. Jerome Christensen, *Romanticism at the End of History* (Baltimore, MD: Johns Hopkins University Press, 2000), p. 78.
55. Iain McCalman notes that the coalition earned the title 'All the Talents' because of its political diversity, but that it 'quickly became ironic, especially after an influential satire by that name had been produced by [...] Eaton Stannard Barrett[.]' *An Oxford Companion to the Romantic Age: British Culture 1776–1832*, ed. Iain McCalman (Oxford: Oxford University Press, 1999), p. 606.
56. *English Bards and Scotch Reviewers*, 123–4. *CPW*, I, 233.
57. Thomas Moore, *The Poetical Works*, 10 vols (London: Longman, Orme, Brown, Green, & Longmans, 1840–1841), IX, 240–3.
58. Raymond Williams, *Culture and Society: 1780–1950* (London: The Hogarth Press, 1958; 1993), p. 32.
59. Erickson concludes, 'The estrangement that writers felt from the reception of their writing had its foundation in the economic changes in the publishing industry created by technological improvements in printing'. *The Economy of Literary Form*, p. 189.
60. Thomas De Quincey, *Confessions of an English Opium Eater and Other Writings*, ed. Grevel Lindop (Oxford: Oxford University Press, 1989), p. 134.
61. Ibid.
62. Lucy Newlyn, *Reading, Writing and Romanticism: The Anxiety of Reception* (Oxford: Oxford University Press, 2000), p. 47. See her extended discussion of this passage, pp. 45–8.
63. On the fascinating function of proper names in Enlightenment and Romantic literary culture, see, for example, Jerome Christensen, *Practicing Enlightenment: Hume and the Formation of a Literary Career* (Madison: University of Wisconsin Press, 1987) and Peter T. Murphy, 'Impersonation and Authorship in Romantic Britain', *ELH*, 59 (1992), 625–49.
64. Giles Playfair, *Kean: The Life and Paradox of the Great Actor* (London: Reinhardt & Evans, 1950), p. 326.
65. '*Sardanapalus*, *The Two Foscari*, and *Cain*', *European Magazine*, 81 (January 1822), 58–70 (p. 58).
66. Ibid.
67. Judith Pascoe, *Romantic Theatricality: Gender, Poetry, and Spectatorship* (Ithaca, NY: Cornell University Press, 1997), p. 172.

68. On the performative function of Robinson's pseudonyms, see Pascoe, *Romantic Theatricality*, pp. 173–83. Claire Brock claims that Robinson's 'proliferating disguises were only too transparent' (p. 103), but this underestimates the sophistication of Robinson's multiple authorial performances. Paula Byrne more convincingly describes Robinson's later life as an attempt to replace her early celebrity profile with a small but distinguished circle of admirers who valued her literary talents. Paula Byrne, *Perdita: The Life of Mary Robinson* (London: Harper Collins, 2004).
69. Reprinted in Letitia Elizabeth Landon, *Selected Writings*, ed. Jerome McGann and Daniel Riess (Peterborough, ON: Broadview, 1997), p. 331.
70. The collection shares its title with the 1736 volume by the 'thresher poet' Stephen Duck, placing Yearsley in a tradition of celebrated labouring-class poets.
71. See Mary Waldron, *Lactilla, Milkwoman of Clifton: The Life and Writings of Ann Yearsley* (Athens: The University of Georgia Press, 1996), pp. 48–63.
72. On Robinson's visual representation, see Anne K. Mellor, 'Making an Exhibition of Her Self: Mary "Perdita" Robinson and Nineteenth-Century Scripts of Female Sexuality', *Nineteenth-Century Contexts*, 22, no. 3 (2000), 271–304.
73. David Bindman notes that steel plates had mostly replaced copper ones by the 1820s. David Bindman, 'Prints', in *An Oxford Companion to the Romantic Age*, ed. McCalman, pp. 207–13 (p. 211).
74. Cited in Leslie A. Marchand, *Byron: A Biography*, 3 vols (London: John Murray, 1957), II, 635.
75. Pascoe, *Romantic Theatricality*, p. 239.
76. Laetitia-Matilda Hawkins, *Memoirs, Anecdotes, Facts, and Opinions*, 2 vols (London: Longman, Hurst, Rees, Orme, Brown, and Green; and C. & J. Rivington, 1824), II, 24.
77. Mary Robinson, *Perdita: The Memoirs of Mary Robinson* (1894), ed. M. J. Levy (London: Peter Owen, 1994), p. 113.
78. Booth, *Revels History*, p. 104.
79. See Cheryl Wanko, *Roles of Authority: Thespian Biography and Celebrity in Eighteenth-Century Britain* (Lubbock, TX: Texas Tech University Press, 2003).
80. Glennis Stephenson notes that 'rather than distinguishing the various [historical or mythological] figures, [Landon] tends to draw them closer and closer together until they all appear as subtexts of one highly personalised, feminised primary text – a primary text that is, basically, L.E.L.' Glennis Stephenson, 'Letitia Landon and the Victorian Improvisatrice: The Construction of L. E. L.', *Victorian Poetry*, 30, no. 1 (1992), 1–17 (p. 7).
81. John Scott, 'Living Authors, No. IV: Lord Byron', *London Magazine*, 3 (1821), 50–61.
82. 'C', 'Lord Byron', *The Brighton Magazine*, 7 (1822), 45–52 (p. 49).
83. See Sandra M. Gilbert and Susan Gubar, *The Madwoman in the Attic: The Woman Writer and the Nineteenth-Century Literary Imagination* (New Haven, CT: Yale University Press, 1979), and Catherine Gallagher, *Nobody's Story: The Vanishing Acts of Women Writers in the Marketplace, 1670–1820* (Oxford: Clarendon Press, 1994).
84. See Kristina Straub, *Sexual Suspects: Eighteenth-Century Players and Sexual Ideology* (Princeton, NJ: Princeton University Press, 1992).
85. Landon, *Selected Writings*, p. 103.

86. Mary Robinson, *Selected Poems*, p. 153. For a useful analysis of the aesthetics and politics of this volume, and its place in Robinson's career, see Jerome J. McGann, *The Poetics of Sensibility: A Revolution in Literary Style* (Oxford: Clarendon Press, 1996), pp. 94–116.
87. Mary Waldron, '"This Muse-Born Wonder": The Occluded Voice of Ann Yearsley, Milkwoman and Poet of Clifton', in *Women's Poetry in the Enlightenment: The Making of a Canon, 1730–1820*, ed. Virginia Blain and Isobel Armstrong (London: Macmillan, 1999), pp. 113–26.
88. Letitia Landon, 'A History of the Lyre' (175), in *Selected Writings*, p. 120.
89. Cited in James Monaco, ed., *Celebrity: The Media as Image Makers* (New York: Delta Books, 1978), xi.
90. Andrew Wernick, *Promotional Culture: Advertising, Ideology and Symbolic Expression* (London: Sage, 1991), p. 106.
91. Donoghue, *The Fame Machine*, p. 77.
92. A selection of these poems is reprinted in Appendix B to McGann and Riess's edition of Landon's writings.
93. On Robinson's intertextual relationships with her contemporaries, see Stuart Curran, 'Mary Robinson's *Lyrical Tales* in Context', in *Re-Visioning Romanticism: British Women Writers, 1776–1837*, ed. Carol Shiner Wilson and Joel Haefner (Philadelphia, PA: University of Pennsylvania Press, 1994), pp. 17–35; Susan Luther, 'A Stranger Minstrel: Coleridge's Mrs. Robinson', *Studies in Romanticism*, 33, no. 3 (1994), 391–409; Ashley J. Cross, 'From *Lyrical Ballads* to *Lyrical Tales*: Mary Robinson's Reputation and the Problem of Literary Debt', *Studies in Romanticism*, 40, no. 4 (2001), 571–605; and Betsy Bolton, 'Romancing the Stone: "Perdita" Robinson in Wordsworth's London', *ELH*, 64, no. 3 (1997), 727–59.
94. Peter J. Manning, '*Don Juan* and the Revisionary Self', in *Romantic Revisions*, ed. Robert Brinkley and Keith Hanley (Cambridge: Cambridge University Press, 1992), pp. 210–26 (p. 216).
95. John Wilson, '*Childe Harold's Pilgrimage, Canto the Fourth*', *Edinburgh Review*, 30 (June 1818), 87–120 (p. 90).
96. On Byronic encoding see Gary Dyer, 'Thieves, Boxers, Sodomites, Poets: Being Flash to Byron's *Don Juan*', *PMLA*, 116, no. 3 (2001), 562–78.
97. The impression that Byron's poems 'provided an almost unmediated knowledge of his mind' (p. 13) is very well analysed by Andrew Elfenbein's chapter 'Byron and the Secret Self' in his *Byron and the Victorians*, pp. 13–46.
98. Murray Archive, Box B.51. For an analysis of Byron's fan mail, see Corin Throsby, 'Flirting with Fame: Byron's Anonymous Female Fans', *The Byron Journal*, 32 (2004), 115–23.
99. Studying television and radio, Donald Horton and R. Richard Wohl note how 'the technical devices of the media themselves are exploited to create illusions of intimacy' (p. 218) and call the nexus of audience and media personality a 'para-social interaction'. I borrow their term and apply it to an earlier medium (that of print) in order to suggest that similar practices have a long and varied history. D. Horton and R. R. Wohl, 'Mass Communication and Para-social Interaction', *Psychiatry*, 19 (1956), 215–29.
100. Emma Francis, 'Letitia Landon: Public Fantasy and the Private Sphere', *Essays and Studies*, 51 (1998), 93–115 (pp. 101, 102).

101. In Ann Yearsley's case this escape from commodity culture was effected by slightly different means. More's publicity campaign presented subscribing to or purchasing Yearsley's book as an act of charity rather than a commercial transaction. A somewhat anachronistic rhetoric of patronage attempts to displace consumption.
102. *'Don Juan'*, *Edinburgh Monthly Review*, 2 (October 1819), 468–86 (p. 485).
103. [Letitia Elizabeth Landon], 'On the Character of Mrs Hemans's Writings', *New Monthly Magazine*, 44 (1835), 425–33 (p. 425).
104. Mary Robinson, 'The Maniac', in *Selected Poems*, pp. 122–6.
105. Ann Yearsley, 'To Those Who Accuse the Author of Ingratitude' (48), in *Poems on Various Subjects* (London: printed for the author and sold by G. G. J. and J Robinson, 1787), pp. 57–60.
106. Cited in Andrew Rutherford, ed., *Byron: The Critical Heritage* (London: Routledge, 1970), p. 315.

2 'An Ode to the Framers of the Frame Bill'

1. The phrase 'I awoke one morning and found myself famous' was first attributed to Byron by Thomas Moore in his *Letters and Journals of Lord Byron with Notices of his Life*, 2 vols (London: John Murray, 1830), I, 347.
2. As a young peer, Byron had patrician ambitions to shine in the House of Lords. He prepared himself for a career there with Speech Day orations at school, and once delayed his return to Harrow so that he could hear parliamentary speeches on Catholic emancipation (Leslie A. Marchand, *Byron: A Biography*, 3 vols (London: John Murray, 1957), I, 95–7). He was a member of the Whig club at Cambridge, and took his seat in the House of Lords when he reached his majority in 1809. Before going abroad he attended seven sessions of the House (Marchand, I, 313n). Robert Charles Dallas claimed that 'I often spoke to him of the superior and substantial fame, the way to which lay before him through the House of Lords, expressing my hope of one day seeing him an active and eloquent statesman.' Robert Charles Dallas, *Recollections of the Life of Lord Byron* (1824) (Norwood, PA: Norwood Editions, 1977), pp. 189–90. On Byron's Speech Day oratory, see Paul Elledge, *Lord Byron at Harrow School: Speaking Out, Talking Back, Acting Up, Bowing Out* (Baltimore, MD: Johns Hopkins University Press, 2000).
3. *Cobbett's Parliamentary Debates*, vol. 21 (London: T. C. Hansard, 1812), p. 811.
4. D. N. Raymond, *The Political Career of Lord Byron* (New York: Henry Holt, 1924), p. 39.
5. The following narrative of the Bill's progress through parliament draws on the *Journals of the House of Lords*, vol. 48 (London: HMSO, 1812), pp. 593–621; *Cobbett's Parliamentary Debates*, pp. 974–9, and the discussion in Raymond, *The Political Career of Lord Byron*, pp. 44–5.
6. For the text of the speech, see *CMP*, pp. 22–7.
7. Raymond, *The Political Career of Lord Byron*, p. 45. *CPW*, III, 391.
8. *Cobbett's Parliamentary Debates*, p. 1084. Italics added.
9. William Blackstone, *Commentaries on the Laws of England: Fifteenth edition, with the last corrections of the author; and with notes and additions by Edward Christian, Esq.*, 4 vols (London: T. Cadell and W. Davies, 1809), IV, 5n.

10. 'Misdemeanor', Thomas Edlyne Tomlins (with additions by Thomas Colpitts Granger), *The Law Dictionary*, 4th ed., 2 vols (London: J. and W. T. Clarke et al., 1835).
11. Blackstone, *Commentaries on the Laws of England*, IV, pp. 97–8. This understanding was still current in 1835, when Tomlins paraphrased Blackstone closely: '[T]he idea of felony was so generally connected with that of capital punishment, that it seemed hard to separate them: and to this usage the interpretations of law conformed. For if a statute made any new offence felony, the law implied that it should be punished with death.' 'Felony', Tomlins.
12. The rags were first turned into a liquid pulp. This pulp flowed onto a moving wire-mesh belt, where the water drained out of it and was sucked away, leaving a damp paper web. This passed through a series of steam-heated rollers, which dried the paper, and then between heavy calendar rollers, which gave it a smooth finish. Lee Erickson notes, 'Since handmade paper was both harder to work with and had a greater percentage of waste because of defects in individual sheets, machine-made paper not only provided an improvement in the quality of publishing materials but also reduced the costs of printing by about 40 per cent. By 1825 over half of all paper in England was made by machine.' Erickson, *The Economy of Literary Form: English Literature and the Industrialization of Publishing, 1800–1850* (Baltimore, MD: Johns Hopkins University Press, 1996), p. 27.
13. James Moran, *Printing Presses: History and Development from the Fifteenth Century to Modern Times* (Berkeley: University of California Press, 1973), p. 39.
14. Ibid., p. 54.
15. The stamp tax was raised to 2d in 1789, 3½d in 1797 and 4d in 1815. It was reduced to 1d in 1836 and abolished in 1855. G. A. Cranfield, *The Press and Society: From Caxton to Northcliffe* (London: Longman, 1978), p. 89.
16. See A. Aspinall, 'The Circulation of Newspapers in the Early Nineteenth Century', *Review of English Studies*, 22 (1946), 29–43.
17. See Terry Nevett, 'Advertising and Editorial Integrity in the Nineteenth Century', in *The Press in English Society from the Seventeenth to the Nineteenth Centuries*, ed. Michael Harris and Alan Lee (Cranbury, NJ: Associated University Presses, 1986), pp. 149–67.
18. Cited in Cranfield, *The Press and Society*, p. 90.
19. Stanley Morison, *The English Newspaper* (Cambridge: Cambridge University Press, 1932), p. 165.
20. See Ian R. Christie, 'James Perry of the *Morning Chronicle*, 1756–1821', in *Myth and Reality in Late-Eighteenth-Century British Politics and Other Papers* (London: Macmillan, 1970), pp. 334–58.
21. As an index of this growth, raw cotton imports quintupled between 1780 and 1800. See Asa Briggs, *A Social History of England*, 3rd ed. (London: Penguin, 1983; 1999), pp. 206–7.
22. Frank Ongley Darvall, *Popular Disturbances and Public Order in Regency England*, 2nd ed. (Oxford: Oxford University Press, 1934; 1969), p. 33.
23. E. P. Thompson, *The Making of the English Working Class* (London: Gollancz, 1963; 1965), p. 278. In what follows, I have leant heavily on Thompson's account of the textile industry in this period, as it remains the most comprehensive and impressive. His conclusion that Luddism was always

a '*quasi-insurrectionary movement*' (p. 553) is, however, in opposition to Darvall's earlier account, in *Popular Disturbances and Public Order in Regency England*, which sees Luddism as an industrial movement without explicit political aims. The differences are discussed in Angus MacIntyre's introduction to the second edition of Darvall's book. Brian Bailey distinguishes midland from northern Luddites, arguing that there is 'no shred of evidence for any political aims' in the midlands, but that many Luddites in Yorkshire and Lancashire 'were insurrectionary in temper'. Brian Bailey, *The Luddite Rebellion* (Stroud: Sutton Publishing, 1998), pp. 145, 147. See also E. J. Hobsbawm, 'The Machine Breakers', in his *Labouring Men: Studies in the History of Labour* (London: Weidenfeld and Nicolson, 1964), pp. 5–22 and Malcolm I. Thomis, *The Luddites* (Newton Abbot: David & Charles, 1970).
24. Thompson, *The Making of the English Working Class*, p. 543.
25. The 'combination' acts of 1799 and 1800 reinforced laws making it illegal for workers to organise into unions. Brian Bailey notes that '[t]he effectiveness of the legislation varied from trade to trade. Unions were often merely driven underground, or survived in the guise of friendly societies. Many illegal unions continued to exist [...] in the textile industries' (Bailey, *The Luddite Rebellion*, xv).
26. Thompson, *The Making of the English Working Class*, p. 544.
27. Ibid., p. 554.
28. Hobsbawm, for example, makes clear that 'in none of these cases [...] was there any question of hostility to machines as such.' (p. 8).
29. Dallas, *Recollections of the Life of Lord Byron*, p. 203.
30. Jeffrey W. Vail has suggested that Byron might have shown the poem to Samuel Rogers, and discussed it with Thomas Moore. Jeffrey W. Vail, *The Literary Relationship of Lord Byron and Thomas Moore* (Baltimore, MD: Johns Hopkins University Press, 2001), p. 51.
31. Malcolm Kelsall, *Byron's Politics* (Sussex: The Harvester Press, 1987), p. 50.
32. Ibid., pp. 2, 49.
33. Ibid., p. 48.
34. The House of Lords Library was established in 1826. No records exist of newspapers supplied to the House before that date.
35. The *Morning Chronicle*, 2 March 1812, p. 3. It is tempting to speculate that Mr Merle may have arranged this paragraph as publicity for his auction house. On the practice of 'puffing' in newspapers, see Nevett, *The Press in English Society*, 1986.
36. Reported by the House of Commons' Secret Committee, cited in Kelsall, *Byron's Politics*, p. 52.
37. The *Morning Chronicle*, 2 March 1812, p. 2.
38. *Nottingham Review and General Advertiser for the Midland Counties*, 6 March 1812, p. 4.
39. This anonymous poem was called 'Industry Distressed: A True Tale' and appeared on p. 3.
40. E. P. Thompson mentions the weavers' poetry, and quotes at length from one of the 'Jone o' Grinfilt' ballads on pp. 322–3. In a collection of documents reprinted from the public records office, Malcolm I. Thomis provides examples of a Luddite song (pp. 1–2) and poem (pp. 55–6). See *Luddism in Nottinghamshire*, ed. Malcolm I. Thomis (London: Phillimore, 1972). For

a general, Marxist survey across a broad historical span, see John Miller, 'Songs of the Labour Movement', in *The Luddites and Other Essays*, ed. Lionel M. Munby (London: Michael Katanka, 1971), pp. 115–42. See also Kevin Binfield, *Writings of the Luddites* (Baltimore, MD: Johns Hopkins University Press, 2004).

41. Since this reprint of the poem was unknown to Jerome McGann, the variant is not recorded in the textual apparatus in *CPW*, III, 9. As well as incidental textual differences of punctuation, capitalisation and italicisation, the *Nottingham Review* text alters the first line from 'Oh well done Lord E[ldo]n! and better Lord R[yde]r!' to 'Oh! well done Lord El[do]n! and better done R[yd]er!' This corrects Byron's error; Richard Ryder, the Home Secretary, was not a Lord.
42. Moran, *Printing Presses*, pp. 106–7.
43. It has unfortunately not been possible to discover exactly when the *Morning Chronicle* began using the steam press. The two important facts here are that the paper did not use the steam press when it published Byron's 'Ode', but that adopting the new technology soon became essential in the crowded periodical market.
44. Moran, *Printing Presses*, pp. 107–8.
45. *The Times*, 29 November 1814, p. 3.
46. Cited in George Paston and Peter Quennel, *To Lord Byron: Feminine Profiles from Unpublished Letters 1807–1824* (London: John Murray, 1939), p. 101.

3 *Childe Harold's Pilgrimage*

1. The title is followed by a subtitle, epigraph, prose preface, addition to the preface (added in the fourth edition), prefatory poem 'To Ianthe' (added in the seventh edition) and the heading 'Canto One' before, finally, the opening stanza. The dedicatory letter to Hobhouse complicates the beginning still further. First printed with Canto Four, it commends the poem to Byron's friend 'in its completed state' and seems to be retroactive, beginning the poem all over again (*CPW*, II, 124). *Don Juan* begins with similar complications. The title is followed by an epigraph (which was the source of some contention), a prose preface (not published until 1901), a verse dedication (not published until 1833) and the heading 'Canto One' before the first stanza.
2. The second stanza was part of the original draft, begun on 31 October 1809 (*CPW*, II, 266). The first stanza was added in late July 1811 (*CPW*, II, 267). 'To Ianthe' first appeared in the seventh edition (1814). For a full account of the poem's manuscripts and composition, see *CPW*, II, 265–9. Facsimiles are available in David V. Erdman, ed., with the assistance of David Worrall, *Childe Harold's Pilgrimage: A Critical, Composite Edition*, Manuscripts of the Younger Romantics (New York and London: Garland, 1991).
3. David Hill Radcliffe observes that 'Of the better-known eighteenth century poets, only Johnson and Goldsmith did not imitate or burlesque Spenser in verse.' David Hill Radcliffe, *Edmund Spenser: A Reception History* (Columbia, SC: Camden House, 1996), p. 53. Richard Frushell discusses Johnson's and

Goldsmith's reactions to Spenser. Richard Frushell, *Edmund Spenser in the Early Eighteenth Century: Education, Imitation, and the Making of a Literary Model* (Pittsburgh, PN: Duquesne University Press, 1999), esp. pp. 121–6, 139–43.

4. Radcliffe, *Edmund Spenser*, pp. 34, 75.
5. Greg Kucich also notes that 'Byron was reading Vicesimus Knox's *Elegant Extracts*, which includes numerous passages from *The Faerie Queene* and Spenser's eighteenth century imitators, as he began work on *Childe Harold's Pilgrimage*.' Greg Kucich, *Keats, Shelley and Romantic Spenserianism* (University Park: Pennsylvania State University Press, 1991), p. 113.
6. Cf. Mark Storey's comment that '*Childe Harold* announces itself as a curiosity, reaching for some of that medieval quaintness that had already served Coleridge well enough'. Mark Storey, *Byron and the Eye of Appetite* (New York: St. Martin's Press, 1986), p. 82.
7. Before proceeding to an analysis of openings in realist novels, Victor Brombert briefly sketches the 'gradual relegation of the muse to a secondary role, and ultimately [...] her disappearance, until the epic beginning is itself thematized [...] [B]eginning [thus] becomes', for Byron, 'an autonomous literary problem' (p. 493). Victor Brombert, 'Opening Signals in Narrative', *New Literary History*, 11 (1980), 489–502.
8. Edward W. Said, *Beginnings: Intention and Method* (London: Granta Books, 1998), p. 72. Said distinguishes 'transitive' beginnings from 'intransitive' origins. 'Transitive beginnings' are the inaugural moments of human projects: more or less constructed commencements. Origins, or 'intransitive beginnings', incessantly fold back upon themselves in search of an originary moment with nothing before it, a commencement *ex nihilo* which is ultimately not human but divine. See also A. D. Nuttall, *Openings: Narrative Beginnings from the Epic to the Novel* (Oxford: Clarendon Press, 1992).
9. Theodore Redpath notes that '*Childe Harold* was [...] a new *kind* of work, and a number of the critics were puzzled as to what kind of a thing it was.' Theodore Redpath, *The Young Romantics and Critical Opinion, 1807–1824* (London: Harrap, 1973), p. 180. Philip Martin suggests that 'The Preface [...] seems to indicate that Byron is unsure of the kind of poem he has written.' Philip Martin, *Byron: A Poet Before his Public* (Cambridge: Cambridge University Press, 1982), p. 9.
10. Cited in James Sambrook, *James Thomson 1700–1748: A Life* (Oxford: Clarendon Press, 1991), pp. 263, 264.
11. Philip Martin contrasts the first readers of *The Castle of Indolence* and *Childe Harold's Pilgrimage*, suggesting that Byron takes on certain elements of Thomson's style, but without a comparable audience. This view holds for the audience that the published poem found, but does not take account of shifts in the way Byron imagined his audience while writing. Martin, *Byron*, p. 18.
12. See Leslie A. Marchand, *Byron: A Biography*, 3 vols (London: John Murray, 1957), I, pp. 173–4.
13. Stanley Fish, *Is There a Text in this Class? The Authority of Interpretive Communities* (London: Harvard University Press, 1980), p. 48.
14. See Jack Stillinger, 'A Practical Theory of Versions', in *Coleridge and Textual Instability: The Multiple Versions of the Major Poems* (Oxford: Oxford University Press, 1994), pp. 118–40.

15. Jerome McGann advanced this view in *Fiery Dust*, where he writes that 'the theme of Cantos I–II is [...] the painful education of the poet into a more sensitive and reliable subjective moral awareness'. Jerome J. McGann, *Fiery Dust: Byron's Poetic Development* (Chicago: University of Chicago Press, 1968), p. 58. He restated it in his commentary in *CPW*, II, 271.
16. Lucy Newlyn, *Reading, Writing and Romanticism: The Anxiety of Reception* (Oxford: Oxford University Press, 2000), p. 24. Newlyn has drawn attention to the importance of 'communal reading scenes', especially for the first generation of Romantic poets (p. 17). She shows how coterie reading-circles were satirised as 'a method of self-defence' and identifies them as part of 'the persistence of anachronistic systems of reception' (pp. 23, 24).
17. I would therefore amend Philip Martin's claim that 'At the time he wrote *Childe Harold* Byron was a lord with no lordly friends, a gentleman of fashion without a coterie' (Martin, *Byron*, p. 18). This was true by the time the poem was published, but not during the period when most of it was written.
18. Not all of these men were members of the Whig club (according to Hobhouse's list, Marchand, *Byron*, I, 140n), they weren't all present at Newstead, and they had varying degrees of interest in homoerotic practice, but these things linked them to Byron and are relevant to the way in which they are imagined as an audience for his poem.
19. Marchand, *Byron*, I, 174–6.
20. Charles Skinner Matthews to Byron, 30 June 1809. Cited in Louis Crompton, *Byron and Greek Love: Homophobia in Nineteenth-Century England* (Swaffham: The Gay Men's Press, 1985), pp. 128–9.
21. Ibid., p. 129.
22. Jerome Christensen, *Lord Byron's Strength: Romantic Writing and Commercial Society* (Baltimore: Johns Hopkins University Press, 1993), p. 60.
23. Jeffrey N. Cox, *Poetry and Politics in the Cockney School: Keats, Shelley, Hunt and Their Circle* (Cambridge: Cambridge University Press, 1998; 2004), pp. 1–15.
24. Francis Hodgson, *Sir Edgar* (London: J. Mackinlay, 1810, repr. with an introduction by Donald Reiman, New York: Garland, 1977).
25. John Cam Hobhouse, *Imitations and Translations from the Ancient and Modern Classics, Together with Original Poems Never Before Published* (London: Longman, 1809). This miscellany also included nine poems by Byron.
26. *BLJ*, II, 43, 56. See also *BLJ*, II, 33, 45–6.
27. See Crompton, *Byron and Greek Love*, pp. 120–1 and p. 130 on Beckford, p. 131 on the page, and p. 139 on Ali Pasha's court.
28. Byron began the original draft (which survives in fragments, designated MS Y, location: Yale) on 31 October 1809, according to the note he later made on the fair copy (designated MS M, location: Murray Archives). But he kept quiet about his poem, not mentioning it in a (surviving) letter for over a year. He hinted at its existence to his mother on 14 January 1811, and immediately disclaimed any desire to publish:

    > I keep no journal, nor have I any intention of scribbling my travels. – I have done with authorship, and if in my last production I have convinced the critics or the world, I was something more than they took me for, I am satisfied, nor will I hazard *that reputation* by a future effort. – It is true I have some others in manuscript, but I leave them for those who come

after me, and if deemed worth publishing, they may serve to prolong my memory, when I myself shall cease to remember. (*BLJ*, II, 35)

29. 'Citoyen' was another name for Matthews, suggesting his democratic politics. The inconsistent spelling of 'Mat(t)hieu' is Byron's own.
30. Matthews to Byron, 13 January 1811. Cited in Crompton, pp. 160–1. Although it seems unlikely that Byron was explicit in his letters, it is possible that the record is distorted because letters that clearly hinted at homosexual activities were destroyed. All the papers in Matthews's rooms at Cambridge were removed after his death, probably by solicitous friends concerned about their contents.
31. On the materials that make up the book *Childe Harold's Pilgrimage*, and for a critique of their handling in *CPW*, see Roger Poole, 'What Constitutes, and What is External to, the "Real" *Childe Harold's Pilgrimage, A Romaunt: and Other Poems* (1812)?', in *Lord Byron the European: Essays from the International Byron Society*, ed. Richard A. Cardwell (Lampeter: Edwin Mellen, 1997), pp. 149–207. The facsimile of a Romaic letter contained a fawning and obsequious apology from the Bey of Corinth for not having extended his hospitality to the visiting English Lord as protocol required when Byron was stranded in Corinth by bad weather. The Bey's embarrassment could have been translated orally for the amusement of Byron's friends, but was concealed from the purchasing public. The first published translation of the letter appeared in 2001. See Petros Peteinaris, 'The Bey Apologises', *Newstead Abbey Byron Society Review* (July 2000), pp. 13–19; and Peter Cochran, 'The Bey Apologises (II)', *Newstead Abbey Byron Society Review* (January 2001), 35–7.
32. Mrs Byron died at the beginning of August 1811, aged 46, after Byron had arrived in England but before he had seen her. On 3 August, Matthews was drowned while swimming in the Cam. By 10 August, Byron had learnt of Wingfield's death. In October news reached him that Edleston had died in May. Marchand, *Byron*, I, 284–6, 295.
33. The deaths of Matthews and Edleston do not at a stroke wipe out the audience of cognoscenti, but I suggest that they represent that audience for Byron more strongly than any other individuals, and therefore their deaths send his *sense* of the audience into crisis.
34. On death and valediction at the end of Canto Two, see Paul Elledge, 'Chasms in Connections: Byron Ending (in) *Childe Harold's Pilgrimage* 1 and 2', *English Literary History* 62 (1995), 131–44.
35. Robert Charles Dallas, *Recollections of the Life of Lord Byron* (1824) (Norwood, PA: Norwood Editions, 1977), pp. 196–7.
36. Marchand, *Byron*, I, 281–2. Byron rejected Cawthorn because 'he did not then rank high among the brethren of the trade' (Dallas, *Recollections of the Life of Lord Byron*, p. 119). Miller was Lord Elgin's publisher, and declined to publish a poem which criticised Elgin in such strong terms.
37. Murray and Dallas agreed that Murray should print the first edition at his own expense, and that they would share any profits and only then arrange payment for the copyright, if the poem proved to be successful (Dallas, *Recollections of the Life of Lord Byron*, pp. 121–2). Murray would eventually pay Dallas £600 for the copyright.

38. Doris Langley Moore, *Lord Byron: Accounts Rendered* (London: John Murrray, 1974), p. 180.
39. Samuel Smiles, *A Publisher and His Friends: Memoir and Correspondence of the Late John Murray, with an Account of the Origin and Progress of the House, 1768–1843*, 2 vols (London: John Murray, 1891), I, 210. Nicholas Mason has shown the effectiveness of Murray's promotional campaign in 'Building Brand Byron: Early-Nineteenth-Century Advertising and the Marketing of *Childe Harold's Pilgrimage*', *Modern Language Quarterly*, 63 (2002), 411–41.
40. Cf. McGann's summary of the effect: 'Its publisher conceived its audience to be a wealthy one, people interested in travel books and topographical poems, people with a classical education with a taste for antiquarian lore and the philosophical musings of a young English lord. As it turned out, all of England and Europe were to be snared by his book's imaginations.' Jerome J. McGann, *The Beauty of Inflections: Literary Investigations in Historical Method and Theory* (Oxford: Clarendon Press, 1985), p. 259.
41. William St Clair, 'The Impact of Byron's Writings: An Evaluative Approach', in *Byron: Augustan and Romantic*, ed. Andrew Rutherford (London: Macmillan, 1990), pp. 1–25 (esp. p. 6). Thirty shillings is the price for the poem in wrappers; 50 shillings takes into account the cost of binding.
42. This was the audience Robert Southey imagined would read *Madoc*, which was first published in quarto by Longman in 1805. He wrote in a letter, 'In fact, books are now so dear that they are becoming rather articles of fashionable furniture than anything else; they who buy them do not read them, and they who read them do not buy them. [...] If Madoc obtain any celebrity, its size and cost will recommend it among these gentry – *libros consumeri nati* – born to buy quartos and help the revenue.' *The Life and Correspondence of Robert Southey*, ed. Charles Cuthbert Southey, 6 vols (London: Longman, Brown, Green and Longmans, 1849–1850), II, 329–30.
43. This is not to suggest that there was no tradition of homosexual writing, especially for the classically educated, but to acknowledge that a new poem which placed itself in that tradition would be necessarily *sub rosa*. It is also not an argument about Byron's own sexual activities or preferences.
44. Caroline Franklin, 'Cosmopolitan Masculinity and the British Female Reader of *Childe Harold's Pilgrimage*', in Cardwell, *Lord Byron the European*, pp. 105–25 (p. 116).

4 Scopophilia and somatic inscription

1. I adopt Lyotard's term 'libidinal economy' in an effort to move beyond a Marxist base/superstructure analysis and suggest ways in which the desires of individual readers, the economic arrangements of publishers and poetic techniques of an author become intertwined. See Jean-François Lyotard, *Libidinal Economy*, trans. by Iain Hamilton Grant (London: The Athlone Press, 1993); and Geoffrey Bennington, *Lyotard: Writing the Event* (Manchester: Manchester University Press, 1988), esp. pp. 34–9.
2. Most recent criticism of Byron's verse tales has set them in the context of British domestic or imperial politics. See, for example, Daniel P. Watkins,

Social Relations in Byron's Eastern Tales (Rutherford, NJ: Fairleigh Dickinson University Press, 1987); Nigel Leask, *British Romantic Writers and the East: Anxieties of Empire* (Cambridge: Cambridge University Press, 1992), pp. 13–67; Marilyn Butler, 'The Orientalism of Byron's *Giaour*', in *Byron and the Limits of Fiction*, ed. Bernard Beatty and Vincent Newey (Liverpool: Liverpool University Press, 1988), pp. 78–96; and Caroline Franklin, ' "Some Samples of the Finest Orientalism": Byronic Philhellenism and Proto-Zionism at the Time of the Congress of Vienna', in *Romanticism and Colonialism: Writing and Empire*, ed. Tim Fulford and Peter Kitson (Cambridge: Cambridge University Press, 1998), pp. 221–42. Turning to Byron's celebrity should not mean turning away from those contexts, but should further illuminate them.

3. Frank Kermode, *The Sense of an Ending: Studies in the Theory of Fiction* (Oxford: Oxford University Press, 1967).
4. Peter Brooks, *Reading for the Plot* (Oxford: Clarendon Press, 1984), p. 52.
5. J. Hillis Miller, 'Narrative' in *Critical Terms for Literary Study*, ed. Frank Lentricchia and Thomas McLaughlin (Chicago: The University of Chicago Press, 1990), pp. 66–79 (p. 72).
6. David Seed has analysed some of the effects of the fragment form in ' "Disjointed Fragments": Concealment and Revelation in *The Giaour*', *The Byron Journal*, 18 (1990), 14–27. For an argument that aims to connect the fragment form to issues of gender and imperialism, see Joseph Lew, 'The Necessary Orientalist? *The Giaour* and Nineteenth-Century Imperialist Misogyny', in *Romanticism, Race and Imperial Culture*, ed. Alan Richardson and Sonia Hofkosh (Bloomington: Indiana University Press, 1996), pp. 173–202.
7. Marjorie Levinson, *The Romantic Fragment Poem: A Critique of a Form* (Chapel Hill: University of North Carolina Press, 1986), pp. 124–5.
8. George Ellis, 'Review of Lord Byron's *Giaour*, and *Bride of Abydos*', *Quarterly Review*, 10 (January 1814), 331–54 (p. 341); Francis Jeffrey, 'Review of Lord Byron's *Giaour*', *Edinburgh Review*, 21 (July 1813), 299–309 (p. 299).
9. 'Communication in literature, then, is a process set in motion and regulated, not by a given code, but by a mutually restrictive and magnifying interaction between the explicit and the implicit, between revelation and concealment. What is concealed spurs the reader into action, but this action is also controlled by what is revealed; the explicit in its turn is transformed when the implicit has been brought to light. Whenever the reader bridges the gaps, communication begins.' Wolfgang Iser, 'Interaction Between Text and Reader', in *Readers and Reading*, ed. Andrew Bennett (London: Longman, 1995), pp. 20–31 (p. 24).
10. Sales figures from William St Clair, 'The Impact of Byron's Writings: An Evaluative Approach', in *Byron: Augustan and Romantic*, ed. Andrew Rutherford (London: Macmillan, 1990), pp. 1–25 (p. 9). Details of the title pages are from early editions of *The Giaour* in the British Library.
11. Leslie A. Marchand, *Byron: A Biography*, 3 vols (London: John Murray, 1957), I, 257–8. Thomas Medwin and John Galt confirmed the rumours, but Hobhouse prudently claimed that 'the girl whose life lord Byron saved at Athens, was not the object of his lordship's attachment – but that of his lordship's Turkish servant' (ibid., I, 258n).

12. Marchand, *Byron*, I, 409. The key portion of Sligo's letter is in *CPW*, III, 414.
13. Byron's reasons for this manoeuvre are, of course, unclear. He may have been reluctant to discuss the incident, as he wrote in his journal, 'to describe the *feelings* of *that situation* were impossible – it is *icy* even to recollect them' (*BLJ*, III, 230). At the same time, by the time of the fifth edition he may have felt it unnecessary to stir up any more interest in the connection.
14. Ellen Brinks's reading of *The Giaour* and *Lara* shares my concern with tracing secrets on the surface of the body, but for her the secret is a (homo)sexual identity, whereas for me it is a narrative crux that produces a scopophilic desire. See Ellen Brinks, *Gothic Masculinity: Effeminacy and the Supernatural in English and German Romanticism* (Lewisburg, PA: Bucknell University Press, 2003), pp. 68–90.
15. Peter Brooks, *Body Work: Objects of Desire in Modern Narrative* (Cambridge, MA: Harvard University Press, 1993), p. 25.
16. This aspect of the poem would have had particular resonance in Romantic Britain. The armed forces were expanding rapidly in response to the Napoleonic threat, and large numbers of volunteer militia, distinguished by their fine uniforms, drilled regularly around the country. See Linda Colley, *Britons: Forging the Nation, 1707–1837* (London: Vintage, 1992; 1996), pp. 297–337. Tim Fulford argues that the period witnessed a protracted rethinking of the values of chivalric masculinity elegised by Burke. Tim Fulford, *Romanticism and Masculinity: Gender, Politics and Poetics in the Writings of Burke, Coleridge, Cobbett, Wordsworth, De Quincey and Hazlitt* (Basingstoke: Macmillan, 1999). John Tosh provides an overview of research in this area. John Tosh, 'The Old Adam and the New Man: Emerging Themes in the History of English Masculinities, 1750–1850', in *English Masculinities 1660–1800*, ed. Tim Hitchcock and Michèle Cohen (London: Longman, 1999), pp. 217–38.
17. Judith Butler, *Gender Trouble: Feminism and the Subversion of Identity* (New York and London: Routledge, 1990; 1999), xv.
18. Butler, *Gender Trouble*, pp. 177–8. Butler's sense of the subject's agency has often been overstated. In her more recent work, she notes; 'The misapprehension about gender performativity is this: that gender is a choice, or that gender is a role, or that gender is a construction one puts on, as one puts clothes on in the morning.' Judith Butler, *Bodies that Matter: On the Discursive Limits of 'Sex'* (London: Routledge, 1993), p. 94.
19. On Byron's use of classical sources in this transformation and the transformation that follows Selim's death, see Robert B. Ogle, 'The Metamorphosis of Selim: Ovidian Myth in *The Bride of Abydos* II', *Studies in Romanticism*, 20, no. 1 (1981), 21–31.
20. Laura Mulvey, 'Visual Pleasure and Narrative Cinema', *Screen*, 16, no. 3 (1975), 6–18, reprinted in *Feminisms: an Anthology of Literary Theory and Criticism*, ed. Robyn R. Warhol and Diane Price Herndl (Basingstoke: Macmillan, 1991; 1997), p. 442.
21. Murray archive, box B52.
22. St Clair, 'The Impact of Byron's Writings', p. 4 and Table 1.5 on p. 6.
23. Copies of *The Giaour* in wrappers sold for 5 ½ s, to which the cost of binding would normally be added (a volume of several tales cost 22 s in wrappers, 32 s bound). This was a good deal cheaper than the octavo edition of *Childe*

Harold's Pilgrimage (12 s in wrappers, 25 s bound) but still well beyond the reach of the men who printed these books, who were paid 36 s a week. Carpenters were paid about 25 s a week, and the 'gentility' by St Clair's definition had incomes of about 100 s a week. St Clair, 'The Impact of Byron's Writings', Table 1.2 on pp. 3, 4.

24. Lady Mildmay reported by Thomas Moore, Marchand, *Byron*, I, 330.
25. Marchand, *Byron*, II, 692.
26. Ibid., I, 332
27. Cited in Marchand, *Byron*, I, 333.
28. Cited in Marchand, *Byron*, II, 597.
29. See H. Warner Allen, *Number Three Saint James's Street: A History of Berry's the Wine Merchants* (London: Chatto and Windus, 1950), p. 87 on the ledgers, pp. 101–4 on Fox, pp. 137–8 on Brummell, p. 149 on Moore and pp. 149–54 on Byron.
30. Marchand, *Byron*, I, 125.
31. For biographical investigations of Byron's diets, see Jeremy Hugh Baron, 'Byron's Appetites, James Joyce's Gut, and Melba's Meals and *Mésalliances*', *British Medical Journal*, 315, no. 7123 (1997), 1697–703; Arthur Crisp, 'Commentary: Ambivalence toward Fatness and Its Origins', *British Medical Journal*, 315, no. 7123 (1997), 1703; Jeremy Hugh Baron and Arthur Crisp, 'Byron's Eating Disorders', *The Byron Journal*, 31 (2003), 91–100; and Wilma Paterson, *Lord Byron's Relish: The Regency Cookbook* (Glasgow: Dog & Bone, 1990), pp. 131–42.
32. James Makittrick Adair, *An Essay on Diet and Regimen*, 2nd ed. (London: James Ridgway, 1812). Baron suggests that the earlier treatise was [William Wadd], *Cursory Remarks on Corpulence* (London: Printed for J. Callow, Medical bookseller; by J. and W. Smith, 1810).
33. William Stark, *The Works of the late William Stark [...] with experiments, dietetical and statical* (London, 1788); and Sir John Sinclair, *The Code of Health and Longevity*, 4 vols (Edinburgh, 1807). Both books are listed in the 1816 sale catalogue for Byron's library, *CMP*, pp. 231–45.
34. Criticism on Byron and food includes Christine Kenyon Jones, '"Man Is a Carnivorous Production": Byron and the Anthropology of Food', *Prism(s): Essays in Romanticism*, 6 (1998), 41–58; Christine Kenyon Jones, '"I wonder if his appetite was good?" Byron, Food and Culture: East, West, North and South', in *Byron: East and West*, ed. Martin Procházka (Prague: Charles University Press, 2000), pp. 249–62; Carol Shiner Wilson, 'Stuffing the Verdant Goose: Culinary Esthetics in *Don Juan*', *Mosaic*, 24, no. 3–4 (1991), 33–52; Peter W. Graham, 'The Order and Disorder of Eating in Byron's *Don Juan*', in *Disorderly Eaters: Texts in Self-Empowerment*, ed. Lilian R. Furst and Peter W. Graham (University Park: Pennsylvania State University Press, 1992), pp. 113–23; Jane Stabler, 'Byron's World of Zest', in *Cultures of Taste/Theories of Appetite: Eating Romanticism*, ed. Timothy Morton (Basingstoke: Palgrave Macmillan, 2004), pp. 141–60; and Tom Mole, '"Nourished by that Abstinence": Consumption and Control in *The Corsair*', *Romanticism*, 12, no. 1 (2006), 26–34.
35. By 1810, there had been 16 German, 15 French, 2 American, 2 Russian, 1 Dutch, and 20 English editions. See Ellis Shookman, 'Pseudo-Science, Social Fad, Literary Wonder: Johann Caspar Lavater and the Art of Physiognomy',

in *The Faces of Physiognomy: Interdisciplinary Approaches to Johann Caspar Lavater*, ed. Ellis Shookman (Columbia, SC: Camden House, 1993), pp. 1–24 (p. 2). Graeme Tytler provides an analysis of Lavater's impact, which aims to make us 'conscious of the historicity of physical character description in English fiction after 1789'. Graeme Tytler, 'Lavater and Physiognomy in English Fiction 1790–1832', *Eighteenth-Century Fiction*, 7, no. 3 (1995), 293–310 (p. 307).

36. Byron was phrenologised by Spurzheim on 26 September 1814. 'I own he has a little astonished me', he wrote, '[h]e says all [my faculties] are strongly marked – but very antithetical for everything developed in & on this same skull of mine has its *opposite* in great force so that to believe him my good and evil are at perpetual war' (*BLJ*, IV, 182).
37. William Wordsworth, *The Thirteen-Book Prelude*, 2 vols, The Cornell Wordsworth, gen. ed. Stephen Parrish, ed. Mark L. Reed (Ithaca, NY: Cornell University Press, 1991), 12. 161–8.

5 The visual discourse of Byron's celebrity

1. Cited in George Paston and Peter Quennell, *To Lord Byron: Feminine Profiles Based on Unpublished Letters 1807–1824* (London: John Murray, 1939), p. 65. The print in question is an engraving of Thomas Phillips's 'cloak' portrait.
2. Ibid., p. 262.
3. Ibid., p. 264.
4. Jane Austen, *Pride and Prejudice* (1813) ed. Vivien Jones (London: Penguin, 1996), p. 205.
5. Ibid. See Deidre Lynch, *The Economy of Character: Novels, Market Culture, and the Business of Inner Meaning* (Chicago, IL: University of Chicago Press, 1998), pp. 130–3.
6. Annette Peach, 'Portraits of Byron', *The Walpole Society*, 62 (2000), 1–144, cat. no. 4.1.
7. Peach, 'Portraits of Byron', cat. no. 29.1. This image became more widely known when an engraving of it by Samuel Freeman (Peach, cat. no. 29.4) was published as the frontispiece to Leigh Hunt, *Lord Byron and Some of his Contemporaries* (London: Henry Colburn, 1828).
8. David Piper, *The Image of the Poet: British Poets and Their Portraits* (Oxford: Clarendon Press, 1982), p. 1.
9. William Galperin, *The Return of the Visible in British Romanticism* (Baltimore, MD: Johns Hopkins University Press, 1993), p. 19. On the division of knowledge into disciplines in the Romantic period, see Clifford Siskin, *The Work of Writing: Literature and Social Change in Britain, 1700–1830* (Baltimore, MD: Johns Hopkins University Press, 1998), especially Part One, 'Disciplinarity: The Political Economy of Knowledge', pp. 29–103.
10. W. J. T. Mitchell, 'Introduction', in *The Language of Images*, ed. W. J. T. Mitchell (Chicago, IL: The University of Chicago Press, 1974), pp. 1–2.
11. 'It is now time to restore prints to their proper historical context. One of the most important recent developments in historiography has been a new understanding of the significance of print culture and the manner in which it operates. The study of printed images must be integrated into this

account.' Timothy Clayton, *The English Print: 1688–1802* (New Haven, CT: Yale University Press, 1997), p. 284.

12. Gillen D'Arcy Wood, *The Shock of the Real: Romanticism and Visual Culture, 1760–1860* (Basingstoke: Palgrave Macmillan, 2001), p. 8.
13. Patricia Anderson has studied the role of these technologies in producing 'a transformed and expanded popular culture' with an 'increasingly pictorial character'. Patricia Anderson, *The Printed Image and the Transformation of Popular Culture: 1790–1860* (Oxford: Clarendon Press, 1991), p. 2.
14. William St Clair, *The Reading Nation in the Romantic Period* (Cambridge: Cambridge University Press, 2004), pp. 134–5.
15. John Murray to Byron, 19 March 1819, in *The Works of Lord Byron: Letters and Journals*, ed. Rowland E. Prothero, 5 vols (London: John Murray, 1898–1904), IV, 282–3.
16. Richard Westall, *Catalogue of an Exhibition of a Selection of the Works of Richard Westall RA, Including 240 Pictures and Drawings Which Have Never before Been Exhibited* (London: Joyce Gold, 1814).
17. Peach, 'Portraits of Byron', cat. no. 11.1.
18. Ibid., p. 43. Richard Walker, *Regency Portraits*, 2 vols (London: National Portrait Gallery, 1985), I, 82.
19. Peach, 'Portraits of Byron', cat. nos 11.2, 11.3.
20. Ibid., cat. no. 14.1.
21. The will is cited by Malcolm Elwin, *Lord Byron's Family: Annabella, Ada and Augusta, 1816–1824* (London: John Murray, 1975), pp. 227–8. In fact, Ada was allowed to have the portrait when she married in 1835, and at that stage she had the copy made for herself by Phillips, which is now in the National Portrait Gallery, London, ref. 142.
22. Peach, 'Portraits of Byron', cat. no. 13.1.
23. Ibid., cat. no. 13.2.
24. Suzanne K. Hyman, 'Contemporary Portraits of Byron', in *Lord Byron and his Contemporaries: Essays from the Sixth International Byron Seminar*, ed. Charles E. Robinson (Newark: University of Delaware Press, 1982), pp. 204–34 (p. 207). For further criticism on Byron's portraits see Christine Kenyon Jones, 'Fantasy and Transfiguration: Byron and His Portraits', in *Byromania: Portraits of the Artist in Nineteenth- and Twentieth-Century Culture*, ed. Frances Wilson (London: Macmillan, 1999), pp. 109–36; Annette Peach, 'Byron and Romantic Portrayal', in *Lord Byron: A Multidisciplinary Open Forum*, ed. Thérèse Tessier (Paris: The Byron Society, 1999), pp. 193–203; and the essays collected in *Byron: The Image of the Poet*, ed. Christine Kenyon Jones (Newark: University of Delaware Press, forthcoming).
25. See *BLJ*, II, 224–5, 228, 234.
26. The public gaze was not always welcome. Thomas Moore, in his biography of Byron, mentions an occasion when Byron and Samuel Rogers were leaving a ball: '[O]ne of the link-boys ran on before Lord Byron, crying "This way, my lord." "He seems to know you," said Mr. Rogers. "Know me!" answered Lord Byron, with some degree of bitterness in his tone – "everyone knows me, – I am deformed."' Thomas Moore, *Letters and Journals of Lord Byron with Notices of His Life*, 2 vols (London: John Murray, 1830), I, 357n. See also Byron's comment that when he arrived for dinner with Madame de Staël, 'I found the room full of strangers, who had come to stare at me as at

some outlandish beast in a rareeshow.' Cited in Leslie A. Marchand, *Byron: A Biography*, 3 vols (London: John Murray, 1957), II, 635.

27. Cited in Walker, *Regency Portraits*, I, 82.
28. Alan Lang Strout, ed., *John Bull's Letter to Lord Byron* (Norman: University of Oklahoma Press, 1947), p. 80.
29. Leslie Marchand transcribes the addressee of this letter as 'J. Asham Esqre. Cornhill'. Asham's identity was further clouded when Richard Walker, in his *Regency Portraits*, in turn mistranscribed Marchand's transcription as 'Ashaw' (Walker, *Regency Portraits*, I, 82). The painter is referred to only as 'Mr. D.' (Marchand suggests painters called Dawe, Devis, Drew and Dance as possibilities). In fact, 'J. Asham' is James Asperne, editor of the *European Magazine*, whose offices were at 32 Cornhill. This identification is endorsed by the MS, now in the Roe Byron collection at Newstead Abbey, which shows that Byron's 'p', as in 'impatient', does have a distinctive ascender, and that the descender of the 'p' in 'Asperne' is almost non-existent, making it easy to take it for an 'h'. Mr. D. is Samuel Drummond (1765–1844), who painted a number of portraits for the *European Magazine* around this time.
30. Cited in Peach, 'Byron and Romantic Portrayal', p. 44.
31. Peach, 'Portraits of Byron', cat. no. 11.11.
32. Ibid., cat. no. 11.12
33. Ibid., cat. no. 11.13.
34. *Don Juan, with a Preface by a Clergyman* (London: Hodgson & Co., 1823). *Byron* engraved by Archibald Dick, published by W. Sams, Royal Library, St James Street, London, 1824. These two images are discussed by Robert Beevers, *The Byronic Image: The Poet Portrayed* (Abingdon: Olivia Press, 2005), pp. 62–3.
35. Letitia Elizabeth Landon, 'The Portrait of Lord Byron at Newstead Abbey', in *Selected Writings*, ed. Jerome McGann and Daniel Riess (Peterborough, ON: Broadview, 1997), p. 260.
36. Peach, 'Portraits of Byron', cat. no. 13.46.
37. Count Delladecima (Marchand's spelling) was 'Byron's chief adviser among the Greeks on Cephalonia' (see Marchand, III, 1129, and 1115–6). For the Homeric helmets, see Marchand, III, 1078–9.
38. Peach, 'Portraits of Byron', cat. no. 13.47.
39. Lord Byron, *Don Juan* (London: William Benbow at the Lord Byron's Head, Castle Street, Leicester Square, 1822). The frontispiece image is reproduced in Beevers, p. 130; see also Doris Langley Moore, *The Late Lord Byron* (London: John Murray, 1961), p. 113.
40. [John Roby], *The Duke of Mantua* (London: Thomas Davison, 1823). See Samuel Chew, *Byron in England: His Fame and After-Fame* (London: John Murray, 1924), pp. 176–7 and James Sambrook, 'Roby, John (1793–1850)', *Oxford Dictionary of National Biography*, Oxford University Press, 2004. [http://www.oxforddnb.com/view/article/23904, accessed 18 April 2006].
41. Henry Fothergill Chorley, *The Authors of England: A Series of Medallion Portraits of Modern Literary Characters* (London: Charles Tilt [1838]). The authors were Hemans, Scott, Byron, Southey, the Countess of Blessington, Coleridge, Bulwer, Lady Morgan, Shelley, Moore, Lamb, Mary Russell Mitford, Campbell and Wordsworth. For the dating of this book, see Oscar José Santucho, *George Gordon, Lord Byron: A Comprehensive Bibliography of Secondary Materials*

in English, 1807–1974, The Scarecrow Author Bibliographies (Metuchen, NJ: The Scarecrow Press, 1977), p. 234.
42. F. G. Stephens and Mary Dorothy George, *Catalogue of Political and Personal Satires Preserved in the Department of Prints and Drawings in the British Museum*, 11 vols (London: British Museum, 1978), IX, 163 (cat. no. 11941).
43. Reproduced as plates 47 and 50 in Anthony Burton and John Murdoch, *Byron: Catalogue to an exhibition to celebrate the 150th anniversary of his death in the Greek War of Liberation, 19 April 1824* (London: Victoria and Albert Museum, 1974).
44. It remains uncertain whether this illustration is by Richard Westall, who painted Byron's portrait, or his brother William, or is a collaboration between the two.
45. George Cruikshank, *Forty Illustrations of Lord Byron* (London: James Robins and Co. [1825]).
46. Stephens and George, *Catalogue of Political and Personal Satires*, X, 501 (cat. nos 14826 and 14827).
47. [Alexander Kilgour], *Anecdotes of Lord Byron, from authentic sources; with remarks illustrative of his connection with the principal literary characters of the present day* (London: Knight & Lacey, 1825).
48. Kilgour's book does contain anecdotes relating to Byron's sea voyages and eating habits, but the inscriptions on these prints do not appear to be direct quotations.
49. See Julian Rothenstein and Mel Gooding, eds, *The Playful Eye: An Album of Visual Delight* (London: Redstone, 1999), p. 61 and *passim*.
50. 'Desg.d etc on stone by A. Picker; W. Day lith to the King Gate St.' Private Collection.
51. 'Designed and engraved by E. Brookes; London; Published Feb[y] 1st, 1832 for the Engraver; by J. B. Brookes, Book & Print Publisher, 2 New Bond Street'.
52. 'Designed on Stone by H. Burn; Printed by Engelmann and Co.; Published by R. Ackermann, 96 Strand.' Private Collection.

6 The handling of *Hebrew Melodies*

1. George Daniel, *The Modern Dunciad: A Satire* (1814), cited in *Byron: The Critical Heritage*, ed. Andrew Rutherford (London: Routledge, 1970), p. 76.
2. Caroline Franklin notes the extent to which 'The Murray circle [...] mediated between Byron and a mass readership in the years of fame (1812–16).' But from the beginning, poet and publisher came to a series of quiet compromises when their interests or impulses seemed to conflict. Franklin observes that '[Byron] had to make compromises either in self-censorship when composing, or in mutually agreed adjustments to his manuscripts, in order to keep Murray as his publisher as long as he did'. Caroline Franklin, *Byron: A Literary Life* (London: Macmillan, 2000), pp. 54, 44–5.
3. Samuel Smiles, *A Publisher and His Friends: Memoir and Correspondence of the Late John Murray, with an Account of the Origin and Progress of the House, 1768–1843*, 2 vols (London: John Murray, 1891), I, 208.
4. '[To Mr. Murray]' ('Strahan, Tonson, Lintot of the times') 13–16 (*CPW*, IV, 172).

5. Smiles, *A Publisher and His Friends*, I, 266.
6. Ibid., I, 235. Given that Murray's biographer is Samuel Smiles, the Victorian apostle of 'self help', this statement should be read as indicative of Smiles's faith that, in pursuit of laudable ambitions, discouragements must be faced with a positive attitude and unresting industry.
7. See Michel de Certeau, *The Practice of Everyday Life*, trans. by Steven Rendall (Berkeley: University of California Press, 1984), especially '"Making Do": Uses and Tactics', pp. 29–42.
8. There are discussions of *Hebrew Melodies* in Frederick W. Shilstone, *Byron and the Myth of Tradition* (Lincoln: University of Nebraska Press, 1988), pp. 99–112; Bernard Blackstone, *Byron: A Survey* (London: Longman, 1975), pp. 129–45; Gordon K. Thomas, 'The Forging of an Enthusiasm: Byron and the *Hebrew Melodies*', *Neophilologus*, 75 (1991), 626–36; Gordon K. Thomas, 'Finest Orientalism, Western Sentimentalism, Proto-Zionism: The Muses of Byron's *Hebrew Melodies*', *Prism(s): Essays in Romanticism*, 1 (1993), 51–66; Caroline Franklin, '"Some Samples of the Finest Orientalism": Byronic Philhellenism and Proto-Zionism at the Time of the Congress of Vienna', in *Romanticism and Colonialism: Writing and Empire*, ed. Tim Fulford and Peter Kitson (Cambridge: Cambridge University Press, 1998), pp. 221–42; Graham Pont, 'Byron and Nathan: A Musical Collaboration', *The Byron Journal*, 27 (1999), 51–65 and Judith Chernaik, 'The Wild-Dove Hath Her Nest', *Times Literary Supplement*, no. 5265, 27 February 2004, 12–14. Frederick Burwick and Paul Douglass have waged a campaign for the *Hebrew Melodies* to be understood as songs, beginning with Paul Douglass, '*Hebrew Melodies* as Songs: Why we Need a New Edition', *The Byron Journal*, 14 (1986), 12–21; continuing with their contributions to the Paderborn Symposium: Frederick Burwick 'Identity and Tradition in the *Hebrew Melodies*' and Paul Douglass, 'Isaac Nathan's Settings for *Hebrew Melodies*', both in *English Romanticism: The Paderborn Symposium* (Essen: Die Blaue Eule, 1985), pp. 123–38, 139–51; and culminating in their facsimile edition of Nathan's settings: *A Selection of Hebrew Melodies, Ancient and Modern, by Isaac Nathan and Lord Byron*, ed. Frederick Burwick and Paul Douglass (Tuscaloosa: University of Alabama Press, 1988). This edition is hereafter cited as Burwick and Douglass.
9. William Roberts, 'Review of *The Corsair*, by Lord Byron', *British Review*, 5 (February 1814), 506–11 (p. 506). See also Theodore Redpath's comment that '[a]s the series [of Turkish Tales] went on there were [...] grumbles on the score of monotony'. Theodore Redpath, *The Young Romantics and Critical Opinion 1807–1824* (London: Harrap, 1973), p. 181.
10. 'Review of Byron, *The Corsair* (1814)', *Critical Review*, 4th Series, 5 (February 1814), 144–155 (p. 154).
11. For example,'Visionary as the prospect may be, we cannot resist the temptation to indulge ourselves, for a moment, in realizing the glorious emancipation which Christianity would induce on the faculties of so noble a mind. [...] Deeply were it to be regretted, that such a mind should be occupied with anything short of the infinite and the eternal!' Josiah Conder, 'Review of *Byron, The Corsair*, 4th Edition (1814)', *Eclectic Review*, 2nd Series, 1 (April 1814), 416–26 (pp. 424–5).
12. 'H. S. B', 'Lines occasioned by reading *The Bride of Abydos*', *Gentleman's Magazine*, 84, no. 1 (1814), 592.

13. 'Review of Byron, *The Corsair* (2nd Edition, 1814)', *Christian Observer*, 13 (April 1814), 245–57. Byron had earlier written to the editor of that journal to thank him for the 'able and I believe just' review of *The Giaour*, which suggests that he might also have seen the subsequent review (*BLJ*, III, 189–90).
14. 'Review of Byron, *The Corsair* (2nd Edition, 1814)', *Christian Observer*, 13 (April 1814), 245–57 (pp. 250–1).
15. Ibid., pp. 256–7.
16. Cited in Malcolm Elwin, *Lord Byron's Wife* (London: Macdonald, 1962), p. 167.
17. See Elwin, *Lord Byron's Wife*, p. 171, and *BLJ*, IV, 177. Byron and Annabella also discussed the theological writings of Richard Porson (*BLJ*, IV, 168). Bishop Kaye recalled Hodgson and Byron arguing over 'the question, determined by Locke in the negative, whether there is an innate notion of the Deity' (*HVSV*, 95). Sadly, Kaye did not record who took which side.
18. *BLJ*, IV, 167. See also *BLJ*, IV, 164, '[H]er being with child at 65 [*sic*] is indeed a miracle – but her getting any one to beget it – a greater.'
19. Lady Melbourne, Byron's confidante, certainly saw his marriage in this light, and actively helped to bring it about. See *Byron's 'Corbeau Blanc': The Life and Letters of Lady Melbourne*, ed. Jonathan David Gross (Liverpool: Liverpool University Press, 1997).
20. Byron also hinted that this reform would produce a newly serious kind of poetry. At the end of a long letter to Annabella in which he discusses his 'by no means settled' religious opinions and promises that 'I will read what books you please – hear what arguments you please', he writes, 'you shall be "my Guide – Philosopher and friend" ' (*BLJ*, IV, 177). The quotation figures Annabella as Henry St John to Byron's Pope, recalling Pope's assertion in *An Essay on Man* that St John is responsible for a new seriousness in his poetry: 'urged by thee, I turn'd the tuneful art / From sounds to things, from fancy to the heart' (4. 391–2). Alexander Pope, *The Twickenham Edition of the Poems of Alexander Pope*, ed. John Butt, 11 vols (London: Methuen, 1939–1969), III (i): *An Essay on Man*, ed. Maynard Mack (1950), p. 166.
21. Thomas L. Ashton, *Byron's Hebrew Melodies* (London: Routledge and Kegan Paul, 1972), p. 26.
22. 'The Wild Gazelle' 19–24 (*CPW*, III, 292).
23. 'Oh! Weep for Those' 4; 11–12 (*CPW*, III, 292).
24. 'All is Vanity, Saith the Preacher' 15–16 (*CPW*, III, 300).
25. The same ideas return in 'Were My Bosom as False as Thou Deem'st It To Be' (*CPW*, III, 305), but there the painful questioning of 'On Jordan's Banks' is opposed by a sure faith in God's justice hereafter, despite the fact that He seems to permit injustice in this world.
26. Cited in Ashton, *Byron's Hebrew Melodies*, p. 5.
27. Ashton notes that he 'had been anticipated as early as 1812, by the Scots music publisher, George Thomson', p. 11.
28. Byron had already been writing about the Jews in the short poem 'Magdalen', which he dated 18 April 1814 (*CPW*, III, 267–8). Set on Calvary, the poem's anti-Semitism is inescapable and embarrassing. 'Israel's swarthy race' is blamed for the crucifixion; the Jews are presented as having an 'idiot hatred', an 'eagerness of blood' and 'an idle lust of useless gold'. But, like so many

Byronic heroes, they become ennobled by their unrepentant endurance of punishment.

29. Jerome Christensen cites objections to this foreign diction from John Hookham Frere, the *Theatrical Inquisitor*, the *Satirist*, Lady Caroline Lamb and Wordsworth, and to his archaisms from George Ellis, and suggests that these complaints 'reflect a longstanding concern about Lord Byron's style, which begins with Henry Brougham's wicked fun about *pibroch* in "Lachin Y Gair"'. Jerome Christensen, *Lord Byron's Strength: Romantic Writing and Commercial Society* (Baltimore, MD: Johns Hopkins University Press, 1993), pp. 136–7.
30. The *British Review*, for example, objected to the sudden shift from Orientalism to superficial piety: 'The writer ought, in a manner, to come out of the schools of the prophets [in order to imitate Hebrew poetry]. He should know his Bible, believe his Bible, and love his Bible, to write with true feeling upon the subjects of the Bible. Hitherto Lord Byron's Muse has had much more connection with the Koran than with the sacred register of all truth. With her pellise in disorder, her zone unbuckled, her cheek suffused, the Muse of Lord Byron steps forth from the polluted precincts of the seraglio, from her couch of roses and glittering kiosk, into the courts of the Lord's house'. William Roberts, 'Review of Byron, *Hebrew Melodies* (1815)', *British Review*, 6 (August 1815), 200–8 (p. 203).
31. Ibid., p. 201.
32. Joseph Slater, 'Byron's *Hebrew Melodies*', *Studies in Philology*, 49 (1952), 75–94 (p. 76).
33. Roberts, 'Review of Byron, *Hebrew Melodies* (1815)', 200.
34. See Jean Baudrillard, *Simulations* (New York: Semiotext(e), 1983).
35. Rex Butler, *Jean Baudrillard: The Defence of the Real* (London: Sage, 1999), p. 17.
36. Anon., 'The Universal Believer; By Lord Byr*n, In Imitation of his Friend Tommy M**re' ([London(?)]: [n. pub.], [1815]). Preserved as a single sheet in the British Library.
37. For full bibliographical descriptions, see Ashton, *Byron's Hebrew Melodies*, pp. 210–11, and Burwick and Douglass, p. 41.
38. As a collector, Thomas Wise was preoccupied with first editions and 'other necessary Editions' (Thomas J. Wise, *A Bibliography of the Writings in Verse and Prose of George Gordon Noel, Baron Byron*, 2 vols (London: Printed for Private Circulation, 1932–33), I, xix). Wise provides no entry for Nathan's book, nor for the collected editions of Byron's works that Murray published in 1815 and which are crucial to Murray's handling of *Hebrew Melodies*. Thomas Ashton provides details of all the relevant books, and supersedes Wise on this point.
39. Murray to Byron, 'Monday' [2 January 1815?] (Murray archives).
40. Nathan's biographer, Olga Phillips, quotes from a formal legal document, transferring *Hebrew Melodies*' copyright from Byron to Nathan for the sum of 5 shillings, witnessed by Kinnaird and William Hamilton, and dated 20 April 1814. See Olga S. Phillips, *Isaac Nathan, Friend of Byron* (London: Minerva, 1940), pp. 73–6. It has not been possible to locate this document. As I show below, Phillips is not always reliable, but it is clear that an agreement existed between Byron and Nathan, whether written or informal.

41. Murray to Byron [Wednesday] 11 January 1815 (Bodleian Library, Dep. Lovelace Byron 155, f. 110).
42. The tenor John Braham (1777?–1856) was Nathan's business partner in the *Hebrew Melodies* project and collaborated in some of the settings. He and Byron were acquainted through their association with Drury Lane Theatre.
43. Smiles, *A Publisher and His Friends*, I, 351.
44. For full bibliographical descriptions, see Ashton, *Byron's Hebrew Melodies*, pp. 212–13, 200, and Wise, *A Bibliography of the Writings in Verse and Prose*, I, 103–4.
45. Ashton, *Byron's Hebrew Melodies*, p. 213.
46. These title pages exist in two states. In one state they specify the poems to be bound into each volume, with *Childe Harold* and Miscellaneous Poems in the first volume and *The Giaour, The Bride of Abydos, The Corsair, Lara*, 'Ode to Napoleon' and *Hebrew Melodies* in the second.
47. As Wise notes, these advertisements are printed on sig. E4 and are therefore an integral part of the book. Some copies of Murray's edition also have additional leaves of advertisements bound in.
48. This was the impression of the reader who bound his or her Byron books into the 2 vols now in the British Library at 11604 f. 25, using the title pages supplied with Murray's *Hebrew Melodies*. The first volume of this set consists of the tenth edition of *Childe Harold's Pilgrimage*, with appended lyrics, and *Hebrew Melodies*.
49. Donald Reiman, ed., *The Romantics Reviewed*, 9 vols (London: Garland, 1972), part B, 5 vols.
50. Murray ledger, reproduced in Ashton, *Byron's Hebrew Melodies*, p. 213. Note that this is more than twice the amount spent on the first edition of *Childe Harold's Pilgrimage*.
51. Ibid. This does not include the related profit from the collected edition.
52. Olga Phillips, in her biography of Nathan, claims that Nathan's edition sold ten thousand copies and made a profit of five thousand pounds (p. 78). She gives no source for these figures, and neither the number of copies nor the profit margin seems credible. Her inflated figures are reproduced in Ashton, *Byron's Hebrew Melodies*, p. 48, Chernaik, 'The Wild-Dove Hath Her Nest', p. 12, and Franklin, *Literary Life*, p. 112. *DNB* notes that 'This publication brought him a wide reputation, but its success was not sufficient to keep him out of financial difficulties. He had previously been compelled, on account of large debts, to leave London and reputedly spent some time in the west of England and in Wales.' R. H. Legge, 'Nathan, Isaac (1790–1864)', rev. David J. Golby, *Oxford Dictionary of National Biography* (Oxford University Press, 2004) [http://www.oxforddnb.com/view/article/19808, accessed 11 July 2006].
53. See McGann's commentary on the composition of both poems in *CPW*, IV, 476–83 and 488–90.
54. McGann observes that 'It is unlikely that Byron would have given the lines to Nathan to publish as an independent "Hebrew Melody" if he was at the same time aware that he would publish them soon as part of his verse tale.' *CPW*, III, 489.
55. 'Review of Byron, *Siege of Corinth* and *Parisina*', *Augustan Review*, 2 (April 1816), 380–8 (p. 387).
56. Ibid., p. 388.

57. 'Review of Byron, *Siege of Corinth* and *Parisina* (1816)', *British Critic*, 2nd Series, 5 (April 1816), 430–6 (p. 435); William Roberts, 'Review of Byron, *Siege of Corinth* and *Parisina* (1816); and Hunt, *The Story of Rimini* (1816)', *British Review*, 7 (May 1816), 452–69 (p. 463).
58. 'Review of Byron, *Siege of Corinth* and *Parisina* (1816)', *Theatrical Inquisitor*, 8 (April 1816), 276–83 (p. 281)
59. [John Scott?], 'Review of Byron, *Siege of Corinth* and *Parisina* (1816)', *The Champion* (February 11, 1816), 45–6 (p. 46).

7 *Childe Harold* Canto Three

1. 'Epistle to Augusta', 24, *CPW*, IV, p. 35.
2. For a survey of contemporary texts on Byron's separation, see Samuel Chew, *Byron in England: His Fame and After-Fame* (London: John Murray, 1924), especially 'The Pamphlets of the Byron Separation', pp. 19–26.
3. Actual divorce, in the modern sense of dissolving the marriage, was almost a legal impossibility, but couples could obtain a court order for separation 'from bed and board'. For a fascinating legal analysis of the separation centred on Lady Byron's legal adviser, see S. M. Waddams, *Law, Politics and the Church of England: The Career of Stephen Lushington 1782–1873* (Cambridge: Cambridge University Press, 1992), pp. 100–134.
4. Waddams, *Law, Politics and the Church of England*, pp. 106–7.
5. Lawrence Stone, *Road to Divorce: England 1530–1987* (Oxford: Oxford University Press, 1992), p. 196.
6. The court felt it was in the public interest to keep the laws on separation strict. Sir William Scott, who was judge of the London Consistory Court in 1816, had ruled in a judgement in 1790 that 'The general happiness of the married life is secured by its indissolubility [...] Necessity is a powerful master in teaching the duties which it imposes [...] the happiness of some individuals must be sacrificed to the greater and more general good.' Cited in Waddams, *Law, Politics and the Church of England*, p. 103. The ecclesiastical courts also had a very high standard of proof. They demanded two witnesses to establish a fact, and would not admit one of the parties involved in the case as a witness (i.e. in separation cases, the husband, wife or lover). Stone, *Road to Divorce*, p. 197, Waddams, *Law, Politics and the Church of England*, p. 107. It was standard practice for the courts to grant custody of children to the father. In an effort to avoid this outcome, lawyers acting on behalf of Lady Byron applied without Byron's knowledge to have Ada made a ward in Chancery, and Lushington wrote to Byron's Lawyer Hanson to announce that Ada had been made a ward of Chancery on 3 February 1817 (Leslie A. Marchand, *Byron: A Biography*, 3 vols (London: John Murray, 1957), II, 685n).
7. Cited in Malcolm Elwin, *Lord Byron's Wife* (London: John Murray, 1962), p. 400.
8. This is the Lovelace archive, from which Ralph, Earl of Lovelace, produced *Astarte*. Lovelace was Byron's grandson, and was brought up by his grandmother, Lady Byron. Highly selective and polemical in his use of the archival material, he attempted to vindicate Lady Byron and show that incest was

the hidden crime of the separation. The contents of the archive were subsequently made more fully available by Malcolm Elwin's research. See Ralph Milbanke, Earl of Lovelace, *Astarte: A Fragment of Truth Concerning George Gordon Byron, Sixth Lord Byron* (London: the author, 1905; repr. ed. Mary Countess of Lovelace, London: Christophers, 1921).

9. Marchand, *Byron*, II, 581. Waddams, *Law, Politics and the Church of England*, pp. 111–12. See also Sir John C. Fox, *The Byron Mystery* (London: Grant Richards, 1924), pp. 57–60. Lushington destroyed his papers relating to the separation before his death (Marchand, *Byron*, II, 582n).
10. Cited in Fox, *The Byron Mystery*, p. 112, see also Marchand, *Byron*, II, 588, although Marchand does not have this part of the statement.
11. 'Stanzas to [Augusta]' 32, *CPW*, IV, 34.
12. Quoted in Doris Langley Moore, *Lord Byron: Accounts Rendered* (London: John Murray, 1974), p. 444.
13. In the line before this quotation, Byron almost quotes Wordsworth: 'thoughts too deep: –' (3. 89). Cf. 'Ode: Intimations of Immortality from Recollections of Early Childhood' (203–4). Cf. also Byron's 'Prometheus' (1816), where Prometheus's wilful spirit finds even in punishment 'Its own concentr'd recompense' (57), *CPW*, IV, 31.
14. 'Review of Byron, *Childe Harold*, III (1816)', *Christian Observer*, 16 (April 1817), 246–59 (p. 253).
15. Walter Scott to Joanna Baillie, 26 November 1816, cited in Andrew Rutherford, ed., *Byron: The Critical Heritage* (London: Routledge, 1970), p. 84.
16. Sheila Emerson, 'Byron's "One Word": The Language of Self-Expression in *Childe Harold* III', *Studies in Romanticism*, 20, no. 3 (1981), 363–82.
17. Samuel Smiles, *A Publisher and His Friends: Memoir and Correspondence of the Late John Murray, with an Account of the Origin and Progress of the House, 1768–1843*, 2 vols (London: John Murray, 1891), I, 369. Murray sold seven thousand copies of *The Prisoner of Chillon* the same evening.
18. Coleridge asked Byron to use his influence to help him get a publisher for a volume of poems, and it was through Byron's intercession that Murray published 'Kubla Khan'. See *BLJ*, IV, 285–6.
19. The impossibility of actualising such forceful self-expression also had its consolations, as Sheila Emerson has observed. She notes that this stanza ambiguously suggests that complete self-expression might destroy Byron, and that by finding it impossible he 'criticizes a way of life and of writing which would provide him with no escape from his tempestuous emotions' (p. 374). The advantage of failing to express himself fully, Emerson suggests, is that Byron sustains the fascinating mystery of his concealed selfhood.
20. *OED*, sense 5.
21. See the entry for 'Electricity' in Iain McCalman, ed., *An Oxford Companion to the Romantic Age: British Culture 1776–1832* (Oxford: Oxford University Press, 1999), p. 495.
22. 'Review of Byron, *Childe Harold*, III (1816)', *Belle Assemblée*, 2nd Series, 16 (Supplement for 1816), 338–41 (p. 338).
23. 'Review of Byron, *Childe Harold*, III (1816)', *Portfolio* (23 November 1816), 73–7 (p. 74).
24. [John Wilson], 'Review of Byron, *Childe Harold*, IV (1818)', *Edinburgh Review*, 30 (June 1818), 87–120 (pp. 99–100).

25. Lady Byron to Mrs Villiers, 11 November 1818, cited in Malcolm Elwin, *Lord Byron's Family: Annabella, Ada and Augusta, 1816–1824* (London: John Murray, 1975), p. 180.
26. L. E. Marshall, '"*Words* are *Things*": Byron and the Prophetic Efficacy of Language', *SEL*, 25 (1985), 801–22 (p. 818).
27. Cf. Marshall's commentary, 'the poet wishes to maintain the reality of hope, virtue, sympathy, sincerity, goodness, and happiness – words which may be things, not merely names or dreams – in a world which inspires no confidence in their existence, and in which such abstractions have become discredited figures of speech'. Ibid.
28. The Scrope Davies notebook, or MS BM, is now in the British Library. For a full description of the book and facsimile of its contents, see *The Manuscripts of the Younger Romantics*, ed. Donald H. Reiman, Lord Byron VII, *Childe Harold's Pilgrimage Canto III: A Facsimile of the Autograph Fair Copy Found in the 'Scrope Davies' Notebook*, ed. T. A. J. Burnett (New York: Garland, 1988).
29. It appears, however, that Byron did receive payment for some of his earliest poems. See Peter Cochran, 'Did Byron Take Money for His Early Poems?' *The Byron Journal*, 31 (2003), 72–6.
30. Smiles, *A Publisher and His Friends*, I, 367.
31. Ibid.
32. Ibid.
33. For the agreement regarding the final £500, see *BLJ*, V, 105–7. For Byron's second request that Kinnaird arrange payment of the money due, see *BLJ*, V, 158.
34. Murray paid £600 for the first two cantos of *Childe Harold* to Dallas, but Byron received no money (see Caroline Franklin, *Byron: A Literary Life* (Basingstoke: Macmillan, 2000), pp. 18–19). Byron did accept 1000 guineas for *Parisina* and *The Seige of Corinth*, but only because he was in dire financial straits and after he first refused the money and then tried to give it away (ibid., pp. 47–8).
35. Ibid., p. 48.
36. Marcel Mauss, *The Gift: The Form and Reason for Exchange in Archaic Societies*, trans. by W. D. Halls (New York: Norton, 1990).
37. Cf. Christensen's discussion of the *British Review's* reading of *Don Juan*: 'For the *British Review* critical independence is wedded to the commodification of the cultural artefact, which frees the purchasing critic from any reciprocal obligation to the selling poet. If things are bought and sold according to a contract arrived at in the open market, seller and buyer make no contact except through the abstracted medium of money, which, because it entails no consequences, emancipates economics from ethics.' Jerome Christensen, *Lord Byron's Strength: Romantic Writing and Commercial Society* (Baltimore, MD: Johns Hopkins University Press, 1993), p. 227.
38. For a theoretical discussion of these issues, see John Frow, 'Gift and Commodity', in his *Time and Commodity Culture: Essays in Cultural Theory and Postmodernity* (Oxford: Clarendon Press, 1997), pp. 102–217.
39. 'Review of Byron, *Childe Harold*, III (1816); and *Prisoner of Chillon* (1816)', *British Critic*, 2nd Series, 6 (December 1816), 608–17 (p. 610).
40. Ibid., p. 609.

8 *Don Juan*

1. Michel Foucault, *The Order of Things: An Archaeology of the Human Sciences* (London: Routledge, 1970; 1997); Charles Taylor, *Sources of the Self: The Making of the Modern Identity* (Cambridge, MA: Harvard University Press, 1989); Dror Wahrman, *The Making of the Modern Self: Identity and Culture in Eighteenth-Century England* (New Haven, CT: Yale University Press, 2004).
2. Nancy Armstrong, *How Novels Think: The Limits of Individualism from 1710–1900* (New York: Columbia University Press, 2005), p. 3.
3. While categories of identity in the *ancien regime* 'could prove to be mutable, malleable, unreliable, divisible, replaceable, transferable, manipulable, escapable, or otherwise fuzzy round the edges', in the modern regime gender, race and class became 'individual traits stamped on every person'; where previously 'identity [was] *not* characterised by an axiomatic presupposition of a deep inner core of selfhood', in the modern regime, identity 'became personal, interiorized, essential, even innate'. Wahrman, *Making of the Modern Self*, pp. 198, 278, 198, 276.
4. Taylor, *Sources*, p. 305.
5. Andrea K. Henderson, *Romantic Identities: Varieties of Subjectivity, 1774–1830* (Cambridge: Cambridge University Press, 1996).
6. By calling attention to the dialogic nature of *Don Juan*, Philip Martin warns against ascribing to the poem any stable position or consistent argument. See Philip Martin, 'Reading *Don Juan* with Bakhtin', in *Don Juan*, ed. Nigel Wood, Theory in Practice (Buckingham: Open University Press, 1993), pp. 90–121. Refusing or disrupting normative ways of thinking is itself a kind of argument, however, and while it would be anathema to the poem systematically to elaborate any thesis, distinct and complex antagonisms recur throughout.
7. Truman Guy Steffan, *Byron's Don Juan*, 4 vols, I: *The Making of a Masterpiece* (Austin, TX: University of Texas Press, 1957), p. 59.
8. William Blake, *The Ghost of Abel*, copy A (1822), pl. 1, *The William Blake Archive*, ed. Morris Eaves, Robert N. Essick and Joseph Viscomi. Accessed 6 May 2002, http://www.blakearchive.org/.
9. M. K. Joseph asserts that 'Don Juanism has a good deal in common with the Brechtian *Verfremdung*, which likewise "distances" the spectator from the action and provokes his reaction to it by a calculated use of the strange, the unexpected or the discordant.' M. K. Joseph, *Byron the Poet* (London: Victor Gollancz, 1964), p. 323.
10. Leigh Hunt mischievously suggested that although Byron shared Montaigne's aristocracy, 'having fallen with various sorts of ambition upon more independent times, his rank did not sit so easily upon him; and not being quite so wise as Montaigne, he suffered his eye for "universality" to be more obscured with spleen.' [Leigh Hunt], 'Passages Marked in Montaigne's *Essays* by Lord Byron', *New Monthly Magazine and Literary Journal*, 19 (January 1827), 26–32 (p. 26).
11. Philip Davis, ' "I leave the thing a problem, like all things": On trying to catch up with Byron' in *Byron and the Limits of Fiction*, ed. Bernard Beatty and Vincent Newey (Liverpool: Liverpool University Press, 1988), pp. 242–84 (p. 244). André Tournon, 'Self-Interpretation in Montaigne's *Essais*', *Yale French Studies*, 64, Montaigne: Essays in Reading (1983), 51–72 (p. 51).

12. One book was in English and one in French. The English edition listed as item 233 in the catalogue (*CMP*, p. 240) was probably *The Essays of Michael de Montaigne*, trans. by Charles Cotton, 9th ed., 3 vols (London: William Miller et al., 1811). The French edition listed as item 228 in the catalogue (*CMP*, p. 239) was probably the 1802 edition published in Paris. However, this edition was in four volumes, and in the sale catalogue it is recorded as three volumes. This may be an error, or a volume may have gone missing.
13. Cited in Richard Kirkland, 'Byron's Reading of Montaigne: A Leigh Hunt Letter', *Keats–Shelley Journal*, 30 (1981), 47–51 (p. 47).
14. The article was in the form of a letter to the editor, and appeared in two parts. Hunt 'Passages Marked in Montaigne's *Essays*', 19 (January 1827), 26–32 and (March 1827), 240–5. From this article I deduce that the copy Byron used on the boat to Cephalonia was not Hunt's. Although Hunt did not record when and how he got his book back (Kirkland, 'Byron's Reading of Montaigne', p. 49) it seems unlikely that he noted at the time which page-corners Byron turned down and later worked from another copy of the essays when transcribing the passages in 1827. It is more likely that Byron returned the book to Hunt, who then used it to prepare his article in 1827.
15. Hunt, 'Passages Marked in Montaigne's *Essays*', p. 26.
16. They are 'On the Education of Children' (1. 26), 'On Practice' (2. 6), 'On the Useful and Honourable' (3. 1), 'On Repenting' (3. 2), 'On Vanity' (3. 9) and 'On Experience' (3. 13). Kirkland, 'Byron's Reading of Montaigne', p. 48. To this list we can add 'On the Lame' (3. 11) which Byron mentions elsewhere (*CMP*, p. 125).
17. Taylor asserts that it is a 'basic condition of making sense of ourselves, that we grasp our lives in a *narrative*' and that 'making sense of one's life as a story is also, like orientation to the good, not an optional extra' (Taylor, *Sources*, p. 47, italics in original). MacIntyre writes that 'man is in his actions and practice, as well as in his fictions, essentially a story-telling animal'. Alasdair MacIntyre, *After Virtue: A Study in Moral Theory* (London: Duckworth, 1985), p. 216. Daniel Dennett sets out his view in 'Why Everyone is a Novelist', *Times Literary Supplement*, 4459 (16 September 1988), 1016, 1028–9. For a contrary argument, see Galen Strawson, 'Against Narrativity', *Ratio*, 22 (n.s.), no. 4 (2004), 428–52.
18. Clifford Siskin, *The Historicity of Romantic Discourse* (Oxford: Oxford University Press, 1988), pp. 3, 12.
19. Roy Porter puts it like this: '[t]here's a standard way of telling the story of the self, one that embodies and bolsters core Western values. Its climax is in the fulfilment of the cherished ideal of "being yourself" [...] In other words, the secret of selfhood is commonly seen to lie in authenticity and individuality, and its history is presented as a biography of progress towards that goal, overcoming great obstacles in the process.' Roy Porter, 'Introduction', in *Rewriting the Self: Histories from the Renaissance to the Present*, ed. Roy Porter (London: Routledge, 1997), pp. 1–14 (p. 1).
20. Taylor, *Sources*, p. 289. Following Alasdair MacIntyre, I understand this specifically modern understanding of development to be produced when earlier goals for the good life are displaced. The classical ideal of man-as-he-should-be, his *telos*, and the Christian doctrine of salvation as the soul's homecoming and highest aim, lose their normative force in modernity.

MacIntyre, esp. Chapter 5, 'Why the Enlightenment Project of Justifying Morality had to Fail', pp. 51–61. The modern understanding of development answers what Anthony Cascardi describes, in terms similar to MacIntyre's, as the difficulty 'of imagining purposive and coherent possibilities for self-transformation where the ends of action are no longer fixed according to nature and where the terms of transcendence have been rendered suspect'. Anthony J. Cascardi, *The Subject of Modernity* (Cambridge: Cambridge University Press, 1992), p. 7.

21. Anthony Giddens, *Modernity and Self-Identity: Self and Society in the Late Modern Age* (Cambridge: Polity, 1991), p. 75.
22. Taylor, *Sources*, p. 12.
23. Michel de Montaigne, *The Essays of Michael de Montaigne, translated into English with very considerable amendments and improvements from the most accurate French edition of Peter Coste*, trans. by Charles Cotton, 9th ed., 3 vols (London: William Miller et al., 1811), III, 3. It has not been possible positively to identify the edition(s) of Montaigne's *Essays* that Byron read. There were two translations available, by John Florio and Charles Cotton. Hunt's article indicates that Byron used Cotton's translation. The ninth edition, 1811, was the most recent edition to be published before Byron began work on *Don Juan*, and is hereafter cited parenthetically in the text.
24. Cf. Timothy Webb's suggestion that *Don Juan*'s 'own brand of shrewd yet cynical wisdom' is based on 'a code of values which has evolved existentially rather than being generated by the spurious authority of abstractions'. Timothy Webb, 'Byron as a Man of the World', in *L'esilio Romantico: Forme Di Un Conflitto*, ed. Joseph Cheyne and Lilla Maria Crisafulli Jones (Bari: Adriatica Editrice, 1990), pp. 279–301 (p. 292).
25. '[To Lady Caroline Lamb]', 14, *CPW*, III, 17. See also 'woman once falling / Forever must fall', 'When We Two Parted', cancelled stanza, *CPW*, III, 320. Jane Stabler locates a source for the image of a fallen woman as a Paria in De Staël's *De La Littérature*. Jane Stabler, *Byron, Poetics and History* (Cambridge: Cambridge University Press, 2002), p. 159.
26. When I refer to an essay that Byron marked, I mean that he turned down the corner of one of its pages in Hunt's edition. If I quote from an essay that Byron marked, it does not necessarily mean that he marked the page from which I quote. When I quote from a particular page marked by Byron, I will indicate this.
27. Dedication 13; 15. 112.
28. Moyra Haslett and Peter Graham have both located sources for *Don Juan* in the popular versions of the story that flourished in contemporary pantomime and spectacular theatre. Noting that '[t]heatrical Don Juans dominated the London stage between 1817 and 1825', and that 'most readers of Byron's poem probably knew several if not many versions' (p. 4), Haslett encourages us to recognise Don Juan as a legendary and not a novelistic character. Moyra Haslett, *Byron's Don Juan and the Don Juan Legend* (Oxford: Clarendon Press, 1997); Peter Graham, *Don Juan and Regency England* (Charlottesville: University Press of Virginia, 1990), esp. 'All Things – But a Show?' pp. 62–88.
29. Alvin B. Kernan, *The Plot of Satire* (New Haven, CT: Yale University Press, 1965), p. 189.
30. Webb, 'Byron as a Man of the World', p. 292.

31. Bernard Blackstone, *Byron: A Survey* (London: Longman, 1975), p. 314.
32. Haidee is the longest of Juan's affairs according to Jerome McGann's calculations. He counts 222 stanzas for Julia's story, 159 for Gulbeyez, 120 for Dudu, 100 for Catherine and 305 for Haidee. See Jerome J. McGann, *Don Juan in Context* (London: John Murray, 1976), p. 128.
33. Byron jokingly suggested that he would make the poem 50 cantos long (*BLJ*, VI, 105), or perhaps 100 (*BLJ*, X, 150), and that he would go on 'as long as I can write' (*BLJ*, X, 135). He envisaged Juan as 'a Cavalier Servente in Italy and a cause for a divorce in England – and a Sentimental "Werther-faced man" in Germany' but could not decide whether he should conclude his career in the French Revolution, in Hell or in an unhappy marriage: 'the Spanish tradition says Hell – but it is probably only an allegory of the other state' (*BLJ*, VIII, 78). Perhaps Byron's most plausible comment on his plan was 'I *have* no plan – I *had* no plan – but I had or have materials' (*BLJ*, VI, 207).
34. Donald Frame notes that '[h]uman conduct is the central point of all. Keen psychologist though he was, Montaigne was always ultimately a moralist. [...] All he learned about himself and others was only partly an end in itself. It was also a means to his only final end: to live well and appropriately and – when he had learned how – to teach others to do so.' Donald M. Frame, *Montaigne's Discovery of Man: The Humanisation of a Humanist* (New York: Columbia University Press, 1955), p. 10.
35. Wahrman, *Making of the Modern Self*, p. 265.
36. I therefore think Kim Ian Michasiw is mistaken to present *Don Juan* as promoting a social constructivist understanding of the self in opposition to conventionally Romantic essentialism. See Kim Ian Michasiw, 'The Social Other: *Don Juan* and the Genesis of the Self', *Mosaic*, 22, no. 2 (1989), 29–48.
37. Taylor, *Sources*, pp. 363, 365.
38. 'Review of Byron, *Don Juan*, I–II (1819)', *Blackwood's Edinburgh Magazine*, 5 (August 1819), 512–18 (p. 513). See *Blackwood's Magazine, 1817–25: Selections from Maga's Infancy*, gen. ed. Nicholas Mason, 6 vols (London: Pickering & Chatto, 2006), vol 5; *Selected Criticism, 1817–1819*, ed. Tom Mole, pp. 311–22. Byron responded to this attack more fully and specifically in 'Some Observations Upon an Article in *Blackwood's Edinburgh Magazine*', but he did not publish his response. See *CMP*, pp. 88–119.
39. 'Review of Byron, *Don Juan*, I–II (1819)', *Blackwood's Edinburgh Magazine*, 5 (August 1819), 512–18 (p. 514).
40. Ibid., p. 513.
41. Horace, *Satires*, I.iii.107–8, in *Horace: Satires, Epistles and Ars Poetica*, ed. H. Rushton Fairclough, Loeb Classical Library (London: Heinemann, 1926), p. 40.
42. In a letter to Byron, Douglas Kinnaird objected to this passage, but cemented the connection between the two words: 'why blame her for liking fucking? If she had canted as well as cunted, then call her names as long as you please' (Murray Archive, cited in Stabler, *Byron, Poetics and History*, p. 183).
43. Deirdre Lynch suggests how 'the new modes of reading and writing that ushered in round characters were defined through representations of the residual categories – the category of patently significant ("flat") characters, as well as the category of superficial readers who could be counted on to

overvalue those characters'. Deidre Lynch, *The Economy of Character: Novels, Market Culture, and the Business of Inner Meaning* (Chicago, IL: University of Chicago Press, 1998), p. 156.

44. Adeline therefore does not operate as a realist character would, according to Elizabeth Ermarth, who writes, 'in realism, identity becomes series-dependent, which is to say that it becomes abstract, removed from direct apprehension to a hidden dimension of depth' (Elizabeth Deeds Ermarth, *Realism and Consensus in the English Novel* (Princeton, NJ: Princeton University Press, 1983), p. 5). Surface impressions, then, become 'mere concretia that owe their significance to the invisible inner reality they register', and a newly penetrative intelligence is required to sound the subject's depths (p. 20). 'What can be seen is always an aspect, what is essentially there has receded to an abstract realm of conceptualisation that we might call depth and this is inaccessible to direct experience at the same time as it entirely informs it' (p. 24).
45. Wahrman, *Making of the Modern Self*, p. 168.
46. Hunt, 'Passages Marked in Montaigne's *Essays*', p. 26.
47. 'Few contemporary figures', Richard Regosin notes, 'had a stronger sense of the variance of outward appearance and inwardness than Montaigne, particularly in the subject that most interests him, man'. Richard Regosin, *The Matter of My Book: Montaigne's* Essais *as the Book of the Self* (Berkeley: University of California Press, 1977), p. 181.
48. George Ridenour, *The Style of Don Juan* (New Haven, CT: Yale University Press, 1960), p. 152. Ridenour's reading of this passage can be found on pp. 117–18.
49. Francis Jeffrey also described Byron as 'a volcano in the heart of our land' in his review of *Childe Harold* Canto Three (Francis Jeffrey, 'Review of *Childe Harold's Pilgrimage, Canto the Third, The Prisoner of Chillon and Other Poems', Edinburgh Review*, 54 (Dec. 1816), 277–310). See also Letitia Landon's use of the volcano image, p. 84, above.
50. '[P]ast all price' and 'beyond all price' may recall the story of the pearl of great price, told in Matt 13.45–6. But the more relevant allusion is to 1 Pe 3.3–4, 'Whose adorning, let it not be that outward adorning, of plaiting the hair, and of wearing of gold, or of putting on of apparel. But let it be the hidden man of the heart, in that which is not corruptible, even the ornament of a meek and quiet spirit, which is in the sight of God of great price.'
51. Jane Stabler has found a source for the image of frozen champagne that also gives it a political inflection. She shows that George Canning, in a speech reported in *Galignani's Messenger*, used it as a simile for the survival of political principles in dark times. Stabler, *Byron, Poetics and History*, p. 168.
52. The most extended reading of Aurora's significance in *Don Juan* is provided by Bernard Beatty, *Byron's Don Juan* (London: Croom Helm, 1985), pp. 137–219.
53. Jean Hall comments, 'where the other Romantics believe that this turn toward innerness is both possible and desirable, Byron tends to doubt both the feasibility and attractiveness of the interior self. He tends to avoid self-exploration because it appears to him a futile process, an exercise in self-delusion.' Jean Hall, 'The Evolution of the Surface Self: Byron's Poetic Career', *Keats-Shelley Journal*, 36 (1987), 134–57 (p. 135).

54. Jean-Jacques Rousseau, *The Confessions*, trans. by Christopher Kelly, *The Collected Writings of Rousseau*, ed. Christopher Kelly, Roger D. Masters and Peter G. Stillman, vol. 5 (Hanover, NH: University Press of New England, 1995), p. 433. See also: 'Montaigne portrays himself in a good likeness but in profile. Who knows whether some scar on the cheek or an eye put out on the side he hides from us might not totally change his physiognomy' (p. 586). Lionel Trilling writes that Rousseau's 'expressions of scorn for the show of sincerity made by Montaigne are recurrent and unqualified.' Lionel Trilling, *Sincerity and Authenticity* (Oxford: Oxford University Press, 1971), p. 59.
55. See *Don Juan* 7. 14; 8. 53 and 14. 75. Rousseau is also mentioned in the unincorporated stanzas for Canto Two.
56. Jerome Christensen, *Romanticism at the End of History* (Baltimore, MD: Johns Hopkins University Press, 2000), p. 188.

Envoi

1. Among other autobiographies, the transgressive thrill of reading *Don Juan* is recalled in Flora Thompson's memoir of domestic service in rural England at the end of the nineteenth century. See Flora Thompson, *Larkrise to Candleford* (Oxford: Oxford University Press, 1945), p. 427. For the appearance of Byron, or Byronic characters, in nineteenth-century novels, see the online bibliography compiled by G. Todd Davis and hosted by Romantic circles. G. Todd Davis, *Fictions of Byron: An Annotated Bibliography*, Romantic Circles Scholarly Resources, accessed 5 September 2006, <http://www.rc.umd.edu/reference/byron-fictions/index.html>. For Byron's political influence, see Paul Graham Trueblood, ed., *Byron's Political and Cultural Influence in Nineteenth-Century Europe: A Symposium* (London: Macmillan, 1981), and Richard Cardwell, ed., *The Reception of Byron in Europe*, 2 vols (London: Thoemmes Continuum, 2004).
2. For *Mazeppa's* adaptation as an equestrian circus act, see Antony D. Hippisley Coxe, 'Equestrian Drama and the Circus', in *Performance and Politics in Popular Drama: Aspects of Popular Entertainment in Theatre, Film and Television 1800–1976*, ed. David Bradby, Louis James and Bernard Sharratt (Cambridge: Cambridge University Press, 1980), pp. 109–18. For *Manfred's* production on the stage, see Margaret J. Howell, *Byron Tonight: A Poet's Plays on the Nineteenth Century Stage* (Windlesham: Springwood Books, 1982), pp. 97–120.
3. Letitia Elizabeth Landon, *Selected Writings*, ed. Jerome McGann and Daniel Riess (Peterborough, ON: Broadview, 1997), p. 260; Charles Tennyson Turner, *Sonnets* (London: Macmillan, 1864), pp. 34–5; John Cam Hobhouse, *Remarks on the Exclusion of Lord Byron's Monument from Westminster Abbey* (London: The Author, 1844). These texts are all discussed in Tom Mole, 'Impresarios of Byron's Afterlife', *Nineteenth-Century Contexts*, 29, no. 1 (2007), 17–34.

Bibliography

1. Reviews and responses to Byron to 1831

Anon., 'Lord Byron', *The European Magazine and London Review*, 65, no. 2 (1814), 2–4.

——, 'Review of Byron, *The Corsair* (2nd Edition, 1814)', *Christian Observer*, 13 (April 1814), 245–57.

——, 'Review of Byron, *The Corsair* (1814)', *Critical Review, 4th Series*, 5 (February 1814), 144–55.

——, 'Biographical Memoir of the Rt. Hon. George Gordon, Ld. Byron', *Lady's Magazine*, 46 (April 1815), 151–52.

——, "Lord Byr*N, the Universal Believer; by Lord Byr*N, in Immitation of His Friend Tommy M**Re." (London: n.p., 1815).

——, 'Some Account of the Rt. Hon. George Gordon, Ld. Byron', *New Monthly Magazine* (July 1815), 527–30.

——, 'Review of Byron, *Childe Harold* III (1816)', *Belle Assemblée, 2nd Series*, 16 (Supplement for 1816), 338–41.

——, 'Review of Byron, *Childe Harold* III (1816)', *Portfolio* (23 November 1816), 73–7.

——, 'Review of Byron, *Childe Harold* III (1816) and *Prisoner of Chillon* (1816)', *British Critic, Second Series*, 6 (December 1816), 608–17.

——, 'Review of Byron, *Siege of Corinth* and *Parisina* (1816)', *Theatrical Inquisitor*, 8 (April 1816), 276–83.

——, 'Review of Byron, *Siege of Corinth* and *Parisina* (1816)', *British Critic, Second Series*, 5 (April 1816), 430–6.

——, 'Review of Byron, *Siege of Corinth* and *Parisina* (1816)', *Augustan Review*, 2 (April 1816), 380–8.

——, 'Review of *Childe Harold's Pilgrimage*, Canto III', *Portfolio*, 23 (November 1816), 73–77.

——, 'Review of Byron, *Childe Harold* III (1816)', *Christian Observer*, 16 (April 1817), 246–59.

——, 'Review of Byron, *Don Juan* I–II (1819)', *Blackwood's Edinburgh Magazine*, 5 (August 1819), 512–18.

——, 'Review of *Don Juan*', *Edinburgh Monthly Review*, 2 (October 1819), 468–86.

——, 'Review of *Sardanapalus, the Two Foscari* and *Cain*', *European Magazine*, 81 (January 1822), 58–70.

'C', 'Lord Byron', *The Brighton Magazine* (July 1822), 45–52.

'Candidus', 'Byron's Plagiarisms', *Monthly Magazine*, 37 (June 1814), 410–11.

'Cantab, A.', 'Appendix to Letter 1 on Cant', *The Brighton Magazine* (August 1822), 182–84.

Conder, Josiah, 'Review of Byron, *The Corsair*, 4th Edition (1814)', *Eclectic Review, 2nd Series*, I (April 1814), 416–26.

Ellis, George, 'Review of Lord Byron's Giaour and Bride of Abydos', *Quarterly Review*, 10 (January 1814), 331–54.

H. S. B., 'Lines Occasioned by Reading *The Bride of Abydos*', *The Gentleman's Magazine*, 84, no. 1 (1814), 592.

——, 'Lines Occasioned by Reading *The Giaour*', *The Gentleman's Magazine*, 84, no. 1 (1814), 592.

Hunt, Leigh, 'Passages Marked in Montaigne's Essays by Lord Byron', *The New Monthly Magazine and Literary Journal*, 19 (1827), 26–32, 240–45.

——, *Lord Byron and Some of His Contemporaries*, 2 vols (London: Henry Colburn, 1828) Reprint, Hildesheim: Georg Olms, 1976.

Jeffrey, Francis, 'Review of Lord Byron's *The Giaour* (1813)', *Edinburgh Review*, 21 (July 1813), 299–309.

——, 'Review of *Childe Harold's Pilgrimage, Canto the Third, The Prisoner of Chillon and Other Poems', Edinburgh Review*, 54 (Dec. 1816), 277–310.

Kilgour, Alexander, *Anecdotes of Lord Byron, from Authentic Sources; with Remarks Illustrative of His Connection with the Principal Literary Characters of the Present Day* (London: Knight & Lacey, 1825).

Macaulay, Thomas, 'Review of Thomas Moore, *Letters and Journals of Lord Byron with Notices of His Life*', *The Edinburgh Review*, 53 (June 1831), 544–72.

Moore, Thomas, *Letters and Journals of Lord Byron with Notices of His Life*, 2 vols (London: John Murray, 1830).

Nathan, Isaac, *Fugitive Pieces and Reminiscences of Lord Byron* (London: Whittaker, Treacher & Co., 1829).

Roberts, William, 'Review of *The Corsair*, by Lord Byron', *British Review*, 5 (February 1814), 506–11.

——, 'Review of Byron, *Hebrew Melodies* (1815)', *British Review*, 6 (August 1815), 200–8.

——, 'Review of Byron, *Siege of Corinth* and *Parisina* (1816) and Hunt, *the Story of Rimini* (1816)', *British Review*, 7 (April 1816), 276–83.

Scott, John (?), 'Review of Byron, *Siege of Corinth* and *Parisina* (1816)', *Champion* (11 February 1816), 45–6.

Scott, John, 'Living Authors, No. IV: Lord Byron', *London Magazine*, 3 (1821), 50–61.

Scott, Walter, 'Review of *Childe Harold's Pilgrimage*, the Prisoner of Chillon, a Dream, and Other Poems', *Quarterly Review*, 16 (October 1816), 172–208.

Wilson, John, 'Review of *Childe Harold's Pilgrimage*, Canto the Fourth', *Edinburgh Review*, 30 (June 1818), 87–120.

2. Select bibliography

Anon., *Cobbett's Parliamentary Debates*, Vol. 21 (London: T. C. Hansard, 1812).

——, *Journals of the House of Lords*, Vol. 48 (London: Her Majesty's Stationery Office, 1812).

Abelove, Henry, 'Some Speculations on the History of Sexual Intercourse During the Long 18th Century in England', *Genders*, 6 (1989), 125–30.

Abrams, M. H., *The Mirror and the Lamp: Romantic Theory and the Critical Tradition* (Oxford: Oxford University Press, 1953).

Accardo, Peter X., 'Byron in America to 1830', *Harvard Library Bulletin* (n. s.) 9, no. 2 (1998), 5–60.

——, *Byron in Nineteenth-Century American Culture: Catalogue of an Exhibition Organized by the Houghton Library, Harvard University* (Newark, DE: University of Delaware, 2001).
Adair, James M., *An Essay on Diet and Regimen*, 2nd ed. (London: James Ridgway, 1812).
Adorno, Theodor W., *The Culture Industry*, ed. J. M. Bernstein (London: Routledge, 1991).
Allen, H. Warner, *Number Three Saint James's Street: A History of Berry's the Wine Merchants* (London: Chatto and Windus, 1950).
Altick, Richard D., *The English Common Reader: A Social History of the Mass Reading Public, 1800–1900* (Chicago: University of Chicago Press, 1957).
——, *Paintings from Books: Art and Literature in Britain, 1760–1900* (Columbus, OH: Ohio State University Press, 1985).
Anderson, Patricia J., *The Printed Image and the Transformation of Popular Culture, 1790–1860* (Oxford: Clarendon Press, 1991).
Anthony, Andrew, 'Celebrity Is Nothing New', *The Observer*, 27 January 2002, 8.
Armstrong, Nancy, *How Novels Think: The Limits of Individualism from 1710–1900* (New York: Columbia University Press, 2005).
Arnold, Matthew, 'Byron', in *Essays in Criticism, Second Series*, ed. S. R. Littlewood (London: MacMillan, 1960), pp. 97–102
Ashton, Thomas, *Byron's Hebrew Melodies* (London: Routledge and Kegan Paul, 1972).
Aspinall, Arthur, 'The Circulation of Newspapers in the Early Nineteenth Century', *Review of English Studies*, 22 (1946), 29–43.
——, 'The Reporting and Publishing of the House of Commons' Debates 1771–1834', in *Essays Presented to Sir Lewis Namier*, ed. Richard Pares and A. J. P. Taylor (London: Macmillan, 1956), pp. 227–57.
Austen, Jane, *Pride and Prejudice*, ed. Vivien Jones (London: Penguin, 1996).
Backscheider, Paula R., 'Introduction', *Prose Studies*, 18, no. 3 The Intersections of the Public and Private Spheres in Early Modern England, ed. Paula R. Back-sheider and Timothy Dykstal (1995), 1–21.
Bailey, Brian, *The Luddite Rebellion* (Stroud: Sutton Publishing, 1998).
Bainbridge, Simon, 'From Nelson to Childe Harold: The Transformations of the Byronic Image', *The Byron Journal*, 27 (1999), 13–25.
Baker, John F., 'The Rise of the Celebrity Author', in *The Professions of Authorship: Essays in Honor of Matthew J. Bruccoli*, ed. Richard Layman and Joel Myerson (Columbia, SC: University of South Carolina Press, 1996), pp. 41–3.
Bannet, Eve T., *The Domestic Revolution: Enlightenment Feminisms and the Novel* (Baltimore, MD: Johns Hopkins UP, 2000).
Baron, Jeremy H., 'Byron's Appetites, James Joyce's Gut, and Melba's Meals and Mésalliances', *British Medical Journal*, 315, no. 7123 (1997), 1697–703.
Baron, Jeremy H. and Arthur Crisp, 'Byron's Eating Disorders', *The Byron Journal*, 31 (2003), 91–100.
Barthes, Roland, *S/Z*, trans. by Richard Miller (New York: Hill and Wang, 1974).
Barton, Anne, *Don Juan* Landmarks of World Literature (Cambridge: Cambridge University Press, 1992).
Baudrillard, Jean, *Simulations* (New York: Semiotext(e), 1983).
Beatty, Bernard, *Byron's Don Juan* (London: Croom Helm, 1985).
Beatty, Bernard and Vincent Newey, eds., *Byron and the Limits of Fiction* (Liverpool: Liverpool University Press, 1988).

Beevers, Robert, *The Byronic Image: The Poet Portrayed* (Abingdon: Olivia Press, 2005).

Bencivenga, Ermanno, *The Discipline of Subjectivity: An Essay on Montaigne* (Princeton, NJ: Princeton University Press, 1990).

Benjamin, Walter, *Illuminations*, trans. by Harry Zohn (London: Fontana, 1992).

Bennett, Andrew, *Romantic Poets and the Culture of Posterity* (Cambridge: Cambridge University Press, 1999).

Bennett, Shelley M., Robyn Asleson, Mark Leonard and Shearer West, *A Passion for Performance: Sarah Siddons and Her Portraitists* (Los Angeles: J. Paul Getty Museum, 1999).

Bennington, Geoffrey, *Lyotard: Writing the Event* (Manchester: Manchester University Press, 1988).

Berlanstein, Lenard R., 'Historicizing and Gendering Celebrity Culture: Famous Women in Nineteenth-Century France', *Journal of Women's History*, 16, no. 4 (2004), 65–91.

Bidney, Martin, 'Motsas for Lord Byron: The Judaeo-British Literary Persona of Isaac Nathan', *The Byron Journal*, 25 (1997), 60–70.

Bindman, David, 'Prints', in *An Oxford Companion to the Romantic Age: British Culture 1776–1832*, ed. Iain McCalman (Oxford: Oxford University Press, 1999), pp. 207–13.

Binfield, Kevin, *Writings of the Luddites* (Baltimore, MD: Johns Hopkins University Press, 2004).

Blackstone, Bernard, *Byron: A Survey* (London: Longman, 1975).

Blackstone, Sir William, *Commentaries on the Laws of England with the Last Corrections of the Author; and with Notes and Additions by Edward Christian, Esq.*, 4 vols, 15th ed. (London: T. Cadell and W. Davies, 1809).

Blake, William, *The Ghost of Abel, Copy a, Pl. 1*. The William Blake Archive, 1822), accessed 6 May 2002; available from <http://www.blakearchive.org/>.

Bolton, Betsy, 'Romancing the Stone: 'Perdita' Robinson in Wordsworth's London', *ELH*, 64, no. 3 (1997), 727–59.

Bone, J. Drummond, '*Beppo*: The Liberation of Fiction', in *Byron and the Limits of Fiction*, ed. Bernard Beatty and Vincent Newey (Liverpool: Liverpool University Press, 1988), pp. 97–125.

——, *Byron* Writers and Their Work, ed. Isobel Armstrong (Tavistock: Northcote House in association with the British Council, 2000).

——, ed., *The Cambridge Companion to Byron* (Cambridge: Cambridge University Press, 2004).

Boorstin, Daniel J., *The Image, or, What Happened to the American Dream* (London: Weidenfeld and Nicolson, 1961).

Booth, Michael R., ed., *The Revels History of Drama in English: Vol. 4, 1750–1880* (London: Methuen, 1975).

Bordo, Susan, 'Reading the Male Body', in *The Male Body*, ed. Laurence Goldstein (Ann Arbor: University of Michigan Press, 1994), pp. 265–306.

——, 'Reading the Slender Body', in *The Visual Culture Reader*, ed. Nicholas Mirzoeff (London: Routledge, 1998), pp. 214–22.

Borges, Jorge L., *Labyrinths* (London: Penguin, 2000).

Bourdieu, Pierre, *The Field of Cultural Production: Essays on Art and Literature*, ed. Randal Johnson (Cambridge: Polity, 1993).

Braudy, Leo, *The Frenzy of Renown: Fame and Its History* (New York: Vintage Books, 1997).

Brecht, Bertolt, *Brecht on Theatre: The Development of an Aesthetic*, trans. by John Willett (New York: Hill and Wang, 1978).
Briggs, Asa, *A Social History of England* (London: Penguin, 1999).
Briggs, Peter M., 'Laurence Sterne and Literary Celebrity in 1760', *The Age of Johnson: A Scholarly Annual*, 4 (1991), 251–80.
Brinks, Ellen, *Gothic Masculinity: Effeminacy and the Supernatural in English and German Romanticism* (Lewisburg, PA: Bucknell University Press, 2003).
Brock, Claire, *The Feminization of Fame, 1750–1830* (Basingstoke: Palgrave Macmillan, 2006).
Brombert, Victor, 'Opening Signals in Narrative', *New Literary History*, 11 (1980), 489–502.
Brooks, Peter, *Reading for the Plot* (Oxford: Clarendon Press, 1984).
——, *Body Work: Objects of Desire in Modern Narrative* (Cambridge, MA: Harvard University Press, 1993).
Brown, David B., *Turner and Byron* (London: Tate Gallery, 1992).
Burke, Peter, 'Representations of the Self from Petrarch to Descartes', in *Rewriting the Self: Histories from the Renaissance to the Present*, ed. Roy Porter (London: Routledge, 1997), pp. 17–28.
Burnett, T. A. J., *The Rise and Fall of a Regency Dandy: The Life and Times of Scrope Berdmore Davies* (Oxford: Oxford University Press, 1981).
——, ed., *Childe Harold's Pilgrimage Canto III: A Facsimile of the Autograph Fair Copy Found in the 'Scrope Davies' Notebook*, The Manuscripts of the Younger Romantics: Lord Byron vol. 7, gen. ed. Donald H. Reiman (New York: Garland, 1988).
Burton, Anthony and John Murdoch, *Byron: Catalogue to an Exhibition to Celebrate the 150th Anniversary of His Death in the Greek War of Liberation, 19 April 1824* (London: Victoria and Albert Museum, 1974).
Burwick, Frederick, 'Identity and Tradition in the *Hebrew Melodies*', in *English Romanticism: The Paderborn Symposium* (Essen: Die Blaue Eule, 1985), pp. 123–38.
Butler, Judith, *Bodies That Matter: On the Discursive Limits of 'Sex'* (London: Routledge, 1993).
——, *Gender Trouble: Feminism and the Subversion of Identity* (New York and London: Routledge, 1999).
Butler, Marilyn, 'The Orientalism of Byron's *Giaour*', in *Byron and the Limits of Fiction*, ed. Bernard Beatty and Vincent Newey (Liverpool: Liverpool University Press, 1988), pp. 78–96.
——, 'Culture's Medium: The Role of the Review', in *The Cambridge Companion to British Romanticism*, ed. Stuart Curran (Cambridge: Cambridge University Press, 1993), pp. 120–47.
Butler, Rex, *Jean Baudrillard: The Defence of the Real* (London: Sage, 1999).
Byrne, Paula, *Perdita: The Life of Mary Robinson* (London: Harper Collins, 2004).
Byron, George Gordon Noel, Baron Byron, *Hebrew Melodies* (London: John Murray, 1815).
——, *The Works of the Right Hon. Lord Byron*, 2 vols (London: John Murray, 1815).
——, *The Works of the Right Honourable Lord Byron*, 8 vols (London: John Murray, 1815–1820).
——, *Don Juan* (London: William Benbow at the Lord Byron's Head, Castle Street, Leicester Square, 1822).
——, *Don Juan, with a Preface by a Clergyman* (London: Hodgson & Co, 1823).

——, *The Works of Lord Byron: Letters and Journals*, 5 vols, ed. Rowland E. Prothero (London: John Murray, 1898–1904).
——, *Don Juan: A Variorum Edition*, 4 vols, ed. Truman Guy Steffan and Willis W. Pratt (Austin, TX: University of Texas Press, 1957).
——, *Byron's Letters and Journals*, 13 vols, ed. Leslie A. Marchand (London: John Murray, 1973–1994).
——, *Lord Byron: The Complete Poetical Works*, 7 vols, ed. Jerome J. McGann (Oxford: Clarendon Press, 1980–1993).
——, *Lord Byron: The Complete Miscellaneous Prose*, ed. Andrew Nicholson (Oxford: Clarendon Press, 1991).
Calder, Angus, ed., *Byron and Scotland: Radical or Dandy?* (Edinburgh: Edinburgh University Press, 1989).
Calhoun, Craig, ed., *Habermas and the Public Sphere* (Cambridge, MA: MIT Press, 1992).
Calvert, William J., *Byron: Romantic Paradox* (Chapel Hill: The University of North Carolina Press, 1935).
Cardwell, Richard, ed., *The Reception of Byron in Europe*, 2 vols (London: Thoemmes Continuum, 2004).
Carlson, Julie, *In the Theatre of Romanticism: Coleridge, Nationalism, Women* (Cambridge: Cambridge University Press, 1994).
Cascardi, Anthony J., *The Subject of Modernity* (Cambridge: Cambridge University Press, 1992).
Cave, Richard Allen, ed., *The Romantic Theatre: An International Symposium* (Gerrards Cross: Colin Smythe, 1986).
Cawelti, John G., 'The Writer as a Celebrity: Some Aspects of American Literature as Popular Culture', *Studies in American Fiction*, 5 (1977), 161–74.
Certeau, Michel de, *The Practice of Everyday Life*, trans. by Steven Rendall (Berkeley: University of California Press, 1984).
Cheeke, Stephen, *Byron and Place: History, Translation, Nostalgia* (Basingstoke: Palgrave Macmillan, 2003).
Chernaik, Judith, 'The Wild-Dove Hath Her Nest', *Times Literary Supplement*, 27 February 2004, 12–14.
Chew, Samuel, *Byron in England: His Fame and After-Fame* (London: John Murray, 1924).
Chorley, Henry F., *The Authors of England: A Series of Medallion Portraits of Modern Literary Characters* (London: Charles Tilt [1838]).
Christensen, Jerome, *Practicing Enlightenment: Hume and the Formation of a Literary Career* (Madison: University of Wisconsin Press, 1987).
——, *Lord Byron's Strength: Romantic Writing and Commercial Society* (Baltimore, MD: Johns Hopkins University Press, 1993).
——, *Romanticism at the End of History* (Baltimore, MD: Johns Hopkins University Press, 2000).
Christie, Ian R., 'James Perry of the Morning Chronicle, 1756–1821', in *Myth and Reality in Late-Eighteenth-Century British Politics and Other Papers*, ed. Ian R. Christie (London: Macmillan, 1970), pp. 334–58.
Clayton, Timothy, *The English Print 1688–1802* (New Haven, CT: Yale University Press, 1997).
Cochran, Peter, 'The Bey Apologises II', *The Newstead Abbey Byron Society Review* (January 2001), 35–7.

——, 'Did Byron Take Money for His Early Poems?' *The Byron Journal*, 31 (2003), 72–6.

Coleridge, Samuel Taylor., *Biographia Literaria*, 2 vols, ed. James Engel and Walter Jackson Bate (Princeton, NJ: Princeton University Press, 1985).

Colley, Linda, *Britons: Forging the Nation, 1707–1837* (London: Vintage, 1992; 1996).

Conrad, Peter, 'Images of Byron', *Times Literary Supplement*, 31 May 1974, 584.

Cooke, Michael G., *The Blind Man Traces the Circle: On the Patterns and Philosophy of Byron's Poetry* (Princeton, NJ: Princeton University Press, 1969).

Cowen, Tyler, *What Price Fame?* (Cambridge, MA: Harvard University Press, 2000).

Cox, Jeffrey N., *Poetry and Politics in the Cockney School: Keats, Shelley, Hunt and Their Circle* (Cambridge: Cambridge University Press, 2004).

Coxe, Antony D. Hippisley, 'Equestrian Drama and the Circus', in *Performance and Politics in Popular Drama: Aspects of Popular Entertainment in Theatre, Film and Television 1800–1976*, ed. David Bradby, Louis James and Bernard Sharratt (Cambridge: Cambridge University Press, 1980), pp. 109–18.

Cranfield, G. A., *The Press and Society: From Caxton to Northcliffe* (London: Longman, 1978).

Crisp, Arthur, 'Commentary: Ambivalence toward Fatness and Its Origins', *British Medical Journal*, 315, no. 7123 (1997), 1703.

Crompton, Louis, *Byron and Greek Love: Homophobia in Nineteenth-Century England* (Swaffham: The Gay Men's Press, 1998).

Cross, Ashley J., 'From *Lyrical Ballads* to *Lyrical Tales*: Mary Robinson's Reputation and the Problem of Literary Debt', *Studies in Romanticism*, 40, no. 4 (2001), 571–605.

Cruikshank, George, *Forty Illustrations of Lord Byron* (London: James Robins and Co. [1825]).

Curran, Stuart, 'Mary Robinson's *Lyrical Tales* in Context', in *Re-Visioning Romanticism: British Women Writers, 1776–1837*, ed. Joel Haefner and Carol Shiner Wilson (Philadelphia: University of Pennsylvania Press, 1994), pp. 17–35.

Dallas, Robert C., *Recollections of the Life of Lord Byron* (Norwood, PA: Norwood, Editions, 1977).

Dalton, Kevin A., 'Middle-Class Celebrity and the Public Sphere, 1763–1844: John Wilkes, Olaudah Equiano, Walter Scott and Charles Dickens.' Ph.D. Thesis, University of Virginia, 1994.

Darvall, Frank O., *Popular Disturbances and Public Order in Regency England*, 2nd ed. (Oxford: Oxford University Press, 1969).

Davis G. Todd, *Fictions of Byron: An Annotated Bibliography* accessed 5 September 2006; available from http://www.rc.umd.edu/reference/byron-fictions/index.html.

Davis, Philip, '"I Leave the Thing a Problem, Like All Things": On Trying to Catch up with Byron', in *Byron and the Limits of Fiction*, ed. Vincent Newey and Bernard Beatty (Liverpool: Liverpool University Press, 1988), pp. 242–84.

Davis, Tracy C., *The Economics of the British Stage, 1800–1914* (Cambridge: Cambridge University Press, 2000).

De Quincey, Thomas, *Confessions of an English Opium Eater and Other Writings*, ed. Grevel Lindop (Oxford: Oxford University Press, 1989).

Dennett, Daniel, 'Why Everyone Is a Novelist', *Times Literary Supplement*, 16 September 1988, 1016, 28–9.

D'Israeli, Isaac, *An Essay on the Manners and Genius of the Literary Character* (London: T. Cadell and W. Davies, 1795).

Donelan, Charles, *Romanticism and Male Fantasy in Byron's Don Juan: A Marketable Vice* (London: Macmillan, 2000).
Donoghue, Frank, *The Fame Machine: Book Reviewing and Eighteenth-Century Literary Careers* (Stanford, CA: Stanford University Press, 1996).
Douglass, Paul, 'Isaac Nathan's Settings for *Hebrew Melodies*', in *English Romanticism: The Paderborn Symposium* (Essen: Die Blaue Eule, 1985), pp. 139–51.
——, '*Hebrew Melodies* as Songs: Why We Need a New Edition', *The Byron Journal*, 14 (1986), 12–21.
Douglass, Paul and Frederick Burwick, eds, *A Selection of Hebrew Melodies, Ancient and Modern by Isaac Nathan and Lord Byron* (Tuscaloosa: University of Alabama Press, 1988).
Drinkwater, John, *The Pilgrim of Eternity: Byron, a Conflict* (London: Hodder and Stoughton, 1925).
Dyer, Gary, 'Thieves, Boxers, Sodomites, Poets: Being Flash to Byron's *Don Juan*', *PMLA*, 116, no. 3 (2001), 562–78.
Dyer, Richard, *Stars* (London: British Film Institute, 1998).
Dyson, A., *Pictures to Print, the Nineteenth-Century Engraving Trade* (London: Farrand Press, 1984).
Elfenbein, Andrew, *Byron and the Victorians* (Cambridge: Cambridge University Press, 1995).
Elledge, Paul, 'Chasms in Connections: Byron Ending (in) *Childe Harold's Pilgrimage* 1 and 2', *English Literary History*, 62 (1995), 131–44.
——, *Lord Byron at Harrow School: Speaking out, Talking Back, Acting up, Bowing Out* (Baltimore, MD: Johns Hopkins University Press, 2000).
Elwin, Malcolm, *Lord Byron's Wife* (London: Macdonald, 1962).
——, *Lord Byron's Family: Annabella, Ada and Augusta 1816–1824* (London: John Murray, 1975).
Emerson, Sheila, 'Byron's "One Word": The Language of Self-Expression in *Childe Harold* III', *Studies in Romanticism*, 20, no. 3 (1981), 363–82.
England, A. B., 'Byron's *Don Juan* and the Quest for Deliberate Action', *Keats-Shelley Journal*, 47 (1998), 33–62.
Erdman, David V., 'Byron's Stage Fright: The History of His Ambition and Fear of Writing for the Stage', *English Literary History*, 6 (1939), 219–43.
——, 'Lord Byron and the Genteel Reformers', *PMLA*, 56 (1941), 1065–94.
Erdman, David V., with the assistance of David Worrall, ed., *Childe Harold's Pilgrimage: A Critical, Composite Edition*, Manuscripts of the Younger Romantics (New York and London: Garland, 1991).
Erickson, Lee, *The Economy of Literary Form: English Literature and the Industrialisation of Publishing, 1800–1850* (Baltimore, MD: Johns Hopkins University Press, 1996).
——, '"Unboastful Bard": Originally Anonymous English Romantic Poetry Book Publication, 1770–1835', *New Literary History*, 33 (2002), 247–78.
Ermarth, Elizabeth D., *Realism and Consensus in the English Novel* (Princeton, NJ: Princeton University Press, 1983).
Fish, Stanley, *Is There a Text in This Class? The Authority of Interpretive Communities* (London: Harvard University Press, 1980).
Foucault, Michel, *The Order of Things: An Archaeology of the Human Sciences* (London: Routledge, 1970) Reprint, 1997.
——, *The Birth of the Clinic: An Archaeology of Medical Perception*, trans. by A. M. Sheridan Smith (New York: Vintage Books, 1975).

——, *Power/Knowledge: Selected Interviews and Other Writings 1972–1977*, ed. Colin Gordon (Brighton: Harvester, 1980).
Fox, Sir John C., *The Byron Mystery* (London: Grant Richards, 1924).
Frame, Donald M., *Montaigne's Discovery of Man: The Humanization of a Humanist* (New York: Columbia University Press, 1955).
Francis, Emma, 'Letitia Landon: Public Fantasy and the Private Sphere', *Essays and Studies*, 51 (1998), 93–115.
Franklin, Caroline, *Byron's Heroines* (Oxford: Clarendon Press, 1992).
——, 'Cosmopolitan Masculinity and the British Female Reader of *Childe Harold's Pilgrimage*', in *Lord Byron the European: Essays from the International Byron Society*, ed. Richard A. Cardwell (Lampeter: Edwin Mellen, 1997), pp. 105–25.
——, '"Some Samples of the Finest Orientalism": Byronic Philhellenism and Proto-Zionism at the Time of the Congress of Vienna', in *Romanticism and Colonialism: Writing and Empire*, ed. Tim Fulford and Peter Kitson (Cambridge: Cambridge University Press, 1998), pp. 221–42.
——, *Byron: A Literary Life* (London: Macmillan, 2000).
Frow, John, 'Gift and Commodity', in *Time and Commodity Culture: Essays in Cultural Theory and Postmodernity* (Oxford: Clarendon Press, 1997), pp. 102–217.
Frushell, Richard, *Edmund Spenser in the Early Eighteenth Century: Education, Imitation, and the Making of a Literary Model* (Pittsburgh, PN: Duquesne University Press, 1999).
Fulford, Tim, *Romanticism and Masculinity: Gender, Politics and Poetics in the Writings of Burke, Coleridge, Cobbett, Wordsworth, De Quincey and Hazlitt* (Basingstoke: Macmillan, 1999).
——, 'The Electrifying Mrs Robinson', *Women's Writing*, 9, no. 1 (2002), 23–35.
Gabler, Neal, *Winchell: Gossip, Power, and the Culture of Celebrity* (New York: Knopf, 1994).
Gallagher, Catherine, *Nobody's Story: The Vanishing Acts of Women Writers in the Marketplace, 1670–1820* (Oxford: Clarendon Press, 1994).
Galperin, William H., *The Return of the Visible in British Romanticism* (Baltimore, MD: Johns Hopkins University Press, 1993).
Gamson, Joshua, *Claims to Fame: Celebrity in Contemporary America* (Berkeley: University of California Press, 1994).
Garber, Frederick, *Self, Text, and Romantic Irony: The Example of Byron* (Princeton, NJ: Princeton University Press, 1988).
Garside, Peter, 'The English Novel in the Romantic Era: Consolidation and Dispersal', in *The English Novel 1770–1829, a Bibliographical Survey of Prose Fiction Published in the British Isles*, ed. Peter Garside, James Raven and Rainer Schöwerling, 2 vols (Oxford: Oxford University Press, 2000), 2, pp. 15–103.
Garside, Peter, James Raven and Rainer Schöwerling, eds, *The English Novel 1770–1829, a Bibliographical Survey of Prose Fiction Published in the British Isles*, 2 vols (Oxford: Oxford University Press, 2000).
George, Laura, 'Byron, Brummell and the Fashionable Figure', *The Byron Journal*, 24 (1996), 33–41.
Giddens, Anthony, *Modernity and Self-Identity: Self and Society in the Late Modern Age* (Cambridge: Polity Press, 1991).
Giles, David, *Illusions of Immortality: A Psychology of Fame and Celebrity* (London: Macmillan, 2000).
Giuliano, Cheryl F., 'Marginal Discourse: The Authority of Gossip in *Beppo*', in *Rereading Byron: Essays Selected from Hofstra University's Byron Bicentennial*

Conference, ed. Alice Levine and Robert N. Keane (New York: Garland, 1993), pp. 151–63.

Glass, Loren, 'Blood and Affection: The Poetics of Incest in *Manfred* and *Parisina*', *Studies in Romanticism*, 34 (1995), 211–26.

Gleckner, Robert F., *Byron and the Ruins of Paradise* (Baltimore, MD: Johns Hopkins University Press, 1967) Reprint, Westport, CT: Greenwood Press,1980.

Gledhill, Christine, ed., *Stardom: Industry of Desire* (London: Routledge, 1991).

Goldberg, Leonard S., 'Centre and Circumference in Byron's *Lara*', *Studies in English Literature*, 26, no. 4 (1986), 655–73.

Goode, Clement T., 'A Critical Review of Research', in *George Gordon, Lord Byron: A Comprehensive Bibliography of Secondary Materials in English, 1807–1974*, ed. Oscar José Santucho (Metuchen, NJ: The Scarecrow Press, 1977), pp. 3–166.

Goode, Clement T., *George Gordon, Lord Byron: A Comprehensive, Annotated Research Bibliography of Secondary Materials in English, 1973–1994* (Lanham, MD: Scarecrow Press, 1997).

Graham, Peter, ed., *Byron's Bulldog: The Letters of John Cam Hobhouse to Lord Byron* (Columbus, OH: Ohio State University Press, 1984).

——, *Don Juan and Regency England* (Charlottesville: University Press of Virginia, 1990).

——, 'The Order and Disorder of Eating in Byron's *Don Juan*', in *Disorderly Eaters: Texts in Self-Empowerment*, ed. Lilian R. Furst and Peter Graham (University Park, PA: Pennsylvania State University Press, 1992), pp. 113–23.

Granger, James, *A Biographical History of England, from Egbert the Great to the Revolution: Consisting of Characters Disposed in Different Classes, and Adapted to a Methodical Catalogue of Engraved British Heads: Intended as an Essay Towards Reducing Our Biography to System, and a Help to the Knowledge of Portraits: Interspersed with Variety of Anecdotes, and Memoirs of a Great Number of Persons, Not to Be Found in Any Other Biographical Work: With a Preface, Shewing the Utility of a Collection of Engraved Portraits to Supply the Defect, and Answer the Various Purposes of Medals*, 3rd ed. (London: J. Rivington and Sons, B. Law, J. Robson, G. Robinson, T. Cadell, T. Evans, R. Baldwin, J. Nicholl, W. Oteridge, and Fielding and Walker, 1779).

Gross, Jonathan David, ed., *Byron's "Corbeau Blanc": The Life and Letters of Lady Melbourne* (Liverpool: Liverpool University Press, 1997).

——, *Byron: The Erotic Liberal* (Lanham, MD: Rowman & Littlefield, 2001).

Gubar, Susan and Sandra M. Gilbert, *The Madwoman in the Attic: The Woman Writer and the Nineteenth-Century Literary Imagination* (New Haven, CT: Yale University Press, 1979).

Habermas, Jürgen, *The Structural Tranformation of the Public Sphere: An Inquiry into a Category of Bourgeois Society*, trans. by Thomas Burger, with the assistance of Frederick Lawrence (Cambridge: Polity Press, 1989).

Haefner, Joel, ' "The Soul Speaking in the Face": Hazlitt's Concept of Character', *Studies in English Literature*, 24, no. 4 (1984), 655–70.

Hagelman, Charles W. and Robert J. Barnes, eds, *A Concordance to Byron's Don Juan* (Ithaca, NY: Cornell University Press, 1967).

Hall, Jean, 'The Evolution of the Surface Self: Byron's Poetic Career', *Keats-Shelley Journal*, 36 (1987), 134–57.

Harris, Cheryl and Alison Alexander, eds, *Theorizing Fandom: Fans, Subculture and Identity* (Cresskill, NJ: Hampton Press, 1998).

Haslett, Moyra, *Byron's Don Juan and the Don Juan Legend* (Oxford: Clarendon Press, 1997).

Hawkins, Laetitia-Matilda, *Memoirs, Anecdotes, Facts, and Opinions*, 2 vols (London: Longman, Hurst, Rees, Orme, Brown, and Green; and C. & J. Rivington, 1824).

Hazlitt, William, *The Complete Works of William Hazlitt*, 21 vols, ed. P. P. Howe (London and Toronto: J. M. Dent and Sons, 1930).

Henderson, Andrea K., *Romantic Identities: Varieties of Subjectivity, 1774–1830* (Cambridge: Cambridge University Press, 1996).

Higashinaka, Itsuyo, 'Byron and William Gifford', *The Byron Journal*, 30 (2002), 21–8.

Higgins, David, *Romantic Genius and the Literary Magazine: Biography, Celebrity, Politics* Routledge Studies in Romanticism (London: Routledge, 2005).

Hillis Miller, J., 'Narrative', in *Critical Terms for Literary Study*, ed. Frank Lentricchia and Thomas McLaughlin (Chicago: The University of Chicago Press, 1990), pp. 66–79.

Hirst, Wolf, ed., *Byron, the Bible and Religion: Essays from the Twelfth International Byron Seminar* (Newark, DE: University of Delaware Press, London and Toronto: Associated University Presses, 1991).

Hoagwood, Terence A., *Byron's Dialectic: Skepticism and the Critique of Culture* (Lewisburg, PA: Bucknell University Press, 1993).

Hobhouse, John C., *Imitations and Translations from the Ancient and Modern Classics, Together with Original Poems Never before Published* (London: Longman, 1809).

——, *Remarks on the Exclusion of Lord Byron's Monument from Westminster Abbey* (London: The Author, 1844).

Hobsbawm, E. J., 'The Machine Breakers', in *Labouring Men: Studies in the History of Labour* (London: Weidenfeld and Nicolson, 1964), pp. 5–22.

Hodgson, Francis, *Sir Edgar*, ed. Donald Reiman (New York: Garland, 1977).

Hoffmann, George, *Montaigne's Career* (Oxford: Clarendon Press, 1998).

Hofkosh, Sonia, *Sexual Politics and the Romantic Author* (Cambridge: Cambridge University Press, 1998).

Horace, *Satires, Epistles and Ars Poetica* Loeb Classical Library, ed. H. Rushton Fairclough (London: Heinemann, 1926).

Horton, D. and R. R. Wohl, 'Mass Communication and Parasocial Interaction', *Psychiatry*, 19 (1956), 215–29.

Howell, Margaret J., *Byron Tonight: A Poet's Plays on the Nineteenth Century Stage* (Windlesham: Springwood Books, 1982).

Howes, Alan B., ed., *Sterne: The Critical Heritage* (London: Routledge and Kegan Paul, 1974).

Hyman, Suzanne K., 'Contemporary Portraits of Byron', in *Lord Byron and His Contemporaries: Essays from the Sixth International Byron Seminar*, ed. Charles E. Robinson (Newark, DE: University of Delaware Press, 1982), pp. 204–36.

Ingersoll, Earl, 'Byron's *Don Juan* and the Postmodern', *Forum for Modern Language Studies*, 33 (1997), 302–14.

Iser, Wolfgang, 'Interaction between Text and Reader', in *Readers and Reading*, ed. Andrew Bennett (London: Longman, 1995), pp. 20–31.

Jackson, J. R. de J., *Annals of English Verse, 1770–1835: A Preliminary Survey of the Volumes Published* (New York: Garland, 1985).

——, *Romantic Poetry by Women: A Bibliography, 1770–1835* (Oxford: Clarendon Press, 1993).

Jewsbury, Maria J., *Phantasmagoria: Or, Sketches of Life and Literature*, 2 vols (London: Hurst, Robinson and Co., 1825).
Johnson, Samuel, *The Rambler*, ed. Alex Chalmers, 4 vols (Philadelphia PA: E. Earle, 1812), IV, 42.
Johnson, Samuel, *Letters of Samuel Johnson Ll.D.*, 2 vols, ed. George Birbeck Hill (Oxford: Clarendon Press, 1892).
Jordan, John O. and Robert L. Patten, eds, *Literature in the Marketplace: Nineteenth-Century British Publishing and Reading Practices* (Cambridge: Cambridge University Press, 1995).
Joseph, M. K., *Byron the Poet* (London: Victor Gollancz, 1964).
Kelly, Ian, *Cooking for Kings: The Life of Antonin Careme, the First Celebrity Chef* (London: Walker, 2004).
Kelsall, Malcolm, *Byron's Politics* (Brighton: Harvester, 1987).
Kenyon Jones, Christine, '"Man Is a Carnivorous Production": Byron and the Anthropology of Food', *Prism(s): Essays in Romanticism*, 6 (1998), 41–58.
——, 'Fantasy and Transfiguration: Byron and His Portraits', in *Byromania: Portraits of the Artist in Nineteenth- and Twentieth-Century Culture*, ed. Frances Wilson (London: Macmillan, 1999), pp. 109–36.
——, '"I Wonder If His Appetite Was Good?": Byron, Food and Culture: East, West, North and South', in *Byron: East and West*, ed. Martin Procházka (Prague: Charles University Press, 2000), pp. 249–62.
——, ed., *Byron: The Image of the Poet* (Newark, DE: University of Delaware Press, 2007).
Kermode, Frank, *The Sense of an Ending: Studies in the Theory of Fiction* (Oxford: Oxford University Press, 1967).
Kernan, Alvin B., *The Plot of Satire* (New Haven, CT: Yale University Press, 1965).
Kirkland, Richard I., 'Byron's Reading of Montaigne: A Leigh Hunt Letter', *Keats-Shelley Journal*, 30 (1981), 47–51.
Kucich, Greg, *Keats, Shelley and Romantic Spenserianism* (University Park, PA: Pennsylvania State University Press, 1991).
Labbe, Jacqueline M., 'Selling One's Sorrows: Charlotte Smith, Mary Robinson, and the Marketing of Poetry', *The Wordsworth Circle*, 25, no. 2 (1994), 68–71.
——, 'Mary Robinson', *Women' s Writing*, 9, no. 1 (2002), 3–15.
Landon, Letitia E., 'On the Character of Mrs Hemans's Writings', *New Monthly Magazine*, 44 (1835), 425–33.
——, *Selected Writings*, eds. Daniel Riess and Jerome McGann (Peterborough, ON: Broadview, 1997).
Leask, Nigel, *British Romantic Writers and the East: Anxieties of Empire* (Cambridge: Cambridge University Press, 1992).
Lebrun, Charles, *A Method to Learn to Design the Passions*, trans. by John Williams, Augustan Reprint Society, Introduction by Alan T. Mackenzie (Los Angeles: William Andrews Clark Memorial Library, University of California, 1980).
Lee, Debbie, 'The Wild Wreath: Cultivating a Poetic Circle for Mary Robinson', *Studies in the Literary Imagination*, 30, no. 1 (1997), 23–34.
Legge, R. H., 'Nathan, Isaac (1790–1864)', rev. David J. Golby, *Oxford Dictionary of National Biography* (Oxford: Oxford University Press, 2004) [http://www.oxforddnb.com/view/article/19808, accessed 10 April 2007].
Levine, Alice and Robert N. Keane, eds., *Rereading Byron: Essays Selected from Hofstra University's Byron Bicentennial Conference* (New York: Garland, 1993).

Levinson, Marjorie, *The Romantic Fragment Poem: A Critique of a Form* (Chapel Hill: University of North Carolina Press, 1986).

Lew, Joseph, 'The Necessary Orientalist? *The Giaour* and Nineteenth-Century Imperialist Misogyny', in *Romanticism, Race and Imperial Culture*, ed. Alan Richardson and Sonia Hofkosh (Bloomington: Indiana University Press, 1996), pp. 173–202.

Lewis, L., ed., *The Adoring Audience: Fan Culture and Popular Media* (London: Routledge, 1992).

Little, David M. and George M. Kahrl, eds, *The Letters of David Garrick*, 3 vols (London: Oxford University Press, 1963).

Lovelace, Ralph Milbanke Earl of Lovelace, *Astarte: A Fragment of Truth Concerning George Gordon Byron, Sixth Lord Byron* (London: For the Author, 1905) Reprint, ed. Mary Countess of Lovelace, London: Christophers, 1921.

Lovell, Ernest J., ed., *His Very Self and Voice: Collected Conversations of Lord Byron* (New York: Macmillan, 1954).

Luckhurst, Mary and Jane Moody, eds., *Theatre and Celebrity in Britain, 1660–2000* (Basingstoke: Palgrave Macmillan, 2005).

Luther, Susan, 'A Stranger Minstrel: Coleridge's Mrs. Robinson', *Studies in Romanticism*, 33, no. 3 (1994), 391–409.

Lynch, Deidre, *The Economy of Character: Novels, Market Culture, and the Business of Inner Meaning* (Chicago: University of Chicago Press, 1998).

Lyotard, Jean-François, *Libidinal Economy*, trans. by Iain Hamilton Grant (London: The Athlone Press, 1993).

MacCarthy, Fiona, *Byron: Life and Legend* (London: John Murray, 2002).

MacIntyre, Alasdair, *After Virtue: A Study in Moral Theory*, 2nd ed. (London: Duckworth, 1985).

Maltby, Richard, *Hollywood Cinema* (Oxford: Blackwell, 1995).

Manning, Peter J., *Byron and His Fictions* (Detroit, MI: Wayne State University Press, 1978).

——, '*Childe Harold* in the Marketplace: From Romaunt to Handbook', *Modern Language Quarterly*, no. 52 (1991), 170–90.

——, '*Don Juan* and the Revisionary Self', in *Romantic Revisions*, ed. Keith Hanley and Robert Brinkley (Cambridge: Cambridge University Press, 1992), pp. 210–26.

Marchand, Leslie A., *Byron: A Biography*, 3 vols (London: John Murray, 1957).

Marchi, Dudley M., *Montaigne among the Moderns: Receptions of the Essais* (Providence, RI: Berghahn Books, 1994).

Marshall, L. E., '"Words Are Things": Byron and the Prophetic Efficacy of Language', *Studies in English Literature*, 25, no. 4 (1985), 801–22.

Marshall, P. David, *Celebrity and Power: Fame in Contemporary Culture* (Minneapolis: University of Minnesota Press, 1997).

Martin, Philip W., *Byron: A Poet before His Public* (Cambridge: Cambridge University Press, 1982).

——, 'Reading *Don Juan* with Bakhtin', in *Don Juan*, ed. Nigel Wood (Buckingham: Open University Press, 1993), pp. 90–121.

Mason, Nicholas, 'Building Brand Byron: Early-Nineteenth-Century Advertising and the Marketing of *Childe Harold's Pilgrimage*', *Modern Language Quarterly*, 63 (2002), 411–41.

Mauss, Marcel, *The Gift: The Form and Reason for Exchange in Archaic Societies*, trans. by W. D. Halls (New York: Norton, 1990).

McCalman, Iain, ed., *An Oxford Companion to the Romantic Age: British Culture 1776–1832* (Oxford: Oxford University Press, 1999).

McDayter, Ghislaine, 'Conjuring Byron: Byromania, Literary Commodification and the Birth of Celebrity', in *Byromania: Portraits of the Artist in Nineteenth- and Twentieth-Century Culture*, ed. Frances Wilson (London: Macmillan, 1999), pp. 43–62.

McDonald, Paul, *The Star System: Hollywood's Production of Popular Identities* (London: Wallflower, 2000).

McGann, Jerome J., *Fiery Dust: Byron's Poetic Development* (Chicago: University of Chicago Press, 1968).

——, *Don Juan in Context* (London: John Murray, 1976).

——, *The Romantic Ideology: A Critical Investigation* (Chicago: University of Chicago Press, 1983).

——, *The Poetics of Sensibility: A Revolution in Literary Style* (Oxford: Clarendon Press, 1996).

——, *The Beauty of Inflections: Literary Investigations in Historical Method and Theory* (Oxford: Clarendon Press, 1998).

——, *Byron and Romanticism*, ed. James Soderholm (Cambridge: Cambridge University Press, 2002).

McKendrick, Neil, John Brewer and J. H. Plumb, *The Birth of a Consumer Society: The Commercialization of Eighteenth-Century England* (London: Europa, 1982).

McPherson, Heather, 'Picturing Tragedy: *Mrs Siddons as the Tragic Muse* Revisited', *Eighteenth-Century Studies*, 33, no. 3 (2000), 401–30.

Medwin, Thomas, *Conversations of Lord Byron*, ed. Ernest J. Lovell (Princeton, NJ: Princeton University Press, 1966).

Mellor, Anne K., 'Making an Exhibition of Her Self: Mary "Perdita" Robinson and Nineteenth-Century Scripts of Female Sexuality', *Nineteenth-Century Contexts*, 22, no. 3 (2000), 271–304.

——, *Mothers of the Nation: Women's Political Writing in England 1780–1830* (Bloomington, IA: Indiana University Press, 2002).

Michasiw, Kim I., 'The Social Other: *Don Juan* and the Genesis of the Self', *Mosaic*, 22, no. 2 (1989), 29–48.

Miller, John, 'Songs of the Labour Movement', in *The Luddites and Other Essays*, ed. Lionel M. Munby (London: Michael Katanka, 1971), pp. 115–42.

Mitchell, W. J. T., ed., *The Language of Images* (Chicago: The University of Chicago Press, 1974).

Mole, Tom, 'Narrative Desire and the Body in *the Giaour*', in *Byron: A Poet for All Seasons*, ed. M. B. Raizis (Messolonghi: Messolonghi Byron Society, 2000), pp. 90–7.

——, 'Byron, Westall, Asperne, Blood: An Early Engraved Portrait', *The Byron Journal*, 29 (2001), 98–102.

——, 'The Handling of *Hebrew Melodies*', *Romanticism*, 8, no. 1 (2002), 18–33.

——, 'Byron's "An Ode to the Framers of the Frame Bill": The Embarrassment of Industrial Publishing', *The Keats-Shelley Journal*, 52 (2003), 97–115.

——, ed., *Blackwood's Magazine, 1817–25: Selections from Maga's Infancy*, gen. ed. Nicholas Mason, Vol. 5: *Selected Criticism, 1817–19*, 6 vols (London: Pickering & Chatto, 2006).

——, '"Nourished by That Abstinence": Consumption and Control in *The Corsair*', *Romanticism*, 12, no. 1 (2006), 26–34.

——, 'Impresarios of Byron's Afterlife', *Nineteenth-Century Contexts*, 29, no. 1 (2007), 17–34.

Monaco, James, ed., *Celebrity: The Media as Image Makers* (New York: Delta Books, 1978).

Montagu, Jennifer, *The Expression of the Passions: The Origins and Influence of Charles Le Brun's "Conférence Sur L'expression Générale Et Particulière"* (New Haven, CT: Yale University Press, 1994).
Montaigne, Michel de, *The Essays of Michael De Montaigne: Translated into English with Very Considerable Amendments and Improvements from the Most Accurate French Edition of Peter Coste*, trans. by Charles Cotton, 3 vols, 9th ed. (London: W. Miller [et al.], 1811).
Moore, Doris L., *The Late Lord Byron* (London: John Murray, 1961).
——, *Lord Byron: Accounts Rendered* (London: John Murray, 1974).
Moore, Thomas, *The Poetical Works*, 10 vols (London: Longman, Orme, Brown, Green, & Longmans, 1840–1841).
Moran, James, *Printing Presses: History and Development from the 15th Century to Modern Times* (Berkeley: University of California Press, 1973).
Moran, Joe, *Star Authors: Literary Celebrity in America* (London: Pluto Press, 2000).
Morison, Stanley, *The English Newspaper* (Cambridge: Cambridge University Press, 1932).
Mozer, Hadley J., '"I Want a Hero": Advertising for an Epic Hero in *Don Juan*', *Studies in Romanticism*, 44, no. 2 (2005), 239–60.
Mulock Craik, D., *The Ogilvies* (New York and London: Harper and Brothers, 1878).
Mulvey, Laura, 'Visual Pleasure and Narrative Cinema', *Screen*, 16, no. 3 (1975), 6–18.
Murphy, Peter T., 'Impersonation and Authorship in Romantic Britain', *ELH*, 59 (1992), 625–49.
Murray, Venetia, *High Society in the Regency Period: 1788–1830* (London: Penguin, 1999).
Nevett, Terry, 'Advertising and Editorial Integrity in the Nineteenth Century', in *The Press in English Society from the Seventeenth to the Nineteenth Centuries*, ed. Michael Harris and Alan Lee (Cranbury, NJ: Associated University Presses, 1986), pp. 149–67.
Newbury, Michael, 'Celebrity Watching', *American Literary History*, 12, no. 1–2 (2000), 272–83.
Newlyn, Lucy, *Reading, Writing and Romanticism: The Anxiety of Reception* (Oxford: Oxford University Press, 2000).
Nicoll, Allardyce and Sybil Rosenfeld, *The Garrick Stage: Theatres and Audience in the Eighteenth Century* (Manchester: Manchester University Press, 1980).
Nuttall, A. D., *Openings: Narrative Beginnings from the Epic to the Novel* (Oxford: Clarendon Press, 1992).
Ockman, Carol, Kenneth E. Silver, Janis Bergman-Carton and Karen Levitov, *Sarah Bernhardt: The Art of High Drama* (New Haven, CT: Yale University Press, 2005).
O'Donoghue, Freeman, *Catalogue of Engraved British Portraits Preserved in the Department of Prints and Drawings in the British Museum*, 6 vols (London: British Museum, 1908).
Ogle, Robert B., 'The Metamorphosis of Selim: Ovidian Myth in *The Bride of Abydos* II', *Studies in Romanticism*, 20, no. 1 (1981), 21–31.
Oliver, Susan, *Scott, Byron and the Poetics of Cultural Encounter* (Basingstoke and New York: Palgrave Macmillan, 2005).
Pascoe, Judith, *Romantic Theatricality: Gender, Poetry, and Spectatorship* (Ithaca, NY: Cornell University Press, 1997).

Paterson, Wilma, *Lord Byron's Relish: The Regency Cookbook* (Glasgow: Dog & Bone, 1990).

Peach, Annette, 'Byron and Romantic Portrayal', in *Lord Byron: A Multidisciplinary Open Forum*, ed. Therese Tessier (Paris: The Byron Society, 1999), pp. 193–203.

——, 'Portraits of Byron', *The Walpole Society*, 62 (2000), 1–144.

Peteinaris, Petros, 'The Bey Apologises', *Newstead Abbey Byron Society Review* (July 2000), 13–19.

Phillips, Olga S., *Isaac Nathan: Friend of Byron* (London: Minerva, 1940).

Piper, David, *The Image of the Poet: British Poets and Their Portraits* (Oxford: Clarendon Press, 1982).

Playfair, Giles, *Kean: The Life and Paradox of the Great Actor* (London: Reinhardt & Evans, 1950).

Ponce de Leon, Charles L., *Self-Exposure: Human Interest Journalism and the Emergence of Celebrity in America, 1890–1940* (Chapel Hill and London: University of North Carolina Press, 2002).

Pont, Graham, 'Byron and Nathan: A Musical Collaboration', *The Byron Journal*, 27 (1999), 51–65.

Poole, Roger, 'What Constitutes, and What Is External to, The "Real" *Childe Harold's Pilgrimage, a Romaunt: And Other Poems* (1812)?', in *Lord Byron the European: Essays from the International Byron Society*, ed. Richard A. Cardwell (Lampeter: Edwin Mellen, 1997), pp. 149–207.

Pope, Alexander, *The Twickenham Edition of the Poems of Alexander Pope*, Vol. 3 (i) *An Essay on Man* ed. Maynard Mack (1950), 11 vols, gen. ed. John Butt (London: Methuen, 1939–1969).

Porter, Roy, ed., *Rewriting the Self: Histories from the Renaissance to the Present* (London: Routledge, 1997).

Postle, Martin, ed., *Joshua Reynolds: The Creation of Celebrity* (London: Tate, 2005).

Quennell, Peter, *Byron: The Years of Fame* (London: The Reprint Society, 1943).

Quennell, Peter and George Paston, *To Lord Byron: Feminine Profiles Based on Unpublished Letters 1807–1824* (London: John Murray, 1939).

Radcliffe, David H., *Edmund Spenser: A Reception History* (Columbia, SC: Camden House, 1996).

Raven, James, *Judging New Wealth: Popular Publishing and Responses to Commerce in England, 1750–1800* (Oxford: Clarendon Press, 1992).

——, 'The Anonymous Novel in Britain and Ireland, 1750–1830', in *The Faces of Anonymity: Anonymous and Pseudonymous Publication from the Sixteenth to the Twentieth Century*, ed. Robert J. Griffin (London: Palgrave Macmillan, 2003), pp. 141–66.

Raymond, D. N., *The Political Career of Lord Byron* (New York: Henry Holt, 1924).

Redpath, Theodore, *The Young Romantics and Critical Opinion 1807–1824* (London: Harrap, 1973).

Regosin, Richard L., *The Matter of My Book: Montaigne's 'Essais' as the Book of the Self* (Berkeley and London: University of California Press, 1977).

Reiman, Donald, ed., *The Romantics Reviewed Part B*, 5 vols (London: Garland, 1972).

Reynolds, John Hamilton, 'Popular Poetry', in *Selected Prose of John Hamilton Reynolds*, ed. Leonidas M. Jones (Cambridge, MA: Harvard University Press, 1966), pp. 70–6.

Ridenour, George, *The Style of Don Juan* (New Haven, CT: Yale University Press, 1960).

Rider, Frederick, *The Dialectic of Selfhood in Montaigne* (Stanford, CA: Stanford University Press, 1973).
Robbins, Bruce, ed., *The Phantom Public Sphere* (Minneapolis: University of Minnesota Press, 1993).
Robinson, Charles E., *Shelley and Byron: The Snake and Eagle Wreathed in Fight* (Baltimore, MD: Johns Hopkins University Press, 1976).
Robinson, Mary D., *Sappho and Phaon* (London: Hookham and Carpenter, 1796).
——, *Perdita: The Memoirs of Mary Robinson*, ed. M. J. Levy (London: Peter Owen, 1994).
——, *Selected Poems*, ed. Judith Pascoe (Peterborough, ON: Broadview, 2000).
——, *A Letter to the Women of England, on the Injustice of Mental Subordination* accessed 5 January 2004; available from http://www.rc.umd.edu/editions/contemps/robinson/cover.htm.
Roby, John, *The Duke of Mantua* (London: Thomas Davison, 1823).
Rojek, Chris, *Celebrity* (London: Reaktion, 2001).
Roper, Derek, *Reviewing before the Edinburgh: 1788–1802* (London: Methuen, 1978).
Rose, Jacqueline, 'The Cult of Celebrity', *London Review of Books*, 20, no. 16 (1998) accessed 26 April 2007; available from http://www.lrb.co.uk/v20/n16/rose01_.html.
Rose, Mark, *Authors and Owners: The Invention of Copyright* (Cambridge, MA: Harvard University Press, 1993).
Ross, Ian Campbell, *Laurence Sterne: A Life* (Oxford: Oxford University Press, 2002).
Rothenstein, Julian and Mel Gooding, eds, *The Playful Eye: An Album of Visual Delight* (London: Redstone, 1999).
Rousseau, Jean-Jacques, *The Confessions*, trans. by Christopher Kelly, Vol. 5 The Collected Writings of Rousseau, eds Christopher Kelly, Roger D. Masters and Peter G. Stillman (Hanover, NH: University Press of New England, 1995).
Rutherford, Andrew, ed., *Byron: The Critical Heritage* (London: Routledge, 1970).
——, ed., *Byron: Augustan and Romantic* (London: Macmillan in association with the British Council, 1990).
Said, Edward W., *Beginnings: Intention and Method* (London: Granta Books, 1997).
Salmon, Richard, 'Signs of Intimacy: The Literary Celebrity in The "Age of Interviewing" ', *Victorian Literature and Culture*, 25, no. 1 (1997), 159–77.
Sambrook, James, *James Thomson 1700–1748: A Life* (Oxford: Clarendon Press, 1991).
——, 'Roby, John (1793–1850)', *Oxford Dictionary of National Biography* (Oxford: Oxford University Press, 2004) [http://www.oxforddnb.com/view/article/23904, accessed 10 April 2007].
Santucho, Oscar J., *George Gordon, Lord Byron: A Comprehensive Bibliography of Secondary Materials in English, 1807–1974*. The Scarecrow Author Bibliographies (Metuchen, NJ: The Scarecrow Press, 1977).
Schickel, Richard, *Intimate Strangers: The Culture of Celebrity* (New York: Doubleday, 1985) Reprint, Chicago: Ivan R. Dee, 2000.
Seed, David, ' "Disjointed Fragments": Concealment and Revelation in *The Giaour*', *The Byron Journal*, 18 (1990), 14–27.
Sennett, Richard, *The Fall of Public Man* (London: Faber and Faber, 1986).
Setzer, Sharon, 'Mary Robinson's Sylphid Self: The End of Feminine Self-Fashioning', *Philological Quarterly*, 75, no. 4 (1996), 501–20.
Shaddy, Robert A., 'Grangerizing: "One of the Unfortunate Stages of Bibliomania" ', *Book Collector*, 49, no. 4 (2000), 535–46.

Shilstone, Frederick W., *Byron and the Myth of Tradition* (Lincoln: University of Nebraska Press, 1988).

Shookman, Ellis, 'Pseudo-Science, Social Fad, Literary Wonder: Johann Caspar Lavater and the Art of Physiognomy', in *The Faces of Physiognomy: Interdisciplinary Approaches to Johann Caspar Lavater*, ed. Ellis Shookman (Columbia, SC: Camden House, 1993), pp. 1–24.

Shumway, David R., 'The Star System in Literary Studies', *PMLA*, 112, no. 1 (1997), 85–100.

——, 'The Star System Revisited', *Minnesota Review: A Journal of Committed Writing*, no. 52–4 (2001), 175–84.

Sinclair, Sir John, *The Code of Health and Longevity*, 4 vols (Edinburgh, 1807).

Siskin, Clifford, *The Historicity of Romantic Discourse* (Oxford: Oxford University Press, 1988).

——, *The Work of Writing: Literature and Social Change in Britain, 1700–1830* (Baltimore, MD: Johns Hopkins University Press, 1998).

Slater, Joseph, 'Byron's *Hebrew Melodies*', *Studies in Philology*, 49 (1952), 75–94.

Smiles, Samuel, *A Publisher and His Friends: Memoir and Correspondence of the Late John Murray, with an Account of the Origin and Progress of the House, 1768–1843*, 2 vols (London: John Murray, 1891).

Soderholm, James, *Fantasy, Forgery and the Byron Legend* (Lexington: The University Press of Kentucky, 1996).

Solly, Edward, 'Indexes of Portraits in the *European Magazine, London Magazine* and *Register of the Times*', in *Report of the First Annual Meeting of the Index Society* (London: Longmans, Green and Co., 1879), pp. 73–95.

Southey, Charles C., ed., *The Life and Correspondence of Robert Southey*, 6 vols (London: Longman, Brown, Green and Longmans, 1849–1850).

St Clair, William, 'The Impact of Byron's Writings: An Evaluative Approach', in *Byron: Augustan and Romantic*, ed. Andrew Rutherford (London: Macmillan, 1990), pp. 1–25.

——, *The Reading Nation in the Romantic Period* (Cambridge: Cambridge University Press, 2004).

Stabler, Jane, *Byron, Poetics and History* (Cambridge: Cambridge University Press, 2002).

——, 'Byron's World of Zest', in *Cultures of Taste/Theories of Appetite: Eating Romanticism*, ed. Timothy Morton (Basingstoke: Palgrave Macmillan, 2004), pp. 141–60.

Staiger, Janet, 'Seeing Stars', in *Stardom: Industry of Desire*, ed. Christine Gledhill (London: Routledge, 1991), pp. 3–16.

Stark, William, *The Works of the Late William Stark [. . .] with Experiments, Dietetical and Statical* (London, 1788).

Stephens, F. G. and Mary Dorothy George, *Catalogue of Political and Personal Satires Preserved in the Department of Prints and Drawings in the British Museum*, Vol. IX, 11 vols (London: British Museum, 1978).

Stephenson, Glennis, 'Letitia Landon and the Victorian Improvisatrice: The Construction of L. E. L.' *Victorian Poetry*, 30, no. 1 (1992), 1–17.

Stillinger, Jack, *Coleridge and Textual Instability: The Multiple Versions of the Major Poems* (New York: Oxford University Press, 1994).

Stone, George Winchester and George M. Kahrl, *David Garrick: A Critical Biography* (Carbondale, IL: Southern Illinois University Press, 1979).

Stone, Lawrence, *Road to Divorce: England 1530–1987* (Oxford: Oxford University Press, 1992).
Storey, Mark, *Byron and the Eye of Appetite* (New York: St. Martin's Press, 1986).
Straub, Kristina, *Sexual Suspects: Eighteenth-Century Players and Sexual Ideology* (Princeton, NJ: Princeton University Press, 1992).
Strawson, Galen, 'Against Narrativity', *Ratio*, 22 (n.s.), no. 4 (2004), 428–52.
Strout, Alan Lang, ed., *John Bull's Letter to Lord Byron* (Norman: University of Oklahoma Press, 1947).
Taylor, Charles, *Sources of the Self: The Making of the Modern Identity* (Cambridge, MA: Harvard University Press, 1989).
Taylor, Desmond Shawe and Rosie Broadley, *Every Look Speaks: Portraits of David Garrick. An Exhibition at the Holburne Museum of Art, Bath* (Bath: Holburne Museum of Art, 2003).
Thomas, Gordon K., 'The Forging of an Enthusiasm: Byron and the *Hebrew Melodies*', *Neophilologus*, 75, no. 4 (1991), 626–36.
——, 'Finest Orientalism, Western Sentimentalism, Proto-Zionism: The Muses of Byron's *Hebrew Melodies*', *Prism(s): Essays in Romanticism*, 1 (1993), 51–66.
Thomis, Malcolm I., *The Luddites: Machine-Breaking in Regency England* (Newton Abbot: David & Charles, 1970).
——, ed., *Luddism in Nottinghamshire* (London: Phillimore, 1972).
Thompson, E. P., *The Making of the English Working Class* (London: Penguin, 1965).
Thompson, Flora, *Larkrise to Candleford* (Oxford: Oxford University Press, 1945).
Thomson, James, *Liberty, the Castle of Indolence, and Other Poems*, ed. James Sambrook (Oxford: Clarendon Press, 1986).
Thorslev, Peter L., *The Byronic Hero: Types and Prototypes* (Minneapolis: University of Minnesota Press, 1962).
Throsby, Corin, 'Flirting with Fame: Byron's Anonymous Female Fans', *The Byron Journal*, 32 (2004), 115–23.
Tomlins, Thomas E., *The Law Dictionary (with Additions by Thomas Colpitts Granger)*, 2 vols (London: J. and W. T. Clarke et al., 1835).
Tosh, John, 'The Old Adam and the New Man: Emerging Themes in the History of English Masculinities, 1750–1850', in *English Masculinities 1660–1800*, ed. Tim Hitchcock and Michèle Cohen (London: Longman, 1999), pp. 217–38.
Tournon, André, 'Self-Interpretation in Montaigne's *Essais*', *Yale French Studies*, 64 Montaigne: *Essays* in Reading (1983), 51–72.
Trelawney, E. J., *Recollections of the Last Days of Shelley and Byron* (Williamstown, MA: Corner House, 1858) Reprint, 1975.
Trilling, Lionel, *Sincerity and Authenticity* (Oxford: Oxford University Press, 1971).
Trueblood, Paul Graham, ed., *Byron's Political and Cultural Influence in Nineteenth-Century Europe: A Symposium* (London: MacMillan, 1981).
Turner, Charles T., *Sonnets* (London: MacMillan, 1864).
Turner, Graeme, *Understanding Celebrity* (London: Sage, 2004).
Tytler, Graeme, 'Lavater and Physiognomy in English Fiction 1790–1832', *Eighteenth-Century Fiction*, 7, no. 3 (1995), 293–310.
Vail, Jeffrey W., *The Literary Relationship of Lord Byron and Thomas Moore* (Baltimore, MD: Johns Hopkins University Press, 2001).
Vargo, Lisa, 'Tabitha Bramble and the Lyrical Tales', *Women' s Writing*, 9, no. 1 (2002), 37–52.

Veylit, Alain, *Some Statistics on the Number of Surviving Printed Titles for Great Britain and Dependencies from the Beginnings of Print in England to the Year 1800* English Short Title Catalogue Website, accessed 16 October 2003; available from http://www.cbsr.ucr.edu/ESTCStatistics.html.

Vicario, Michael, 'The Implications of Form in *Childe Harold's Pilgrimage*', *Keats-Shelley Journal*, 33 (1984), 103–29.

Wadd, William, *Cursory Remarks on Corpulence* (London: J and W Smith, for J Callow, Medical Bookseller, 1810).

Waddams, S. M., *Law, Politics and the Church of England: The Career of Stephen Lushington 1782–1873* (Cambridge: Cambridge University Press, 1992).

Wahrman, Dror, *The Making of the Modern Self: Identity and Culture in Eighteenth-Century England* (New Haven, CT: Yale University Press, 2004).

Waldron, Mary, *Lactilla, Milkwoman of Clifton: The Life and Writings of Ann Yearsley* (Athens: The University of Georgia Press, 1996).

——, '"This Muse-Born Wonder", the Occluded Voice of Ann Yearsley, Milk-woman and Poet of Clifton', in *Women's Poetry in the Enlightenment: The Making of a Canon, 1730–1820*, ed. Isobel Armstrong and Virginia Blain (London: Macmillan, 1999), pp. 113–26.

Walker, Alexander, *Stardom: The Hollywood Phenomenon* (London: Michael Joseph, 1970).

Walker, Richard, *Regency Portraits*, 2 vols (London: National Portrait Gallery, 1985).

Wanko, Cheryl, *Roles of Authority: Thespian Biography and Celebrity in Eighteenth-Century Britain* (Lubbock, TX: Texas Tech University Press, 2003).

Ward, Aileen, '"That Last Infirmity of Noble Mind": Keats and the Idea of Fame', in *The Evidence of Imagination: Studies of Interactions between Life and Art in English Romantic Literature*, ed. Donald H. Reiman, Michael C. Jaye and Betty T. Bennett (New York: New York University Press, 1978), pp. 312–33.

Watkins, Daniel P., *Social Relations in Byron's Eastern Tales* (Rutherford, NJ: Fairleigh Dickinson University Press, 1987).

Watson, Nicola J., 'Trans-Figuring Byronic Identity', in *At the Limits of Romanticism: Essays in Cultural, Feminist and Materialist Criticism*, ed. Nicola J. Watson and Mary A. Favret (Bloomington and Indianapolis: Indiana University Press, 1994), pp. 185–206.

Webb, Timothy, 'Byron as a Man of the World', in *L'esilio Romantico: Forme Di Un Conflitto*, ed. Joseph Cheyne and Lilla Maria Crisafulli Jones (Bari: Adriatica Editrice, 1990), pp. 279–301.

Wernick, Andrew, *Promotional Culture: Advertising, Ideology and Symbolic Expression* (London: Sage, 1991).

West, Paul, *Byron and the Spoiler's Art* (New York: Lumen Books, 1992).

Westall, Richard, *Catalogue of an Exhibition of a Selection of the Works of Richard Westall RA, Including 240 Pictures and Drawings Which Have Never before Been Exhibited* (London: Joyce Gold, 1814).

Wilkes, Joanne, *Lord Byron and Madame De Staël: Born for Opposition* (Aldershot: Ashgate, 1999).

Williams, Keith, *The English Newspaper: An Illustrated History to 1900* (London: Springwood, 1977).

Williams, Raymond, *Culture and Society, 1780–1950* (London: The Hogarth Press, 1993).

Wilson, Carol S., 'Stuffing the Verdant Goose: Culinary Esthetics in *Don Juan*', *Mosaic*, 24, no. 3–4 (1991), 33–52.

Wilson, Frances, ed., *Byromania: Portraits of the Artist in Nineteenth- and Twentieth-Century Culture* (London: Macmillan, 1999).

Wilson, Lisa M., 'Pen Names: Marketing Authorship in a Romantic "Age of Personality," 1780–1830.' Ph.D. Thesis, SUNY Buffalo, 1999.

Wilson, Michael S., 'Garrick, Iconic Acting, and the Ideologies of Theatrical Portraiture', *Word and Image*, 6 (1990), 368–94.

Wise, Thomas J., *A Bibliography of the Writings in Verse and Prose of George Gordon Noel, Baron Byron*, 2 vols (London: Printed for Private Circulation, 1932–33).

Wolfson, Susan, '"The Mouth of Fame": Gender, Transgression, and Romantic Celebrity', in *Essays in Transgressive Readings: Reading over the Lines*, ed. Georgia Johnston (Lewiston, NY: The Edwin Mellen Press, 1997), pp. 3–34.

Wood, Gillen D'Arcy, *The Shock of the Real: Romanticism and Visual Culture, 1760–1860* (Basingstoke: Palgrave, 2001).

Woodmansee, Martha and Peter Jaszi, eds, *The Construction of Authorship: Textual Appropriation in Law and Literature* (Durham and London: Duke University Press, 1994).

Wordsworth, William, *The Thirteen-Book Prelude*, 2 vols The Cornell Wordsworth, gen. ed. Stephen Parrish, ed. Mark L. Reed (Ithaca, NY: Cornell University Press, 1991).

Yearsley, Ann, *Poems on Various Subjects* (London: Printed for the author and sold by G. G. J. and J. Robinson, 1787).

Young, Ione D., ed., *A Concordance to the Poetry of Byron*, 4 vols (Austin, TX: The Pemberton Press, 1965).

Zachs, William, *The First John Murray and the Late-Eighteenth Century London Book Trade* (Oxford: Oxford University Press for The British Academy, 1998).

Index